Ocean of Time

The Making of a Mariner

Robert A. Duke
with Shearlean H. Duke

Ocean of Time

The Making of a Mariner

Robert A. Duke
with Shearlean H. Duke

Sidekick Press
Bellingham, Washington

Copyright © 2021 by Robert A. Duke

All rights reserved. No part of this publication may be reproduced, distributed, or transmitted in any form or by any means, including photocopying, recording, digital scanning, or other electronic or mechanical methods, without the prior written permission of the publisher, except in the case of brief quotations embodied in critical reviews and certain other noncommercial uses permitted by copyright law. For permission requests, please address Sidekick Press.

This memoir represents the author's recollection of his past. These true stories are faithfully composed based on memory, photographs, diary entries, and other supporting documents. Some names, places, and other identifying details have been changed to protect the privacy of those represented. Conversations between individuals are meant to reflect the essence, meaning, and spirit of the events described.

Published 2021
Printed in the United States of America
ISBN: 978-1-7365358-5-1
LCCN: 2021913096

Sidekick Press
2950 Newmarket Street, Suite 101-329
Bellingham, Washington 98226
sidekickpress.com

Robert A. Duke, 1938-
Ocean of Time: The Making of a Mariner

Cover design by Spoken Designs (https://www.spokendesigns.com)

CONTENTS

Prologue 1
Elusive Lady 3
A Step Backward 13
Learning to Sail 19
Making a Mariner... 27
1983, A Pivotal Year.. 39
Sailing to Baja 57
Cruiser's Baja... 77
Going Home... 93
Boating Writer.. 105
Cheyenne Summer – Panama Canal 117
Lilli Sohex, Cook Islands to Tonga 121
Gang's All Here, A Group Charter 125
Lake Powell, Colorado River... 129
Bay Islands, Honduras 139
Whitsunday Islands and the Great Barrier Reef..................... 163
Bahamas: Cheyenne Summer and Bareboating 169
Writing Myself to Tahiti 175
Yacht Club History Project 179
Marine Highway Ferry to Alaska.. 185
Gray Whales in My Living Room... 195
Reconnoitering with Captain Kyle 199
Alone to Alaska.. 211
Glacier Bay 223
Sweetie Pie Survives a Landslide.. 231
Salmon, $0.12/Pound... 235
Alaska on the *Home Shore* 239
Shearlean to Alaska and Africa... 259
Swallowing the Anchor... 263
Time is Money 265
About the Author 283

Illustrations
   Map of the Baja Coast.. 56
   Bob and Shearlean with *Elusive Lady*................................. 149
   Elusive Lady's sister ship, *Mañana*.................................... 150
   Bob and Shearlean on the eve of the Baja Departure.......... 151
   Bob Duke on writing assignment at Bora Bora, Tahiti 152
   Sweetie Pie sister-ship underway, Gulf Islands 153

Shearlean at *Sweetie Pie's* helm in an Alaskan fjord 154
Captain Jim Kyle, *Home Shore* 155
Home Shore, coastal Alaska 156
Bob Duke grilling kabobs aboard *Home Shore* 157
End of the training cruise on *Home Shore* 158
Bob Duke at *Home Shore*'s helm, Alaska 159
Sea Change, 2015 160
Symbiont 161
Map of the Inside Passage 184

Appendix
Islander 36 Specs 267
List of Improvements to *Symbiont* 268
Sweetie Pie's Specs and Improvements 273
Inside Passage Voyage Statistics 274
Getting Underway Daily Checklist 275
Single-Handing Lessons Learned 276
Song: So You Don't Surprise Bears 276
IPTC Abridged Curriculum, Learning Objectives and Labs 277
Radar 279
Electronic Charting 279
GPS 279
Depth Finder 280
Steering 280
VHF Radio 280
Cuisine 281
Family Cruising Books 282

Prologue

From the perspective of forty-five years of boating, it was no wonder my first outing on my first boat was becoming a tragedy. Just thirty minutes after leaving the safety of the harbor, our boat was filling with water, we were sinking, and I was a helpless bystander. We were going to die right here in full view of an audience in the homes lining the clifftop of Corona del Mar, California, overlooking the Pacific Ocean. I could visualize the severe black headline in the *L.A. Times Orange County Edition* reporting our misfortune. I saw the lifeless body of my wife, Shearlean—youthful, tall, blond, and beautiful—grey and mangled in death, surging back and forth in the surf. I knew nothing about boats or the ocean, and so my persistent dream of seeing the world from the deck of a boat might end right here, right now.

As I watched the beach growing ever nearer, I now appreciated the paralysis that had kept me in Newport harbor until today, when a professional mariner had agreed to accompany me.

Elusive Lady

In my early thirties, I was discovering about myself that I seemed to come to things slower, later in life, than other men. I was doing things my peers had done in their twenties, like wandering around Europe the summer of '67, nearing thirty. I was unsure about what I might be seeking, sometimes chasing a fast-track will-o'-the-wisp stock option job, hoping for riches; other times chasing the swinging-singles California lifestyle. Though I was continually searching for something vague, the notion of seeing the world from the deck of my own boat or sailing across the Pacific to Tahiti would pop into view and off I would go mentally, sometimes physically, looking for that boat with the globe-girdling deck I thought I had to find.

This time, I convinced my wife of two years we should sell our house on the Orange County border with Los Angeles County—a dream house by our standards, having both grown up in ugly mill towns, her in Tennessee and me in Pennsylvania. The house I wanted to trade in for a "well-loved" motor yacht was in suburban Orange County: a former model home with swimming pool, on an olive-tree-covered cul-de-sac lot. The yacht of my dreams would one day be slipped in Dana Point Marina, so far south in Orange County that we'd be halfway to

San Diego from there. We'd keep our jobs and our friends, for now, and simply commute from our floating home. We'd seemed so normal, settled, and established that our friends and colleagues were stunned.

We acquired the boat through a yacht broker who worked out of a tiny green curbside shack alongside the section of Pacific Coast Highway (PCH) in Newport Beach, located between archaic Larson's marine railway shipyard and the always busy harborside Rusty Pelican restaurant. My "new" boat had six berths in three cabins; at the center of the boat was the saloon, beneath which were two V-8 gasoline engines. Three steps up from the saloon led to the helm on the bridge deck. Alternatively, three steps led down to the master stateroom and the cockpit at the stern. *Elusive Lady* had belonged to a family of house painters, so her hull and superstructure paint looked great, but it hid the accumulated deterioration brought on by caring for a boat as though it were a house.

Instead of selecting pricey marine hardware of bronze and stainless steel, and rather than choosing coatings formulated for the corrosive marine environment and applying them with regard to waterfront conditions, house painters chose material suited to structures in benign residential communities they knew well.

Elusive Lady had been hauled out for inspection at Larson's Shipyard, which performed deferred maintenance and essential repairs to make her safe and seaworthy. With the work completed, the boat was launched and tied up temporarily at a vacant shipyard dock next door to the Rusty Pelican. This was where Shearlean and I first came aboard to live, literally on the doorstep of the Rusty Pelican, the width of the sidewalk away from the parade of cars congesting the PCH. In the evening, while we watched TV in the saloon, the sliding cabin door would suddenly skid open and several cheery faces would look in, with the obvious intention of coming aboard (probably while waiting for their table) until they frowned in unison to see us there.

We were expected to take the boat to its permanent slip at M-Dock in the east basin of Dana Point's new marina, just thirteen nautical miles south of Newport Beach. Aside from the din of traffic and lack of privacy, every additional day at Larson's was expensive.

Taking a boat to Dana Point should be a simple, three-hour, coastwise voyage. We could go, any day, weather permitting. So, why not just go? The answer boiled down to me not comprehending how to *just go* in a boat, because I'd never *just gone* anywhere in a forty-six-foot boat, out on the actual Pacific Ocean. I grossly underestimated my role in my dream. A seaworthy skipper was an even greater prerequisite than a boat.

Days passed, and I found myself paralyzed with indecision. I would have to leave the harbor in order to see the world. If my dream were not incentive enough, the boatyard was threatening me with eviction to get its slip back.

In mounting shame and desperation, I asked Pike Putnak, the marine surveyor and licensed skipper, who had earlier inspected the *Lady* for me and recommended repairs, to accompany Shearlean and me to Dana Point. To Pike this must have seemed a frivolous request, but he reluctantly agreed and we set a date and time. I wanted to hug him, but Pike Putnak was not huggable unless he'd had enough to drink. Then, he might also sing sea shanties and play his concertina, and ooze fathomless charm, even warmth, until he passed out. (Pike got his name as a teenager on salmon seiners fishing Icy Strait in Southeast Alaska using the proverbial ten-foot-pole [or pike] to enthusiastically fend off hazardous chunks of disintegrating icebergs that threatened nets and boats in the strait.)

We got the *Lady* underway on a weekday morning, about 10:00 a.m. About a hundred feet behind the *Lady's* stern, blue water glinted in the sun as the wakes of small boats smacked wet kisses against waterfront pilings. Tense as I was with getting underway for Dana Point, I couldn't resist marveling at my joy to merely be standing at the helm controls of my own boat—the *Lady's* one helm, on the bridge deck, with two sets of engine instruments, their markings printed in stark black-and-white contrast, and mounted in chrome-rimmed protective lenses set in a gloss-varnished dark mahogany cabinet mounted to the bridge deck. It reminded me of my parents' console radio from vacuum tube days. A spoked, carved wood steering wheel was mounted in the center with the kingpin wrapped with marine twine and varnished for preservation to identify the wheel position where the rudders were centered. In the middle of the flat shelf of the top of the console was a flush-mounted compass. To the right of the console, adjacent to the companionway, were two highly polished chrome-plated half-cylinders covering a pair of black-and-red-knob-topped chrome levers attached to cables that controlled the engines' throttles and gears.

An impatient Pike hovered at my shoulder. Shearlean gathered the last loose dock line into neat loops around the bow deck cleat. She looked at me expectantly, and I looked back with all the encouragement I could muster. Her blond hair was piled and pinned atop her head and covered tightly with a black wool watch cap, and she moved athletically, at ease with the boat's motion and her duties.

At this end of crowded Newport Harbor, at Larson's Shipyard, the instant a boat exits its slip it is in heavy boat traffic. This area is a turning basin, small-craft commercial traffic is speeding about, rental boats are knocking around, and large yachts are maneuvering in the channel. I must be instantly ready and alert.

"Leave the wheel alone. Don't touch the throttles. Put both engines in reverse," Putnak ordered, his New Jersey accent sounding more like a threat than a command. *Elusive Lady* shuddered and started easing backward, slowly, evenly. There was nothing to do but watch aft to see if we were clear on both sides. "Out of gear," Putnak said from behind a stream of cigarette smoke. Sensing the boat was picking up speed and seeing the end of the slip we'd been tied to slide by I heard Pike bark, "Port engine reverse." I obediently pulled the nearest lever back and the boat's stern angled to port as the bow cleared the end of the dock. We were in the channel now. "Starboard engine forward," said Pike.

Because we were now gaining sternway, shifting the starboard engine forward slowed us a bit and brought the bow around to port and straightened the *Lady* in the channel. "Port engine forward," he commanded. "A little wheel, to keep us on our side of the channel," Putnak muttered, adding, "not too close. Watch for boats backing into the channel." He took a seat on the lid of the storage locker built into the bridge coaming, just below and behind my right shoulder, and lit another cigarette. With a trace of irritation, Putnak told me I should have sounded my horn when backing into the busy channel.

I was sweating profusely with nervous tension, while at the same time I was giddy with the pleasure of being underway at last. I looked aft and saw I was causing only a small wake (no danger to anyone's boat) and drew a soothing breath. Shearlean was sitting in the mate's helm chair, next to me, calmly returning friendly waves from the shore and other boaters.

As we neared the harbor exit, *Elusive Lady* began to pitch gently with the ocean swell entering the harbor. And there, ahead of me, the open ocean awaited—where I fantasized only Tahiti lay over the horizon. Passing the jetty riprap, a mild roll began. Watching the tachometers, I eased both engines up a few hundred RPM, then jiggled the red knobs of the throttles a little, as Pike had showed me on our sea trial, to synchronize both engines by ear. I eased myself into the captain's chair, grinning across at Shearlean. Pike puffed on his cigarette and stared noncommittally at our wake, probably analyzing our engine exhaust for any signs of engine problems. As long as he was sober, Pike was all business, all the time.

We passed through a swarm of arriving and departing boats for about a half-mile before turning to port for Dana Point.

With the boat moving gently, Shearlean suggested some beer and snacks, and went down the aft ladder into the cockpit, probably to use the master stateroom toilet, before going forward through the boat to the galley. She suddenly reappeared, eyes wide, choking on her words, "The boat's full of water!" As she pulled herself up the ladder, I saw that her jeans were soaked around her ankles.

Pike sprang from the locker lid he was sitting on and gathered both red throttle lever knobs in one big hand and yanked them closed, idling the engines. He ripped the black-knobbed port and starboard gear handles upright into neutral, and instantly leaped through the companionway into the saloon. The mild, onshore breeze immediately pushed the bow around toward the shore, not a half-mile away. I remained in my chair, paralyzed by thoughts that this was our home and everything we owned was in it. I was useless, a captain without a clue, wondering how long it would take us to drift onto the beach. Shearlean looked frantic but was also immobilized. We each moved at the same instant and followed Putnak below.

Because of the prevailing northwest wind, the entire west coast of the United States is a lee shore—a boat's worst enemy. Land is what generally sinks boats, open water is usually safety, though counter intuitive to landlubbers. California boats are rarely anchored and so anchors and ground tackle are minimal equipment, seldom ready for immediate use. Most Southern California boating is marina-to-marina or to moorings at Catalina and other Channel Islands. Otherwise, boats are continuously underway, sportfishing or yacht racing or day sailing. Anchoring in surf would be suicidal and only delay the inevitable as the surf would dislodge the best anchor and as soon as the hull touched bottom, the boat would begin breaking up.

My thoughts about our potential fate were not nearly so logical as I watched Shearlean watching me. With no thrust at the propellers, the boat no longer squatted in the trough of its wake and now floated level, allowing the flooding waters to flow forward into the rest of the boat. The biggest openings in the bottom of a boat are in the stern: the propeller shafts, rudder shafts, engine cooling water intakes, and engine exhausts.

All Shearlean and I could do was watch as Putnak flung saloon floor access hatches onto the saloon sofa, exposing engines idling smoothly, but water had risen a foot to the engine mounts.

Pike, both arms submerged to his elbows, was furiously feeling for something underwater and needed only a moment to dismiss one thing and move to another. At the rate water was entering the boat, I guessed the hull was still intact, but the leak was big enough to see the water level rising. With a shout to me to stop both engines, Pike kneeled in the water behind one engine and then the other as he thrashed around, apparently having gotten hold of something. I still had no idea what he was doing. Stooped over behind the engines he calmly said, over his shoulder, "I found it. You two go keep an eye on the shore."

The shore was a lot closer now, closer than any prudent skipper would venture on purpose, but the surf line was barely visible, indicating the water was deep almost to the beach, below the clifftop homes of Corona del Mar. Moments later, soaked to his waist, his hands bleeding, Putnak emerged onto the bridge deck and looked over the side to satisfy himself that the bilge pump was discharging water. His wet and bleeding hands fumbled with a cigarette, which was more wet than dry, and lit it. He sucked hard on it, held the smoke momentarily and then spewed it out along with his command to start the engines and resume our course.

Back on his locker seat, his sodden cigarette drooping from his lips, he muttered, shaking his head, "That asshole, Larson."

Larson's shipyard had removed both propeller shafts in order to replace the worn strut bearings that support the shafts between the engines and the propellers—a routine and ordinary boatyard job. When the shafts were reinstalled, the lock nuts had not been tightened against the packing glands. Not locked in place, the screw-in packing glands were unscrewed by the rotation of the shafts, creating two three-inch openings in the bottom of the boat.

"Asshole" Larson, Pike later explained, had failed to inspect the boat before and after launching it to ensure it was watertight. Any incidental leakage had been handled by the bilge pump. An experienced skipper—not me—would have done his own check or noticed the bilge pump running too frequently, or would have known, as Pike did, where to look for a leak.

I was stunned, immobilized, by my utter lack of response to our potential peril. It had happened and was over, and I had failed to act, I was helpless out here on the ocean in my boat. This was unacceptable.

Shearlean carried on with what she had started to do before the crisis and put a beer into my hand. I couldn't look at her, but I was relieved that she felt calm enough to reenter the boat's galley and witnessed, to her satisfaction, that we were no longer sinking. Pike continued smoking and muttering to himself, perhaps more outraged over the event than me. Pike was notorious in the harbor for criticizing brokers and tradesmen who didn't meet his standards.

With additional help from Pike, for maneuvering in the confines of Dana Point's busy harbor and close quarters of a marina, we found our way to M-dock, east basin, and settled into our live-aboard slip.

I never considered legal action against Larson. Shearlean and I bought Pike a gift, a pair of Craftsman toolboxes, each with a commemorative brass plaque bearing Pike's name and the title of "captain," and the date of our near tragedy. The *Lady* suffered no real damage, and while the incident dampened my enthusiasm for ocean voyaging, it didn't extinguish it. With *Elusive Lady,* my first step toward seeing the world by boat was now behind me, which brought my ultimate goal into sharper focus. However timorous my actions were, I had severed my lifelong connection with the land, and whatever happened next couldn't undo what was done.

I got to work transforming the *Lady* from a traditional '50s motor yacht to a comfortable '70s liveaboard yacht. Instead of two single berths in the master stateroom, I wanted a cozy, queen-sized berth, I wanted generously proportioned homestyle toilets instead of the original, tiny, squatting-height fixtures, and a proper, stainless steel *marine* galley range was a must. On the exterior, neglected trim and fittings needed to be re-bedded and refastened to stop rain leaks that would ultimately cause wood rot.

Working on the boat helped redeem my self-respect as a would-be boater, but no dockside chores or tasks could heal the tear ripped in my confidence by our near sinking.

Still, I was content with our new lifestyle and progressed smoothly from project to project, but we never took *Elusive Lady* anywhere. Oh, we took her out of her slip and idled around the harbor, over to the fuel dock, across to the boatyard and into the turning basin, but not even over to Catalina Island, about thirty miles away. The world would have to wait.

Choosing is sometimes seemingly all it takes to create change.

A Step Backward

If my first outing with my first boat didn't prove I didn't know what I was doing, the coming year would make it perfectly clear. Meanwhile, the lifestyle was exhilarating, surrounded as I was with all things nautical, a real boat to focus on and the comradeship of like-minded adventurers.

Ours was one of two liveaboard boats on M-dock, and we soon realized the forlorn existence we'd adopted. At our jobs all day, we were effectively weekenders like most other boaters. We were far down M-dock, near the main channel, and our general daily impression was one of desolation with moaning wind, crying gulls, and creaking dock lines.

I nevertheless enjoyed the boat because it kept me connected to my dream of seeing the world and I liked working with tools and my hands to repair and maintain the boat. It was a therapeutic and satisfying diversion from my intensely intellectual profession of writing and publishing computer documentation seated at a desk all day.

Here I was, at the western edge of the North American continent, afloat on the Pacific Ocean. I had sea lions snorting noisily in the channel and otters crunching crabs on a nearby boat's swim step, while gulls circled noisily overhead as proof there was a more appealing world at the fringe of the mayhem of the grasping, striving, chaotic continental United States.

I found this littoral area, where tides were a daily phenomenon, was populated with places, people, and activities blessed with an aura which reached inland only as far as the sea breeze. It provided bars open at 4:00 a.m. for returning fishermen, catch-of-the-day restaurants, floating gas stations, no-wake speed limits, sheriff's deputies patrolling in boats, Coast Guard helicopters rising noisily and darting off on a mission, surfers trudging across grassy dunes with their boards held high, and piers lined with sport fishermen there to catch the sound of the surf and maybe a fish.

We had joined a society for whom a boat was more than a hull and propulsion system. It symbolized a particular way to travel and see the world. For my fellow boaters, though, I discovered boats symbolized many things: the status and prestige of a yacht, the sport of big game fishing, yacht racing competition, escape from unpleasant home life, a safe place to sleep off too much to drink, a place to party, or the key to solitary or family adventure.

To me, the words "boat" and "adventure" were synonymous. A glance at adventure literature and reading age-of-discovery history proved that. By wanting to see the world from the deck of my own boat, I had blundered into a popular dream which sustained many seeking hope in their life of "quiet desperation," or nourishment of an imagination that promised escape from drudgery or burdensome responsibility. How many of us—because I was in that cohort—would actualize their dream and achieve their escape?

I found I admired my fellow boaters, liveaboard or not, because most seemed to have this sense of adventure that owning a boat represented, which positively affected each boater's outlook on life. It was an eclectic group, with owning a boat being the only common denominator, but it proved to be enough.

On L-dock, across the fairway directly opposite my slip, was the ferro-cement hull (yes, a concrete boat, a then-popular method of amateur boatbuilding) that a family of six (the youngest a boy of ten) had constructed in a nearby vacant lot. The fifty-foot hulk had been trucked from its building site to Dana Point Shipyard, where it was launched and towed to its marina slip. The family was living aboard while they worked from dawn to dusk to finish and commission what was intended to be a ketch-rigged motor sailor. Their goal, their adult daughter told Shearlean, was to sail to the "South Seas" and to eventually immigrate to Australia "before all the kids were grown."

On the west side of the main channel, side-tied to the end of the dock, was what appeared to be a kit-built sailing trimaran (three hulls) with a lone middle-aged man who shared the boat with a large, muscular female Rottweiler that, from a distance, looked to me like a pig on a leash. Such boats, usually amateur-built of lightweight plywood, were notoriously fragile and ill-suited to heavy weather, relying on speed to find shelter before things got too rough. His vintage, grass-green pickup truck had the word MOWING painted on each door and the bed contained four lawn mowers. Reputedly, the boat only moved annually to prove it was "seaworthy" as a condition of his lease.

Much more conventional and practical was the Islander 36 sailboat of my M-dock neighbor in the slip at the foot of the access ramp (wisely close to the restrooms). They were a lively, gregarious, and handsome fifty-ish couple, whose goal was to be in Baja in a year or so. They seemed to have a flair for a carefree lifestyle, both (I speculated) got by on their looks and charm. He was a part-time car salesman, when he needed the money, and she was a cocktail waitress when it suited her. They had a very practical side, I thought, exemplified by their choice in a boat for cruising to Baja. As proof of their serious intentions, both were taking community college Spanish language classes.

Their Islander 36 represented the endless stream of Baja-bound production fiberglass sailboats that ventured down the west coast of North America in the 1970s and '80s, and beyond. Realistically, any fiberglass sailboat in decent condition and prudently skippered was capable of safely making the coast-wise passage. Some of those same boats continued on to the Marquesas Islands and elsewhere in the South Pacific, with a few circling the Earth—something I hoped to do one day. I would soon discover this was the sort of boat I needed for seeing the world.[1]

After all the excitement of buying a boat and living in a marina had faded, even I had to confess there were huge impracticalities to living aboard. If you were still connected to the land by a job, dressing and grooming for work daily in a public restroom was cumbersome and problematic. Just getting from the boat slip to a parking lot restroom on windy or rainy days was challenging. For Shearlean, a *Times, Orange County* staff writer, with high heels, hose, hair, makeup and all, it was especially hard, and when she was done primping, she had to go back outside into the wind and rain to get to her car. Dressing or finishing grooming at work left you feeling vulnerable about your image with your boss and colleagues.

Other realities quickly wrecked my liveaboard fantasy. To marina operators, liveaboards are a mixed blessing. Liveaboards offered great security and cared for other boats when the wind picked up and canvas covers started flapping, loose halyard flailed masts, and old dock lines broke. But liveaboards knew everything going on in the marina, were quick to report problems, and demand attention.

Resentments developed between liveaboards and weekenders as excited weekend kids and dogs turned the docks into playgrounds, bathrooms became dirty and littered, and security gates were propped open for arriving guests, but invited trespassers to climb aboard unattended vessels.

Jane, our lilac Siamese cat, forced us to face the difficulties of the liveaboard life we'd adopted. With her demanding voice, she daily insisted on getting off the boat to roam the dock. Jane routinely walked on all twenty boats on M-dock, leaving paw prints in morning dew, which remained after the dew evaporated. Her ramblings left the deck of each boat looking as though a cat stampede had passed through since

---

[1] See "Islander 36 Specs" in the Appendix.

the boats' owners had last visited. The climax came, though, by Jane continually falling into the harbor and being brought back to us, with her rescuer remarking, "Is this yours?" as he thrust forward his fist, full of wet fur.

Dana Point Marina was so constructed that there was no easy way for a person or cat to get out of the water. The perimeter of the marina basin was a sheer, unclimbable concrete wall and the floating docks were too high to climb onto.

When I accepted that my Plan A, big financial success—stock options, my own company, or dumb luck—wasn't going to happen for me, it was something of a relief: I could stop trying so hard.

Plan B wasn't much clearer than Plan A, but was at least a different direction.

With the *Lady*, I had grabbed the dream before it slipped away. We had a big boat, one I could fix up and outfit for local cruising, if not world cruising. We were skimming the cream of the best that waterfront living had to offer without the cost of real estate, and had transformed ourselves from being inland tract housing suburbanites to *yachties.*

Resolving to find an inland home for Jane also finally spurred Shearlean and me to rethink a land-based home for ourselves, and after a winter of living aboard, we rented a waterfront apartment in Seal Beach, California, practically back to where we came from on the LA/Orange County line.

When ancient mariners gave up the sea it was called "swallowing the anchor." Reputedly, upon retirement, old salts would declare they were going to shoulder an oar and start walking inland until someone asked what it was they were carrying, and that's where they would settle down.

Our change wasn't as colorful and serious as that, but it was a pretty big step back from the brink of my dream.

There is not usually a Plan C in most tales, but a more capable boat and part-time world travel might be a practical alternative plan. Creating big chunks of free time could make a boat more affordable and ensure opportunities to use it. Outfitting and maintaining a boat yourself, and overseeing professional work would save money. In the bargain, it would make me a knowledgeable and self-sufficient skipper. As I thought it through, time took on greater value than I anticipated as I considered how slow long-distance travel by boat is—under a hundred miles a day—and then, when you reached your hard-won destination, you needed the time to leisurely enjoy it thoroughly. After years of struggling with the money/time dichotomy, it had dawned on me that to continue pursuing wealth was squandering my time (the one resource I already possessed) and that I needed only money enough to assemble my dream. Dragging my dream around behind my pursuit of money had been putting the cart before the horse, and ultimate success meant going all-in for the boat and a nautical life.

But, by deciding not to rely on becoming wealthy, Shearlean and I would have to continually make enough money to sustain ourselves and our boat indefinitely, and do so while taking huge blocks of time away from work to use our boat to see the world. That could be as tricky as figuring out how to get wealthy. We had made small discoveries in both our professional and personal lives that making changes and achieving goals could sometimes be as simple as resolving to do or not to do something. As Shearlean liked to say, "Thinking makes it so."

Learning to Sail

Suitable only for navigating sheltered waters, *Elusive Lady's* worst shortcoming was severely limited range, about two hundred miles. But it was an essential learning experience. From reading numerous boating books, it was clear that sail power was what provided unlimited range for cruising the world. (It wouldn't be until decades later that the combination of fuel-efficient, affordable diesel engines and relatively inexpensive fiberglass trawler yachts, mainly from Taiwan, would make long-distance powerboat cruising a reality.)

Seal Beach was an out-of-the-way beach town, located in the westernmost corner of Orange County. It, like La Palma, was off the beaten path and was somewhat neglected—some would argue to its benefit. Our apartment was on the top floor of the three-story, L-shaped, twelve-unit building facing the beach across Ocean Avenue. Old Town, as the business district was called, was six blocks east where a recreational pier reached into the ocean. It was incongruously notorious for its drunken St. Patrick's Day celebrations, when crowds gathered to cheer on public sex, usually accomplished nearly out of sight atop a van or RV outside a bar. Apart from endless competition for on-street parking, it was a quiet, pleasant, and safe beach town.

Shearlean discovered a waterfront condominium project, Marina Pacifica, being constructed in nearby Long Beach, so we made a deposit on a ground-floor studio and prepared to move when it was completed. Slips were available to homeowners, so I rented one with the intention of putting a small sailboat into it and learning to sail.

Sailing is as much an art as a practical skill, and I had never before sailed—that is, maneuvered or controlled a boat under sail. So, I decided that I had to learn to sail if I was going to proceed beyond reading about it.

Shearlean's gnomish colleague at the *Times*, county lifestyle reporter Gordon Grant, she told me, had done some sailing and so I asked him, "How long does it take to learn to sail?"

Slow to respond, as though musing about an answer, he said, "Somewhere between three hours and a lifetime." So, I asked Gordon, one day, if he had three hours to spare on a coming weekend.

With promising interest in the sale of *Elusive Lady*, I decided to risk buying a small sailboat to learn to sail, but not just any small sailboat. In fact, not really small at all.

The city of Long Beach's recreation facility nearby in Alamitos Bay offered free sailing lessons, and now working in a home office, I had time for lessons. Small sailboats populated Alamitos Bay, most ranging from eight to fourteen feet, a majority being the tiny, square-bowed, eight-foot, Sabot dinghies. Even if a beginner avoided capsizing, the Sabot sailor got wet. At age thirty-six, I was unwilling to get wet and cold, or to fold my seventy-six-inch frame into a ninety-six-inch boat.

I wanted to be comfortable while learning to sail, and I wanted a cuddy cabin for storage and a toilet, and I wanted an outboard motor for getting around the expansive bay. I chose a fiberglass Victory 21 sloop, designed by Carpentier and built by Coronado Yachts. Twenty-one feet long, with a ballast keel, an outboard motor, and a cuddy cabin, I named it *Wing* (Wing(ed) Victory, get it?).

I showed up at the Long Beach Recreation department's waterfront facility the first morning, along with about a dozen boys and girls, eight-to-twelve years old, there to learn to sail the department's Sabots or their own Sabot. Though open to adults, I was the only grownup present, attending three two-hour sessions, much to the delight of the young sea lawyers (whom I referred to collectively as "little shits," due to their loud protests and overdeveloped sense of right-of-way and other sailing rules).

Between a weekend sail with Gordon, teaching me to tack and jibe, explaining how to read and correct luffing, and instructing me on reading the wind and trimming sails, I received my three-hour initiation into lifetime sailing. With six hours of practice under the tutelage of the recreation department, I refined my skills, and built enough confidence to venture out into the open ocean beyond Alamitos Bay, relying on my substantial *Wing* to forgive my blunders and novice mistakes. As I would learn and pass on to others, in any ocean and in any boat, a boat rarely fails its crew, more often the crew fails its boat.

I was finally sailing and the world was opening to me now, but Shearlean and I confined ourselves and *Wing* to fair weather in the local offshore area from Long Beach to Huntington Beach, which was plenty of sailing for us both, and ensured that we had only good experiences on the water as we built our confidence. I passed along to Shearlean the rudiments of sailing I had learned, but she was content to be a passenger and to leave the work of sailing to me.

The area from Long Beach to Huntington Beach was a '70s California-version of a boating paradise, boasting sights, facilities and attractions—all making learning to sail great recreation. Founded in 1911, the Port of Long Beach covers thirty-one miles of shoreline with ships arriving from all over the world. A short distance offshore from the port were four man-made "islands," actually offshore oil wells disguised as islands with palm trees, waterfalls, colorful lights, and interesting structures. The islands were named to honor four astronauts killed in training: the Apollo 1 crew of Ed White, Gus Grissom, and Roger Chaffee, who died in a fire during a training exercise, and Ted Freeman, who died in a plane crash while in training.

Down the coast a couple of miles was Surf City, otherwise known as Huntington Beach, outfitted with all of the legendary accoutrements of Southern California life on display at the water's edge and peopled with the youngest and oldest surfers to be found anywhere.

Before I'd given up tatters of Plan A, I had taken one more shot at getting rich by joining Precision Publication Inc. (PPI), a then technical publishing firm in Los Angeles, with a staff of writers, editors, and illustrators writing computer manuals for Fortune 500 companies. I was hired as vice president of operations to oversee writing and publishing the technical manuals we were contracted to deliver to our clients. Wealth was not to be. Our business wasn't what is called today "scalable;" we could never do better than just get by. We decided to close the doors.

As the only company officer financially able (thanks to Shearlean's income) to take care of closing down our publishing operations, I undertook the legal and financial obligations of the business, and inherited the remaining prospective clients, which ultimately proved profitable.

I started working from my Marina Pacifica home, unwittingly making myself a pioneer (in 1976) in the newly invented "home office" phenomenon that would become commonplace with the advent of personal computers and the internet. Upon closing PPI, I started doing business as Peopleware, and subsequently as Good Enough Publishing and Duke Communications, and others of what was nautically known as "flags of convenience."

As beneficiary of PPI's estate, I was able to profitably continue writing and publishing computer documentation for about two years but made no effort to find new clients. Working at home, I developed a proprietary software documentation product, accepted a consulting contract with Chase Bank, requiring me to live in Manhattan for three months, and spent January and February in Hopkins, Minnesota, solving a computer management problem for SuperValu stores.

Having given up on getting rich writing and publishing computer documentation, I wanted to be done with that part of my life in order to get on with investing my time in the boating lifestyle I was so committed to. Having written all day, every day, for fifteen years, I stopped. Not only, it turned out, was I done writing software documentation, I was done writing professionally for years to come. Talk about burnout.

I wanted something physical to do, outside an office, away from a desk, and definitely something to do with boats. *Now!*

Carefully managed, money wasn't a problem. We had savings, no boat at the moment. *Elusive Lady* had sold while I was at Chase Bank in New York and I had sold *Wing* in just two days to a Marina Pacifica neighbor. Shearlean's job at the *Times* was secure and I felt I could always find a way to make at least a little money doing something.

Desiring more hands-on and practical boat knowledge, I contacted Pike Putnak, to ask if I could accompany him occasionally on boat surveys. Putnak wasn't enthusiastic about it, suggesting I'd be in the way and a talkative nuisance, but he finally agreed. I think he saw me as someone with grit when I didn't go to pieces when *Elusive Lady* was sinking or perhaps thought he might benefit somehow from the arrangement.

Surveys are inspections of a boat's condition and appraisals of its value, required to insure and finance a boat. Marine surveyors inspect boats from stem to stern, inside and out, usually in dry dock, and inventory all of the boat's gear and equipment. They write a lengthy report describing the boat and stating its value based on its condition and equipment. Surveyors have an extensive, though superficial, knowledge of everything a boat comprises and good understanding of whether components and systems are serviceable, appear properly maintained, and conform to legal and safety standards. If in doubt, the surveyor recommends further inspection and testing by an expert. Surveyors are the supreme marine generalist: they know a little bit about nearly everything, but are seldom experts in anything. A surveyor is not a diesel mechanic, sailmaker, rigger, electrician, plumber, electronics technician, etc.

Learning surveying looked to me to be the shortest, fastest possible route for learning as much about everything to do with boats and boating, and it required the one thing I was already expert at—technical report writing.

I was still reading extensively about boats and boating, and had been moving toward reading about yacht design, marine metals, fiberglass boat construction standards, sail-making, and diesel mechanics. It all came rather easily to me, because I had worked with engineers and manufacturers for years writing test, maintenance, and operation procedures for every sort of electromechanical device, from spacecraft to submarines. Fortunately, I was a keen observer and articulate enough to express whatever I observed in useful and accurate terms. The writing of survey reports would be easy for me; the challenging part would be interpreting telltale signs of deterioration and defect, but Pike had my back with his reviews of my reports.

Putnak was separated from his "nagging" wife, alienated from his "sissy" son, and had disowned the daughter who "married the Jap," but was on speaking terms with his other daughter, the one resembling him in most ways. He was living with his alcoholic girlfriend, Joanie, in the loft above his diesel engine shop in a business center in Costa Mesa, adjoining Newport Beach. Putnak was known around the waterfront as a good diesel engine mechanic, but a generally spiteful and cantankerous individual, with a long list of hatreds along racial and ethnic lines, and with special hell reserved for yacht brokers, all other salesmen in general, and incompetent work (as he was with "asshole" Larson for nearly sinking my boat).

I don't know why he liked or tolerated me, but he did, and I managed to avoid his abuse for two years and even found something to like and admire if I looked at him narrowly. After shadowing Putnak on a dozen surveys, he offered me a job working for him surveying boats for $0.50 on the dollar, payable by the job. I accepted his offer and worked for him and sometimes with him (on yacht deliveries) several times a week. He made sure I got the simplest surveying jobs and reviewed all of my reports before Joanie typed and mailed them.

Everything about Putnak was tough: tough talk, tough posture, tough on others, and tough on himself, yet we never had a confrontation. When we finally had a falling out, he wasn't even present. He and Joanie were traveling together for an expenses-paid survey in Florida commissioned by one of Putnak's many "fans" who knew he couldn't be bought or corrupted by yachting's unsavory fringe or scammers.

By the time I departed, Putnak felt he was getting too old to be wrangling the heavy parts of diesel engines around and had closed his shop and moved to a conventional office where I had my own desk. He and Joanie had found an apartment.

Shortly after Pike and Joanie left for Florida, Putnak's favorite daughter arrived to do some office paperwork, during which she said her father had told her to keep an eye on me. I said nothing in reply, but was incensed that anyone should think they needed to "keep an eye on me"—least of all Putnak's uncouth daughter. I called a friend who worked with Shearlean at the nearby *Times* building, who had a pickup truck, and asked him to meet me at noon at Putnak's office address to move a desk. Tim pulled up at the door on time and we lifted my desk and chair into the truck and drove off. I was now self-employed: Bob Duke, Marine Surveyor.

I never spoke to Putnak again after that and neither of us made any effort to contact the other. Even now, I can't think of any better way for things to have ended, especially when more came to light over time. Putnak provided me with great experience and a terrific grounding in seamanship and nautical knowledge, he really knew his stuff and I've always been grateful for the apprenticeship he provided to a raw landlubber. But he had managed to keep secret from me the most lucrative part of his surveying business, which was his claims and loss work with insurance companies. As he grew older, Putnak took in other partners or apprentices, offering to sell them his well-established business on more than one occasion.

Putnak's fierce independence had earned the confidence of lenders and insurers, some of which rubbed off on me. Yacht insurance agents, marine underwriters, and banks I had contacted about my new independence continued providing me with surveying jobs because Putnak couldn't handle all the work he was offered.

Compared to many of the surveyors I knew, most of whom I admired greatly, I was merely a dilettante, looking for boating knowledge and experience, but not seeking a profession. Most of the best surveyors I knew grew up in and managed boatyards and had experience (many with the construction and repair of boats) far greater than I could acquire in the way I came to the profession. I was never accepted within the ranks of professional surveyors, but I never applied, realizing I lacked the foundation required to function at the top of the profession; I was merely adequate.

Making a Mariner

With Shearlean content in her dream job as an editor with one of the nation's most prestigious daily newspapers, she provided the credit and capital needed to free me to explore options.

I found an office to share with the U.S. representative of a Taiwan sailmaker at a new boatyard on PCH in Newport Beach. I began doing business as "Bob Duke, Boat Detective."

I wasn't eligible to join the surveyor's professional association, because members were required to have five years of experience surveying, and I had only two. But other boating professions required only a license, and I determined that taking those licensing tests were an expeditious way to enhance my credentials.

Yacht brokers sell used boats, usually for a ten percent commission, and what little I knew about brokerage was what I had learned buying *Elusive Lady*. It was brokers who most often arranged for the survey.

To get practical brokerage experience I worked part-time as a salesman for Jerry Helrung, a power boat broker/dealer, for one year. I sold only one-half of a boat, earning the seller's half of the brokerage commission. Half of my half went to Jerry, so my share of the commission was only a few hundred dollars. My only part in the transaction was to have answered the phone one day, which made me the salesman of record because Jerry's office had the listing for that boat.

I did no real sales work, no prospecting, cold-calling, price negotiating, or securing of financing: I'd learned long ago I was no salesman. I preferred making myself useful by attending to sales support—unpaid tasks that the real salesmen avoided because it took them away from tasks that paid serious money. My willingness to do the drudge work, and being no threat in competing for sales commissions, I was welcome and popular at the brokerage. What was a nuisance to everyone else was fun and valuable experience for me. I did no surveys for boats in which I or an associate had any sales interest, as it would have been unethical.

Most of what I learned about brokerage was what I read by studying for the broker's test—laws and practices governing purchasing and selling boats. I also learned a lot about marine insurance, marine finance, and about the network of services, individuals and facilities that support boat sales and ownership. I learned a lot by operating many boats, moving them around from harbor to harbor and slip to slip as a service to buyers and sellers. Gratis, I had access to a fleet of boats with no cost involved, it only required my time. What a great way to spend my days.

Anyone at the helm of a boat rates being call "skipper," but to be called "captain" requires a license.

In the early '80s, controversy loomed over the financial and legal status of yachts, as owners looked to earn income from their costly boats and to shelter them from taxes. State and federal authorities challenged owners about the legality of the "boat businesses" they had created and whether people aboard those boats were guests, clients, or passengers. The key question was whether the person skippering the boat was qualified to transport people, and, consequently, what was the owner's legal liability for insurance, safety requirements, and taxes?

Few persons skippering boats back then had formal training unless the vessel was officially designated a passenger-carrying vessel. (The heart of this conflict was that many vessels were represented to be bareboat charters, meaning the charterer was skippering the boat, when in fact a hired skipper was often at the helm.) If the charterer wasn't the skipper, a U.S. Coast Guard-licensed captain was required, and it wasn't a legitimate bareboat charter. Now, what had before been viewed as benign recreational use was forcing boat owners to seek licenses for themselves or their hired hands in order to avoid liability and jeopardy in case of an accident or enforcement violation. Until now, the only formal training for recreational boaters had been courses by the Coast Guard Auxiliary or U.S. Power Squadrons.

Responding to this crisis, a maritime training company was offering U.S. Coast Guard (USCG) license training courses in Newport Beach. Thinking I should know what other boating professionals know, I took the course. I got a USCG 50-Ton Ocean Operators license, called a six-pack license, which permitted me to operate a commercial vessel with a maximum of six passengers onboard. The course taught the test, so everyone passed. And why not, it was a textbook knowledge test, with nothing practical, no boat operation or handling.

A USCG license taught me little about seamanship or navigation and nothing about sailing. Mainly, I learned about the COLREGs, which stands for the International Regulations for Preventing Collisions at Sea 1972, otherwise known as the rules of the road.

When my license came up for renewal, I let it expire. I wasn't operating passenger carrying vessels.

Ham radio was often the preferred means of long-range communication for long distance cruisers, blue-water sailors, and circumnavigators—those crossing oceans to remote destinations—such as I hoped to do one day.

So, while I was in a training mood, I decided I should get a Ham license, because there was a convenient marine-oriented course being taught by Gordon, in Orange County. I'd had friends who were enthusiastic Ham operators, but I was never interested enough to get a license myself. With a boating purpose attached to it now, I decided to take the plunge.

Common two-way maritime radio is Marine VHF, a low-power line-of-sight service. Mariners who like to talk a lot typically also have a Citizen Band (CB) radio onboard, such as truckers and many others use.

I got a license for Morse code and voice. I let it expire the first time it came up for renewal. I found I had no desire to speak to anyone over great distances from remote locations, which seemed to be the focus of the Hams I knew. I still recall Gordon saying at the end of our course that when we received our license, which would inform us of our call sign, we would never forget it. And he was right. Though I never spoke my call sign over the radio, I instantly remember it to this day and am forever KA6RSJ.

Local emergency room physician, Dr. Bob Hall, MD, was offering a two-day course, titled: The Intensive Survey of Medical Emergency Care, geared to boaters, mountain climbers, hikers, and such. His press release about his upcoming course caught Shearlean's attention at the *Times, Orange County* and she signed us up.

Few people voluntarily put themselves so far beyond emergency assistance as cruising boaters. Even without traveling great distances, boaters can wend their way into places which create their own highly localized weather, and which block every form of communication, including satellite, such as exploring the fjords of Southeast Alaska. Even if help is available, it may be a long time arriving, and so, besides distance, the speed of proper treatment can be a factor in a medical emergency.

Dr. Bob was hyper serious about his course, and convincing each of his twenty students that his course was the real deal. He impressed me by having all of us give each other saline injections and taking vital signs while pretending to radio them by shouting them to someone across the room who wrote them down and read them back, aloud, to verify they were correct. Upon graduation, Dr. Bob warned us to never play doctor by offering medical treatment to others in anything less than a true emergency (a warning we tested a few times).

Prior to seeking all of this self-contrived training, like most recreational boaters, my first and only boating training had been the *U.S. Coast Guard Auxiliary Boating Safety* course, which Shearlean and I took when we bought *Elusive Lady*. Compared to all other boating courses I was to take, it was undoubtedly the most useful, largely because it was so basic (e.g., the pointy end of the boat is the bow). It was an eight-hour course, offered free to promote boating safety, one of the key missions of the auxiliary since its founding by Congress in 1939.

Yacht clubs are great sources of boating experience, and you don't have to take a test, get a license, or attend classroom instruction.

Yearning to get some serious sailing experience, especially on boats over thirty-five feet, and to learn from seasoned skippers, I wanted to join a yacht club. Though it would strain our budget, Shearlean agreed. Bahia Corinthian Yacht Club (BCYC) was a full-service club with restaurant and bar, slips to rent, and a diversified activities calendar, including cruises and evening beer can-, weekend around the buoys-, and major ocean-sailing races. Also, it had its own parking lot (important in Newport Beach where valet parking was the norm starting at 4:00 p.m.) and its finances were in order. I responded to the application's in-person interview requirement, but always suspected it was Shearlean's role as the *Times, Orange County* lifestyle editor that sealed the deal for our acceptance. I hoped club members might avail themselves of my surveying services to help offset our membership costs.

By now we owned the small sailboat, *Sherry J*, a Gladiator 24, a flush deck sloop, designed by Lapworth and built by Continental Plastics. A trunk cabin version of this boat was sailed around the world by a teenage boy, Robin Graham, departing in 1965. Of the dozen or so boats I had ever owned, I thought *Sherry J* was special. For one thing, to my amazement, Shearlean decided to gather an all-female crew to race it for two seasons, in the newly established Women's Ocean Racing Series (WORS) intended to attract more women to sailing as participants rather than auxiliaries to their husbands. (All areas of boating, now, were attempting to appeal to women, at last recognizing their role in purchase decisions and participants in the sport.) Not designed for performance, *Sherry J* would never win a race (even under the most generous handicap system), but Shearlean was racing for participation, not victory. While Shearlean had always been a most willing and capable first mate, she'd never previously expressed any desire to take the helm. But she was always surprising me (she never discussed how she got her hands-on sailing experience, but I guess it was crewing for various female skippers, such as Mary Longpre aboard *Valentine*).

Shearlean had gone with Gordon Grant and me on my novice sail and participated in learning the basics, but she chose only this once to be a skipper. When she and I raced another boat of ours, I asked Shearlean to take the helm to start the race, because she was a great starter. Otherwise, on our passages in sailboats and powerboats, she stood her helm-watches, alone, with few complaints, but never desired to be at the helm except to relieve me.

The other reason *Sherry J* was special was that, years later, I realized what a practical little "escape-the-rat-race" boat she was. She was simple, inexpensive (I paid cash for her), very capable and proven, and required little maintenance. A boat any competent sailor could take anywhere they wanted to go at minimum cost. I once toyed with the idea of extensive one-way cruising. A cheap series of capable boats to be sailed to destinations, used to liveaboard, and cruise the desired area, and then sold locally for an airline ticket home. Yes, at twenty-four feet, *Sherry J* was tiny, but many such small boats have safely and comfortably circumnavigated the world in the hands of capable sailors: notably Lin and Larry Pardey's twenty-four-foot cutter *Seraffyn*, both east-about and west-about, and John Guzzwell's twenty-foot yawl *Trekka*, 1955 to 1959.

Racing sailboats never appealed to me, though it offered intense lessons in seamanship and how to sail. Sailing to me was the means of getting from one place to another, and as long as I was making progress towards my destination, I wasn't too concerned about technique. Sometimes, though, I paid dearly for my self-imposed ignorance by being unable to solve problems with simply trimming the sails to balancing the rig or changing sails to reduce the effort of steering the boat or to improve speed to arrive at an anchorage before dark. Endurance and brute strength were sometimes my only tools, because sailing finesse wasn't among my skills.

So why would any racing skipper want me for crew? Because, I concluded, I was always available and on time. The really skilled guys were in great demand and often careless about commitments, or they were high-maintenance prima donnas. Also, I couldn't try to tell the skipper how to sail his boat as some lofty crew did. Though I didn't know much, I wasn't asked to do much, because I was too big for many of the boats under forty feet that I crewed on. I weighed about two-hundred-twenty-five pounds, enough weight to affect the boat's trim. I was often told to stay near the center of the boat, usually near the main mast and at the companionway, handling the halyards, and neutral to the boat's trim. I didn't complain—this is where I wanted to be: I was yacht racing, out on a boat on the water.

Cruising was why I was learning to sail and why I wanted a boat in the first place. If you've never been anywhere on a boat of your own, there are plenty of interesting, challenging, and worthwhile destinations locally to be explored and appreciated—even if it is in Southern California. Southern California's cruising reputation is that it offers no cruising, it is said there's no place to go: a mooring at Catalina Island's Avalon Bay, anchoring at a Port of Long Beach oil well island, or a San Diego marina guest slip. There are no palm-fringed lagoons with warm, sparkling water so clear you can see your anchor in the white coral sand bottom, thirty feet beneath your keel, and no other boats in sight. But if you've got a boat you've got to take it somewhere, so you go wherever you can, because you need the practice for that ultimate escape you promised yourself when you bought the boat. That was me (and tens of thousands of other Californians).

An exception to humdrum California cruising were the eight Channel Islands, including rugged and remote Channel Islands National Park, about seventy miles from Los Angeles, an epic voyage by local standards. Cruises to the remoter Channel Islands, San Clemente and Santa Cruz, were more challenging, requiring everything of the skipper and crew of real cruising, but they offered little in return, other than experience with genuine blue-water passage-making.

Not yet wise enough to appreciate all of the qualities of *Sherry J* and exaggerating all the money I would save being my own broker and surveyor, I succumbed to the itch for a bigger and better boat, which eventually led to *Symbiont*.

I wasn't looking for a Fuji 35 when I found *Symbiont*, in fact, I'd never before heard of one, but it was love at first sight.

Aside from her looks, emphasized by her pretty clipper bow, I was impressed with the generous proportions of her accommodations. I had standing headroom throughout, and could stretch out fully in generously sized berths.

I found her in San Diego in 1981, for-sale-by-owner, an attorney, which made me pessimistic about negotiating the purchase price, but he was motivated.

Designed by John G. Alden, for construction by Fuji Yacht Builders of Japan, in 1973, it was thirty-five feet (length overall) long, with a ten-foot beam and five-foot draft, with a long keel and attached rudder. She was cutter-rigged, built in 1976, and equipped with a fifty-horsepower, Perkins 4-109 diesel engine. The Fuji 35s were built from 1973 through 1982. As one ad for the Fuji 35 put it, "If you're going to make the long sail to the South Pacific, you might as well be coddled in a gorgeously warm and wood-filled cabin like that of the Fuji 35." I agreed, hoping when I purchased her that I might be cruising for several years and would one day depart from Baja to the Tuamotus Islands, thirty-eight hundred miles southwest, as many other cruisers anticipated doing.

I don't recall her original name, but Shearlean and I named her *Symbiont* in honor of the sentiment, noted in our ship's log: "*Sym-bi-ont*, noun, 1) to live together, 2) the living together in initiate association."

It was sometimes a regrettable name, because it sounded too "biological" for some people, and others remarked, "I didn't know they had a navy," referring to the 1974 kidnapping of Patty Hearst, the nineteen-year-old granddaughter of newspaper publisher William Randolph Hearst, by the Symbionese Liberation Army (SLA), an American left-wing terrorist organization. But we stuck by *Symbiont*, faithful to our perception of the relationship between boat and crew.

I had no plan or list of improvements before buying *Symbiont*. What I ended up doing was purely extemporaneous, ideas occurring to me with each day I spent with her, based on faults and shortcomings of the many boats I had been on. In hindsight, I would be guilty of only one serious omission I wouldn't fully appreciate until nearly twenty years later—no radar.[2]

Lacking the foundational skills of the best surveyors (boatyard operators, marine architects, master mariners) I decided to return to what I could do better than other surveyors, professional captains, yacht brokers, marine architects, and a host of other marine professionals: writing and teaching.

Orange County's Orange Coast College offered an extensive curriculum of recreational and maritime industry training courses, so I summarized my boating background and proposed a recreational course on how to buy a boat. The college replied with its own proposal, suggesting I offer a summary of "How to Buy A Boat" as a two-hour lecture and also as an in-depth eight-hour classroom course, and asked whether

---

[2] See "List of Improvements to Symbiont" in the Appendix.

I was interested in teaching adult beginning sailing in the upcoming summer recreational program. I agreed to all three.

It was an effort to promote my surveying business that motivated me to start writing about boating. My initial attempt, in 1980, was titled, "Boating With Mac Phail." Mac Phail was to be a nautical Murphy (as in Murphy's law—"If something can go wrong, it will go wrong.") Because it was intended to be instructional humor and no boating magazine I knew of had a nautical humor column, I hoped to earn a place as a columnist and regular monthly check. "Pacific Skipper Magazine" published three Mac Phails, but there was no encouragement to write more, so I switched to feature articles about surveying, which were readily accepted.

With Shearlean's editorial help (I wasn't a proficient feature writer, yet) I submitted articles to a growing list of regional, national, niche, and special interest boating magazines and newspapers.[3]

After about two years, by 1983, my income from writing about boats, sportfishing, boating-related travel, and the marine industry was beginning to equal my income from surveying. I sold everything I wrote. About half of what I wrote were assignments, which meant I was guaranteed acceptance and payment, and the other half were written on speculation, which meant it might not be accepted and even if it were, payment would be slow.

I also took photos to complement my writing, and sometimes the photos paid more than the writing. What made my photography successful was that I often had the only photos available to illustrate what I had written.

Ultimately, I wrote continually until 2007 for over three decades.

Southern California's maritime world was where I now worked and played, so you'd think I would have been satisfied with having all the

---

[3] From the partial list of publications, you can see the breadth of subject matter that my "boating" writing encompassed: *Sail, Motor Boating & Sailing, Cruising World, Sea, Pacific Skipper, UCI Journal, Professional Boat Builder, Pacific Yachting, Marine Business Journal, Los Angeles Times, Sport Fishing, Orange County Magazine, Hot Boats,* and *PassageMaker.*

boating one man could handle. *Symbiont* was a boat that could take me anywhere in the world that I was capable of taking her. Yes, I had made a lot of progress, but coming right down to it, I hadn't been anywhere or done anything truly seafaring.

While living aboard a boat, yacht racing offshore, moving sportfishing boats between San Diego and Newport Beach, and overnight trips to Catalina's Avalon or weekends at the Isthmus were things many Southern Californians were doing, too, weeks-long ocean passages and a foreign home port were not.

The 1983 Transpacific Yacht Race (Transpac) would replace my parochial boating experience and Baja Bob would show me where to take *Symbiont*.

1983, A Pivotal Year

Delivering a big racing yacht from Hawaii to California wasn't something I'd ever imagined doing, but when I was offered the opportunity, I immediately accepted. An image instantly popped into my mind: me at the helm of a speck of a boat on a rimless blue disk under a boundless sky lit by an unnaturally brilliant sun. I'm still suspicious it was my memory of a sunscreen ad, but it remains my symbolic memory of that voyage.

Bob Steel, a recently arrived Australian sailor, managed Maritime Outfitters, and knowing him proved to be the biggest benefit of having my surveying office at the upscale boatyard. Bob displayed a severely erect posture and a patient manner that suggested he was here if you needed him, otherwise he intended to stay out of your way while you got on with your job. Outfitters was doing many interesting projects, using the yard's modern facilities for what I thought of as a "patron" client, one who appreciated Outfitters' superior skills and meticulous service for high-end marine projects where cost was not an issue. When Australia won the 1983 America's Cup, in Perth, Australia, Bob was the handy recipient of my congratulations to his country.

Wealthy perfectionist patron Henry Wheeler was an admirer of naval architect Bill Lapworth and was rumored to own a few Lapworth-designed yachts, which he stored in an industrial park warehouse nearby. Henry regarded Lapworth as a visionary and industrial artist, and his designs as "works of functional art."

In 1983, Henry's fifty-four-foot Lapworth aluminum sloop, *Aorangi*, was chartered to the U.S. Naval Academy for cadets to participate in that year's Transpac from Los Angles to Honolulu, with Steel as one of the watch captains.

The Transpac race occurs every two years, in July. Traditional boats, such as *Aorangi*, are of the monohull class. The distance of the race is approximately twenty-two hundred miles. The record longest time to finish was five minutes short of twenty-four days, but the typical duration of modern races is four-to-five days for the early finishers. The smallest boat to ever participate was twenty-five feet and the largest, a hundred and sixty-five feet.

Aorangi finished seventeenth of eighteen vessels in her class, Class B, and fiftieth overall in a little over eleven days.

Bob had me survey *Aorangi* to establish a record of its condition and for obtaining insurance for the duration of the charter.

When the race finished, the charter ended in Honolulu. The task now was to deliver *Aorangi* back to Newport Beach. Steel put together a delivery crew and offered me a spot among a crew of five. Besides me, this crew consisted of George, an international yacht delivery skipper, George's girlfriend/cook Frauke, Jim, a laid-back fiftyish waterfront gofer and experienced sailor, and a USC student I instantly dubbed "Thing."

Besides being crew, I was to survey *Aorangi* in Honolulu as a condition of accepting it back from charter, and, again, for insurance for the return voyage. For my part, I was getting paid for my expenses and a surveying fee. I had the time and always wanted to make a long passage, and what better way to do it than on a professionally crewed fifty-four-foot sailing yacht.

When I saw *Aorangi* again, in Honolulu's Ala Wai Boat Harbor, I saw a far different boat than the one I'd surveyed in Newport Beach. At first sight, she looked dilapidated and forlorn. She'd been used hard and abandoned at the end of the race. The charter crew was relieved of any responsibility for her, knowing a delivery crew was arriving right behind them. When I first surveyed *Aorangi*, I'd done it with the objective tunnel vision of an impartial surveyor, but now I couldn't help looking at her through the eyes of a prospective crew member. Having the soul of a cruiser, I cared about comfort, convenience, and ease of use—all dispensable to hard-driving, competitive racers pushing the boat to its limits for two hundred and sixty-four hours between Los Angeles and Honolulu. I noted there was only a tiny dodger protecting the companionway hatch opening (nothing spanning the width of the cockpit to protect crew from the wind and sun), there were no seat cushions to ease the bite of the hard cockpit bench seats, or back cushions to soften leaning against the companionway bulkhead. There was no autopilot, but at least the huge wheel would make steering nearly effortless. Below decks, the galley was minimal, and accumulated trash was stuffed in the built-in bin, while the navigation station was immaculate. There were no portlights in the hull, only a few scattered prisms in the deck to illuminate the deep interior, where there were eight berths of taut fabric laced to frames of aluminum pipe. There were no mattresses or bed linen, and the sleeping bags were wet. Also lacking was a deck hatch wind scoop to aerate and cool the interior. At the bow was a mountain of sail bags topped by two folded sails, each too big to be moved by one person.

But, hey, what's a delivery crew for, anyway? Nothing on *Aorangi* appeared broken or damaged, and there was no reason she could not turn right around and head directly back to the mainland. As hospitality and accommodations for Transpac participants, private marina tenants moved their boats to moorage in Keehi Lagoon or temporary dockage. The harbormaster made it obvious we were expected to waste no time exiting our anonymous benefactor's slip. All courtesy, it appeared, ended when the race ended.

We spent the first couple of days in Honolulu provisioning the boat for five persons, uncertain how long the return voyage would take. We cleaned *Aorangi* inside and out, and serviced all the equipment and systems, and paid special attention to the engine because we were going to have to motor several hundred miles north before turning east for California to escape the Pacific High[4].

Meanwhile, Thing was spending days surfing at Waikiki and then experienced a severe toothache that required extraction, so he was more liability than help (but that would eventually prove to be his nature). Frauke stayed in her berth pondering the complexities of provisioning and George seemed preoccupied with intangibles and offered no direction for our preparations. Jim and I teamed up and went to work, doing all of the obvious chores required to make *Aorangi* shipshape for our return voyage. Somehow, momentum built, and we finished the whole preparation process at the end of the week. Jim and I also exchanged some misgivings about our chaotic start for this passage, but we were both mature enough and experienced enough to be confident we could get by, if we had to, on our own.

Designed to minimize weight, *Aorangi's* built-in fuel tanks were small, even by sailboat standards. We bought a dozen six-gallon plastic jerry jugs to carry additional diesel fuel on deck, lashed to the lifelines to extend our motoring range in the High.

For an overnight shakedown cruise, we departed Honolulu, Oahu, for Hanalei Bay, Kauai, before committing to our return passage to California. Entering the expansive bay on the north coast of Kauai, George steered us toward the Hanalei pier, where we dropped anchor, a lot closer to shore than I thought necessary, until he explained that he

---

[4] The High is in the northeastern portion of the Pacific Ocean, northeast of Hawaii and west of California. It is strongest during the northern hemisphere's summer (now), and shifts towards the equator during the winter. It is responsible for California's dry summer and fall, and typically wet winter and spring, as well as Hawaii's year-round trade winds. (Wikipedia)

wanted to be close to the beach; it seemed he had plans to visit Princeville. We had no dinghy, another drawback to a cruising agenda on a racing boat, and within ten minutes of anchoring, George went for a swim toward Princeville, while I stood anchor watch on the minimal ground tackle racing sailors begrudgingly carry aboard their boats.

All went well enough and we deemed everything was ready, so after dinner that first night we departed Hanalei Bay to sail north until we encountered the High, and to then motor through, around, or across the High, until George decided it was time to turn east to sail for California. If we were lucky, we'd find wind before we ran out of fuel and sail to the west coast of the U.S. mainland, and, hopefully, arrive at a point somewhere in the vicinity of Newport Beach.

Confronting a powerful High, one can't help thinking of Coleridge's *The Rime of the Ancient Mariner*: Day after day, day after day/We stuck, nor breath nor motion/As idle as a painted ship/Upon a painted ocean.

The challenge of the Transpac race was to negotiate the semipermanent, subtropical anticyclone, officially titled the "North Pacific High," to reach Honolulu from Los Angeles in the shortest time without disabling your boat in the process. The High is an obstacle, whether racing east to west or merely sailing west to east as we were about to do.

Besides our compass, our two principal navigation aids were SatNav (such as I installed on *Symbiont*) and weather fax, which was a National Weather Service offering, producing a black-and-white meteorological chart of the ocean area we were navigating. We plotted latitude and longitude on a paper chart to record our position and the weather fax enabled us to see the position, outlined in isobars, of the High relative to our course. Exactly when and where we could encounter the High was a matter of speculation, because its size, shape, and location continually changed, but it was tangible enough that we would know it when we ran into it.

George chose a 6-6-4-4-4 watch-keeping system. Jim and I had the first night watch, 7:00 p.m. to 11:00 p.m. George and Thing would relieve us. We each would steer for an hour. Jim had the enviable ability to sleep anywhere and anytime, so he was leaning back against the companionway bulkhead, his chin on his chest and I was at the wheel. My goal of a long passage was happening.

Clothed only in swimming trunks, the trade wind (something I'd never experienced, but read about countless times) immersed me in its sensual embrace. I wanted to experience it more intensely, so I stood on the helm seat, holding onto the backstay, to be enveloped head-to-toe by the wind, and threw back my head to gaze into the utter blackness of the sky, glistening with brilliant stars. I must have moaned ecstatically, because Jim raised his head. I stepped down into the footwell and listened closely to the hissing bow wave, its fluctuations sounding like words whispered from the sea. I looked down at the binnacle compass card dancing sluggishly to the boat's tempo, seeking something tangible to bring me back to the boat from wherever I'd gone.

Jim and I next had the dawn watch, 3:00 a.m. to 7:00 a.m., my favorite time of day, on sea or land, and I was rewarded with a fascinating sunrise. About 4:00 a.m., a faint glow appeared in the east, slowly silhouetting the clouds on the horizon while a shooting star painted a green slash across the still black western sky, marking the boundary between the coming flash of dawn and paling of the stars in the greying sky.

Though we'd only been underway twelve hours, time was already distorted, its rhythm was that of the watch system we'd adopted. As long as we continued north, time remained constant. Dawn, noon, and dusk would occur at their usual hour. "Hawaii time" and "boat time" were the same. When we would eventually turn east, the sunrise would gradually occur earlier and earlier, noon would shift by about two hours. We would all be affected by a form of gradual jet lag, a little disorienting, with noon gradually occurring a little sooner every day.

The day before, we had gained all the northing we could get before running into the High. We entered the High at about 7:00 a.m., and it was so well-defined that it was incredibly real. As a West Coast sailor, I felt as though I were entering a sort of sailing shrine. Overhead, the

High was a stark bright-blue dome unblemished by clouds. At the western edge of the High, we could see the tops of clouds whose puffy bulk was hidden below the horizon. Scanning south, then east along the great arc of the horizon, to due north, off our bow, and then circling west again, there was this wonderful, dark blue surface and brilliant blue sky; we'd been swallowed by the High.

We removed the headsail, sheeted in the main, and started the engine. Based on the latest weather fax, George chose a compass heading he hoped would quickly get us out of the High to where we could find wind, before we ran out of fuel.

We were crossing the shrine at a comfortable four or five knots and water washed along the topsides, yet we lost all sense of motion and progress as the High seemed to expand to keep us enveloped. After about thirty minutes, the engine was merely a pleasant hum in the background of *Aorangi's* throaty wake.

On watch, later in the day, I was surprised by a sudden chill that enveloped the boat and, simultaneously, Jim looked at me quizzically and we locked eyes, expressing our disbelief at the sudden cold. Around the boat, I saw a strange phenomenon, a bright blue, creek-like stream of water flowing across a blue-green, meadow-like ocean. I thought my eyes were playing tricks on me. The bright blue stream reminded me of entering tropical shoal waters over a reflective white sand bottom. It was only about a hundred yards wide and small eddies occurred along its length. I looked back at it, but its defining edges had been dissolved by the sun's glare. It happened so fast I had to ask Jim if he saw what I thought I saw.

I had heard Frauke was prone to severe seasickness, still, when she couldn't get out of her berth the day after Hanalei Bay, I was concerned. The boat's motion had been mild, with little pitching or rolling. As the cook, she had purchased and stored all of our provisions and was the only one who knew what we had and where to find it, so we had a problem. We each looked in on her to wish her well, but to describe her as merely unresponsive would be an understatement, comatose would have been more accurate. George, whom she had accompanied on previous yacht deliveries across the Atlantic, through the Panama Canal, to Newport Beach, at first, was dismissive (I guessed he'd seen it all before). After a couple of days, when George began showing some concern, Jim and I actually wondered if she might die. She wasn't eating or drinking, and George was treating her with anti-nausea suppositories twice a day, but she showed no improvement. George's solution for our meals had been to recommend breaking out the freeze-dried emergency rations, add water, and get by until Frauke recovered. We'd been subsisting on snacks and fruit, but that wasn't good enough for Jim or me, so I volunteered to cook one meal per day with whatever I could find.

Stunningly, George revealed Frauke said she had an inflamed ovary! So, what's she doing on a boat in the middle of the Pacific Ocean? I thought, but kept silent. We had a decent medical kit onboard, but it was aimed at physical injuries and digestive problems. Probably overstepping my emergency medical training (sorry, Dr. Bob), I suggested she take codeine for pain and aspirin for inflammation every four hours and suck on ice cubes for hydration.

As we motored along at five knots, which it seemed we had been doing for an eternity, our first drenching rain squall found us. We all spontaneously stripped off our clothes and had our first good shower in nearly a week, standing on deck around the mast, passing a bar of soap around. We were rinsing off the soap when Frauke appeared, wearing only her underpants, looking like a cadaver, but smiling weakly, and she joined us for a shower. "Frauke" is a German word meaning "little woman (frau)," and she was: maybe five feet tall and I doubt a hundred pounds. She kept her straw blond hair in braids and pinned up. I don't recall ever having a conversation with her, though she spoke unaccented American English (and she may have been American). She and George often spoke German (it sounded like) to each other, annoying Jim and me with their insensitive exclusion.

She cooked a magnificent dinner that night, which everyone (but especially me) appreciated. Though she stayed in her berth sixteen hours a day and seldom came on deck, she seemed to be fully recovered.

George was energetic or nervous, involved or meddlesome, take your pick. He managed to always find something that needed doing on *Aorangi*: mending, inspecting, adjusting, testing, logging data, checking, and re-checking. He was American, mid-thirties, even tempered and sinewy, maybe a hundred and sixty pounds and just under six feet tall. He was too fair, I feared, for a long life under the sun. I haven't a clue why he spoke fluent German. And since we weren't on the same watch, we talked little. Trusting Bob Steel as I had come to do, I figured that if George and Frauke were good enough for Bob, that was good enough for me, so I had never looked into his background.

With fair weather and a good boat, we were more passengers than crew, and I would have been pleased if it remained that way—a cruiser's attitude. I only worried that George would decide one day that we should fly a spinnaker—it's a huge, light fabric sail that requires an unwieldy spar and additional running rigging, and careful attention at the helm. I feared spinnakers because of the numerous fiascos I had witnessed when I crewed for races. Luckily, we had consistently moderate winds and weather for all eighteen days, with steady ten-to-twelve knot winds, for which our one-hundred-fifty-percent genoa headsail was well-suited. It seemed George did know how to relax.

Thing, living on one of Newport Harbor's private islands with his mother (divorced from his real estate developer dad), was awkward physically and socially, verging on shy, twenty-something, blond, and more of a domesticated surfer than a true son of the surf.

He had brought his surfboard with him on the plane to the boat, he threw his wet towels into other people's berths, used up the boat's dry cell batteries for his Walkman, ate all the M&Ms out of the trail mix, sipped a little of our precious, limited water from a full glass and emptied the rest into the sink, set open, half-finished Cokes on the galley counter where they fell over and drained into the refrigerator, and he never participated in galley cleanup. On watch, he would speculate endlessly about arriving in Newport Beach and discovering there had been a nuclear war during our passage and civilization had been eradicated. "Wow!" he would say, as he looked at us intently, hoping for a response.

Aorangi's interior was wide open: the bow was a huge sail locker for storing a big inventory of sails, the main cabin consisted of eight pipe berths, four to a side, with personal storage lockers above each. The galley and navigation station were up a couple of steps at the engine box, and from there, the companionway opened into the cockpit. There was really no place for Thing's surfboard, a long board, which seemed to skid, slide, fall, and get thrown around the interior, always in the way. Thing said he was disappointed in surfing at Waikiki. I think my list of Thing's offenses numbered at least twenty-five, but I am certain he was able to annoy each of his other crewmates in numerous, unique ways. I eventually wrote an article for a boating magazine, titled, "The Thing That Crewed," hoping it might prevent such behavior befalling another boat's crew.

Thanks to the watch system we had, Jim and I seldom spent much time with Thing, though he persistently reminded us of his presence by being late to relieve our watch. My impression was that George was oblivious to Thing, focusing his whole attention on the boat, and sometimes, Frauke.

I don't know how the others felt about our passage, but I think they just wanted to finish this job. Thing frequently checked George's position plots, which he marked on our chart four times per day. Me? I sensed I was gradually falling under the spell of the repetition of days and routine. I thought only of the boat, ocean, and weather, and lacked desire for any change, I was content—blissed out, some would say. This seemed to be all I wanted. I thought I could relate a bit to a legendary French sailor, Bernard Moitessier. Single-handing his boat *Joshua,* in the 1968 Sunday Times Golden Globe Race—the first nonstop, 'round-the-world yacht race—Moitessier famously sailed one-and-a-half times around the world, nonstop. With the fastest circumnavigation time toward the end of the race, he was the likely winner for the fastest voyage, but he elected to continue sailing and not return to the starting line in the United Kingdom (to win the race).

We had motored approximately four hundred miles through oily, smooth seas that glistened like rain-wet stone under the waning full moon. With minor course changes to keep up with the fluctuating edge of the High, we ran out of expendable fuel around midnight, before escaping the High. Our remaining fuel in *Aorangi's* two tanks had to be reserved for refrigeration, recharging the batteries, and maneuvering if we encountered traffic. When the engine died, that was it, so we centered the boom, sheeted in the main as flat as possible, and all went to bed, allowing the boat to drift until some wind came up. Just after first light, the main sail gave rattle in response to a wisp of wind, and we all turned out to make breakfast, set sails, and get underway. The High had shrunk and spit us out into some good wind.

In no time, we were heeled over twenty-five degrees and we had to reduce our headsail. I'd read a lot in the past and talked with people about passages, but failed to really appreciate what it means to sail at a steep angle of heel, day and night. The gimballed galley range was now at shoulder-height, and you fell into your down-side berth and needed a handhold to pull yourself up and out. On deck, you moved about in permanent stoop, practically knuckle-walking. Sailing a single course, day after day, beating to windward to make easting or northing, then gradually losing it all as the wind shifted, was frustrating. Like everything else about sailing long distances, this, too, changed—for the better—and the wind finally moderated. The big swells, occasional confused seas, and winds gusting to thirty knots began to die, leaving us with gentle, undulating seas rippled by an unexpectedly steady ten-to-twelve knot breeze, which lasted until our arrival in Newport Beach.

Our passage took eighteen days, and our first landfall was Catalina Island, a few hours sailing to Newport Beach. Eighteen days and nights all melded into one big chunk of time, like a giant bubble that enveloped us, a nautical, space-time singularity. That first night out had proved worth celebrating, because most night watches were mundane shifts of duty with an occasionally brilliant moon, sometimes overcast skies, temporarily chilling seas, and fleeting mists. Every night, I thought I heard voices from the wake, and there were occasionally startling real sounds: a frightened bird, a pod of whales blowing, and whistling porpoises playing in our bow wave, but they were never visible. In fact, shrouded in the night, I felt less remote than during the day when the sky and sea formed a boundless horizon we could never approach. We saw few birds and no other vessels.

A postscript to Frauke's story concerns her lost watermelon. Frauke had put a watermelon on the boat, but she couldn't find it. Others doubted there was a watermelon, but I'd seen it come aboard. Overtime, each of us searched the boat for the watermelon, but it wasn't found until after we arrived in Newport Beach. The cleaners, readying *Aorangi* for storage, tracked down a foul odor to a decaying watermelon out of sight in a dark corner of the engine bilge.

As satisfying as this passage had been, a high point in my boating experience up to that time, I was to learn later that the journey had only temporarily satisfied my desire for a long passage.

Perhaps no other highway is as important to international boaters as Baja California's Transpeninsular Highway 1, which crosses back-and-forth from the Pacific Ocean to the Sea of Cortez through a thousand miles of wilderness, from the U.S./Mexico border to Cabo San Lucas at the peninsula's southern tip.

The narrow, two-lane highway of tarred gravel threads its way through lush, microclimate valleys of wine grapes, skirts the salt marshes of the California gray whales' haven at Scammon's Lagoon, rises high on vast barren mesas, dips into cool date palm oases, arrows straight to the horizon through cactus wonderlands accented by multi-hued desert rocks, and then bursts over a volcanic mountain ridge to reveal the dazzling sapphire panorama of the Sea of Cortez. From here, south to Cabo, are dazzling, inviting bays, promontories, and islands, inhabited by uncountable sailing and fishing boats, beckoning land-bound journeyers to join them. I found it irresistible.

The highway, which opened in 1973, is difficult, demanding, and hazardous for the unwary. Yet, its admirers become addicted to its unforgiving personality, and for those seeking the natural wonders along Baja California's shores, the isolated road is the only access.

Cabo sportfishing skippers routinely make forty-eight-hour turnaround drives to San Diego for urgently needed parts. Cruisers in the Sea of Cortez make local excursions along the length of the highway and periodic provisioning and parts runs to San Diego (as we would one day do). Trailer boaters towed vessels of every description down to popular Bahía de los Ángeles and beyond for holidays and vacations. Hordes of recreational vehicles endlessly stream up and down the highway carrying aluminum skiffs, inverted on truck roofs, for fishing. Mingled among these conventional boaters are sailboarders, surfers, and the off-road explorer with an inflatable dinghy rolled up in the bed of their truck.

Bob Lonpre was a car dealer, yachtie, and fellow yacht club member who had earned the sobriquet "Baja Bob" in tribute to his many highway trips the length of Baja's Highway 1. He was stocky, a shade under six feet, with thick, black hair, and a perpetual "Hi there, looking for a car" expression on his face that incredibly contradicted his question, suggesting it was okay if you didn't want a car (but he had to ask).

I'd been longing to drive to Cabo as early as 1965, when it could be a grueling survival test, but I failed to find an experienced companion. When Bob asked whether Shearlean and I would like to accompany him on his annual drive, we instantly answered "yes." The adventure would turn out to be, for Shearlean and me, a twenty-four-year romance with the whole of Baja, by sea and by road, covering every inch of the magic peninsula. (Thanks, Baja Bob.)

Our vehicle was nothing special, just one of Bob's Pontiac dealership's new sedans. It restricted places we could go, but as Bob knew from witnessing Baja's taxi drivers' abilities, any sedan could get around Baja with prudent handling and abundant caution. Our leisurely roundtrip to Cabo San Lucas at the tip of the peninsula lasted a week in October, incurring one minor breakdown when something rattled loose in the undercarriage, forcing Bob to get under the car to fix it.

Though it meant little at the time, one of our key visits was to La Paz, where Shearlean and I got to see boating facilities and meet some marina owners and cruising boaters who had made La Paz their home port. Unconscious of it at the time, the trip planted the seed for our cruise to Baja. Bob, a consummate raconteur, shared his decades of Baja history, lore, color, and practical information as we traveled. Whether 1983 or any of the years up to 2007, when Shearlean and I did our final road trip, driving the highway remained a serious undertaking, with real dangers, and requiring serious preparations.

Based on Bob's tutelage and my own Baja highway experience, the following were always our minimum preparations: buy Mexican auto insurance to stay out of jail in case of an accident, exchange dollars for pesos at the border and insist on small denominations to avoid the hassle of making change, carry extra fuel with you, carry lots of water, be prepared to be stranded by flooding rain or stations out of gasoline, bring your own shade because there's none in the desert, and never drive at night because cattle and horses wander the whole length of the highway. Tie down everything you are hauling in case you go off the road. My personal suggestion is to carry a ten-pound bag of small apples to hand out to the boy soldiers with machine guns searching your vehicle at the roadblocks (they're bored and desperate for a treat).

I drove the highway five times between January and June of 1984: four times without incident, other than some mechanical problems with my Ford Ranchero pickup truck, with two hundred thousand miles on it, selected for survivability in Baja. On my fifth trip, I broke one of the survival commandments when driving a borrowed Jeep at night, followed by Shearlean driving our truck.

Shearlean would swear she watched me die that night when driving between La Paz and Puerto Escondido. I'd persuaded the Department of Tourism to lend me a Jeep for a trip into the mountains for a magazine article. We drove our truck to La Paz to pick up the Jeep, and Shearlean was following me back to our boat in Puerto Escondido after dark, despite knowing better. It was a black night on a black road when a black steer suddenly appeared in my headlights as we collided. First, I thought the steer was coming over the open Jeep's hood and into my lap, but it disappeared from view as my headlights went out and I swerved momentarily out of control—it all happened in seconds. I rolled onto the shoulder of the highway and looked over the elevated edge of the road and listened but couldn't detect the steer. The battery had flown off its mounting tray and slammed into the radiator and something was wrong with the steering.

Poor Shearlean, shaking and sobbing at witnessing her husband's death was speechless, even as I hugged her. I was shaking, too, having barely survived death by an open range steer. We left the Jeep there and drove the truck back to La Paz and checked into a hotel for the night.

The next morning, I reported my accident to the tourism official and the Jeep people. The Jeep people immediately sent someone to get it off the highway before it was spotted by the Federales and became an "official" accident. I paid the deductible on my insurance and that was the end of the matter.

But did that stop me from driving at night? No, sorry to say. What the accident did for my driving in Baja for the next twenty years or so was two-fold: on the highway alone at night I never again exceeded thirty miles per hour, but if I had to drive faster, I would get in behind a big truck and stay on its rear bumper. Baja big rigs are heavily armored against steers and I suspect they don't even bother to slow down for them.

Cruising to Baja looked feasible—even inviting. I'd only previously thought of cruising in terms of the whole world, but discovering a destination—a world-class one, at that—practically on my doorstep ignited my desire to depart as soon as possible. Confronting my forty-sixth birthday added fuel to the fire, perhaps it was now or never.

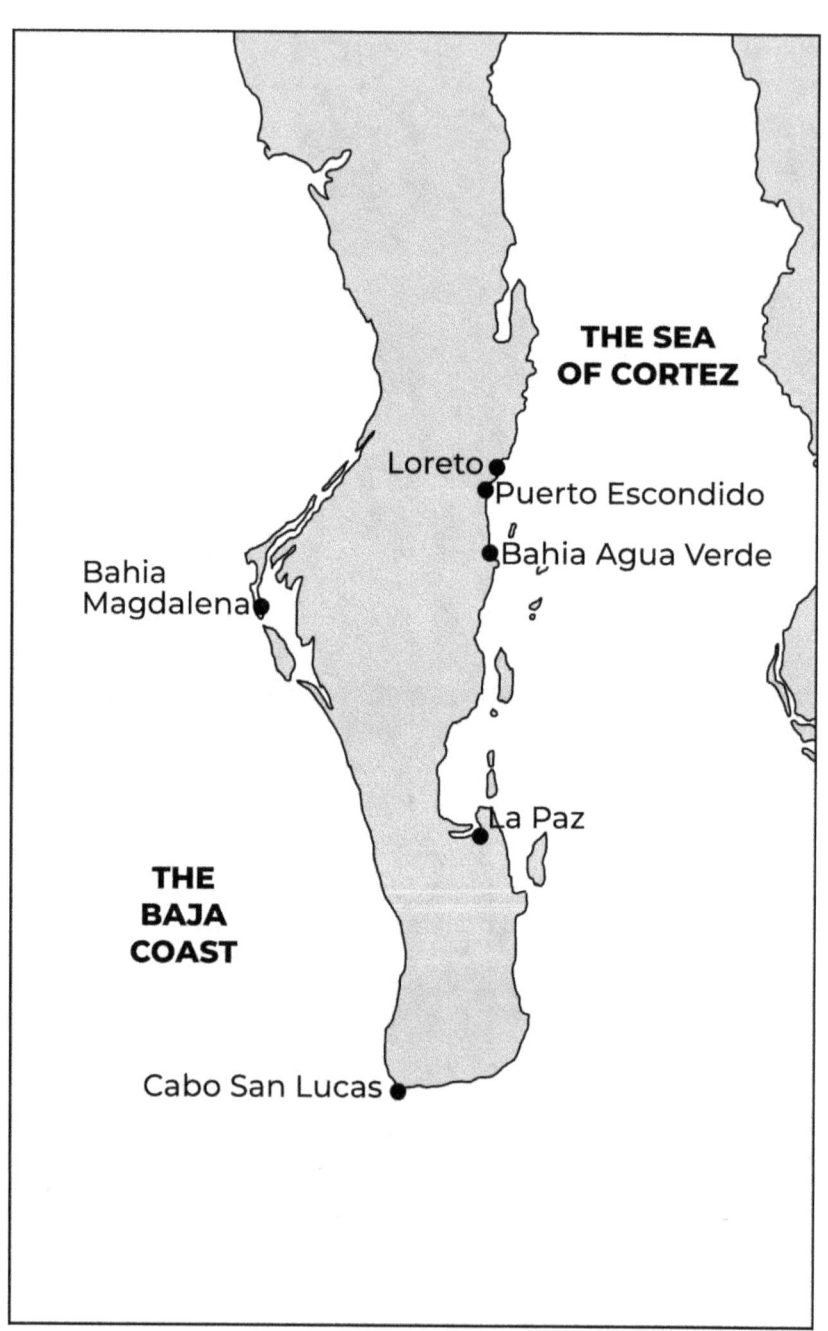

Map of the Baja Coast

Sailing to Baja

Sailing *Symbiont* a thousand miles to La Paz, Baja Sur, was less a decision and more something that happened, as best as I can recall. We seem to have returned from our road trip with Baja Bob with momentum for deciding to sail to La Paz, which continued building to the point where Shearlean resigned her job and we set a departure date to coincide with the start of the 1984 Newport Beach to Ensenada International Yacht Race, the thirty-sixth consecutive race. The first such race was April 23, 1948, with a hundred and seventeen boats.

By this time, we had sailed in the Ensenada race a few times before with *Symbiont* and as crew on other boats. We were also occasional visitors to Ensenada, by road, for its restaurants and scenic drive a few miles south. We had entered *Symbiont* in the 1983 race and were among a record 675 boats in that race, establishing the contest as the world's largest international yacht race. In the 1983 race, we had a guest onboard, Bernadette Brennan, *Cruising World*'s editor, for whom I'd been writing on a regular basis, who wanted to experience this phenomenal event for herself.

I thought of myself now as a good-enough boater, but still technically a poor sailor. I had never cared to learn how to trim sails to perfection for maximum speed, good balance, or an easy helm. I was always willing to start the engine to get where I was going. I was a cruising sailor from the beginning, I told myself, someone who uses a boat to get to places that can't be reached any other way. As long as I eventually got where I was going, safely, and with modest effort, I was satisfied. Mine was not an attitude every cruising sailor shared, but I had come to sailing late in life (and even later to cruising) and with a means-to-an-end purpose in learning to sail. As I had decided in other areas of my life, good-enough sailing skills were "good enough."

I was relieved that our desire for adventure had prevailed over the terror of the near sinking of *Elusive Lady's* maiden voyage ten years ago. We had owned three sailboats in the meantime, voyaging among the far-flung California Channel Islands, from tame Catalina to wild San Miguel, near Point Conception, the reputed Cape Horn of California. Our courage and confidence had grown to the point that we had committed ourselves to leaving our jobs and renting our house to sail Baja's Sea of Cortez to test whether we had the right stuff to cross the Pacific and continue around the world. We planned to write about our journey, as had our new friends, Lin and Larry Pardey, and the many boating authors and writers we had read.

Lin and Larry Pardey circumnavigated the world twice, in thirty years of sailing, on two wooden boats Larry had built, designed by Lyle Hess. Besides their frugal and self-sufficient lifestyle, which Lin made famous in books and magazine articles, their boats were engineless, relying only on sail power.

In 1982, my friend Bill Eisenlohr, who custom-finished bare fiberglass sailboat hulls, such as Westsails and Bristol Channel Cutters, was working with Lyle Hess[5], when he learned the Pardeys were returning to

---

[5] "Even though there are many easier ways to earn a living, all that I ever wanted to do is design boats," Hess said. Lyle Hess was a yacht designer best known for designing the blue-water cruising boats of Lin and Larry Pardey, the Bristol Channel Cutter,

Southern California to build a twenty-nine-foot version of *Seraffyn* they had commissioned Hess to design, again of wood. The boat would be christened *Taleisin of Victoria*; Victoria being Canadian Larry's hometown and the capital of British Columbia.

Bill's skills were used to affordably custom-finish bare production sailboat hulls for frugal buyers. Larry's skills were used to build and finish a whole boat to his uncompromising standards and desire for traditional qualities. The two craftsmen made an interesting contrast, sharing many of the same abilities and values, but pretty much approaching their work from opposite directions. I remember in particular, Bill's and Larry's discussions of building wooden spars (mast and boom), one using power tools and the other using only hand tools. Larry could take as much time and care as he wished, whereas Bill had a client's budget and schedule to meet. Both produced materially identical custom spars for two comparable boats.

Bare hulls were just that: a molded fiberglass hull with stringers, bulkheads and other structural components and a deck, and nothing else: no spars, rigging, engine, furnishings, or fittings. A bare hull was equivalent to about ten percent of the finished value of a cruising sailboat; Bill offered to provide the remaining ninety percent of the work and material to create a finished, cruising-ready sailboat.

Larry sometimes built his own tools, tested materials before applying them, cast many of his one-of-a-kind fittings, and milled his own timber.

Lyle introduced Bill to Larry, and Bill invited me to join them. It was an invitation to a singular boating event. I got to see the construction of

---

and other oceangoing small sailing cruisers. He was a fan of traditional wooden craft, particularly the small yachts of his boyhood, and cut his teeth designing and building wooden boats. The shrinking wooden boat market forced him out of the business in the 1950s, but the burgeoning fiberglass revolution opened the door to his return as a yacht designer in the 1960s. He was a master of creating handsome, spirited, oceangoing small boats, and when asked in an interview what the common quality in his designs was, he thoughtfully replied: "I feel that any boat that points her bow out to sea should be designed so that the crew need not worry about a safe return." Lyle Hess passed away in July 2002 at the age of ninety.

Taleisin from laying the keel up to its naming ceremony. I only missed out on the launching, because Shearlean and I had sailed to Baja before the event.

I had read all of Lin's books about sailing *Seraffyn*, and the couple were sailing celebrities of the highest order to me. We all got along well and spent many happy hours together in "Bull Canyon," where the Pardeys lived and built the boat, the subject and title of a later book Lin wrote about at that time.

As a consequence of Parkinson's disease, Larry was forced to retire from sailing. He was moved to a nursing home in 2009 and died at the age of eighty on July 27, 2020.

The last I heard, at the time of this writing, Lin was still sailing.

Among what we had learned, we understood that if we were taking a small boat onto the ocean, we had to be willing and able to endure whatever came along, because there is no recourse. Life rafts and distress calls are no guarantees of survival, and we shouldn't be venturing where we expected others to risk their lives for ours. This is not a common decision many people are called upon to make for themselves, but one anyone who chooses to risk their own life owes to the rest of humanity if they're to be allowed the luxury of their choice.

The 1984 race started on Saturday, April 28, 1984, under ominous conditions. Black clouds swirling low overhead, sustained winds of twenty knots with gusts to thirty, frigid temperatures with marine radio weather reporting hail in the area, and frequent lightning accompanied by intense thunder: these were the worst conditions imaginable for beginning an ocean voyage. This front had arrived Thursday, April 26, and had built steadily into the weekend. I'd never seen anything like it in twenty-two years in Southern California. Conditions were so severe—so extraordinary—that novices could be forgiven for abandoning hope of venturing out of the harbor.

I was incredibly relieved that I had the foresight to invite crew to join us for this leg of the voyage: best friend Bill Eisenlohr, an excellent sailor, and Shearlean's sister, Janet Jones, who had crewed with her sister for the two seasons Shearlean raced *Sherry J.*

We had left the guest dock at BCYC on April 27, after delaying our departure by one day, hoping the high winds would die down. Our only plan, with one day's head start, was to sail to Ensenada to beat the race fleet in, then to say our goodbyes to everyone there, and to then make our plans for getting to La Paz.

With the wind from the south-southwest and the seas lying down a bit (though atmospheric conditions remained turbulent), we had to sail beyond the southeast end of Catalina before we could tack. At sea late that afternoon, through the night and into the following day, we were surrounded by squalls the likes of which were rare in Southern California. Everyone was dressed in long underwear, with layers of clothes worn under a ski parka or puffy vest under waterproof, foul-weather gear. The ladies' toilet breaks were truly heroic efforts. Conditions gradually turned milder but were never "normal."

Ensenada harbor lies in the northeast corner of Bahia Todos Santos. We arrived before the racers and anchored in the corner of the harbor near the junction of Azueta and Costero Boulevards. Too tired for anything else, we four stayed on the boat and slept until the fleet began to arrive.

For hardy racers among the legion of race entries, this front caused the most spectacular finish of any race when a hundred and eighty boats crossed the Ensenada finish line within ten minutes.

For most, the point of the race is a weekend-long party, often in conjunction with Cinco de Mayo or as a warmup for the upcoming Mexican holiday. Baja Bob and Mary Longpre had an annual reservation for a hotel suite overlooking race headquarters, and Jack and Charlene Johnson always reserved a motel room, with kitchen facilities, outside of

Ensenada for an elaborate fiesta party to which all yacht club members were invited. Shearlean and I partied at the suite and motel kitchen, explaining to friends and strangers about our planned voyage and saying goodbye and accepting bon voyage wishes. For three days, Ensenada was alive with visitors and celebrations.

On the fourth day, Ensenada was abandoned and Shearlean and I felt personally abandoned, having been the object of so many goodbye and good luck messages, and too many unsubtle, worried looks asking, "Why?"

Of particular concern to me was Shearlean's and Janet's intense, teary-eyed, and huddled talk saying their final goodbye. The sisters had lost both parents within a year of each other, and under circumstance neither had yet had time enough to assimilate. And now, here was Shearlean going off on some wild, pointless adventure beyond Janet's understanding. Shearlean recorded their words in her journal. I never read that journal until writing this memoir, and Shearlean's words came as a great relief to me.

It had never been Shearlean's idea to see the world from the deck of a boat, or, specifically, to sail to Baja, but she never opposed the idea. For years, I had assumed that I had dragged Shearlean into accompanying me on my dream and she loved me enough not to refuse or complain and came along without protest. What I found out reading her journal (when writing this memoir) impressed me about her even more than I was impressed by her in forty years of marriage.

To my astonishment, I learned she had her own reasons for wanting to do what we did, though she'd never shared them with me, except by her actions, being a ready and willing participant.

Shearlean's journal entry, May 2, 1984, Quintas Papagayo Hotel, Ensenada, Mexico:

"Heavy weather still plaguing the area. Sunday evening, my sister asked me a question I am still having trouble answering. It hurts me to think of it. I cry. She had tears in her eyes and a pleading quality to her voice: 'Why are you doing this, Shearlean?' she asked me. I felt a real sadness and fear in her voice. And the truth is I did not know what to say. I had told others various things, but for my sister I owed her a true explanation. And the truth is: I do not know. Bob says he is dragging me into it. That I'm going because he is going, but I know there is more to it than that. I am going because I am afraid. I am filled with fear and I must come through it to be able to live with myself. It is the same sort of fear I faced when I left home at eighteen to go to college. I wasn't sure I'd make it, but I did. I became a better person for the experience. It's something I have to do—for me."

If the city of Ensenada felt abandoned by the departure of the race participants, the harbor felt desolate. Ours was the only yacht remaining. I felt the burden of my commitment to myself, to Shearlean, and to hundreds of friends and strangers in whom we'd confided our dream.

Of all the far-out notions, this situation reminded me of my first marriage. Long before the ceremony, but well after the engagement commitment, I started having second thoughts and doubts (yes, as might every groom), which were becoming clearer every day. But being unable to face retracting my proposal and figuring out how to return wedding gifts, I went through with the ceremony, which inevitably led to divorce.

Am I going through with this voyage because of my proven lack of courage to undo what I have done?

Shearlean was tense and nervous, but silent on the subject of leaving. Shearlean had sacrificed her world-class job.

I had committed years of work and effort to reach this point of realizing my dream of seeing the world from the deck of my own boat. The fact that we'd gotten this far without argument or opposition was acceptance enough for me. It was my decision.

Despite gaining so much knowledge and experience, I was not emotionally ready for this. What I thought I wanted so much, I feared to grasp. I felt extremely critical of myself. For all my preparations: learning about boats inside and out, Shearlean and I sailing long distances among the Channel Islands with fellow yacht club members, my eighteen days sailing twenty-two hundred miles across the broad Pacific, and the thoughtful modifications I made to *Symbiont* with every necessity and convenience, and on and on, my mind churning with years of experience, preparation, and practice. Theoretically, I was prepared and capable of everything necessary to sail to Cabo San Lucas, but . . .

Was this how the ancient mariners felt when they feared they might sail off the edge of the flat world? What was waiting out there, exactly?

Maybe tomorrow. Just one more night snuggly anchored behind Ensenada's massive riprap seawall.

What I couldn't seem to let go of was a dirty, dingy, nearly empty commercial shipping harbor where everything was grey and shading to black. The wind was still strong with violent gusts. It was May, but cold. A foreign harbor, another country. Different laws. Different language. Different customs. Different culture. And ahead of me was more of the same.

A few hours back, the way we came was San Diego, California, USA. It was probably warm, the sun shining. But we'd had a going-away party celebrating what we said we intended to do.

I decided not to take my feelings too seriously. Accept this reality, I counseled myself. Let a couple of days pass, there's no hurry. Sort things out. Get used to these conditions. Embrace what brought me to this point and accept the challenge that lies ahead.

On the morning of May 3, 1984, we got the anchor up before dawn, while the wind was still gentle, and motored past the breakwater, raised the main, staysail, and jib, and steered a hundred and eighty degrees to put Ensenada (and everything it stood for) behind us.

We sailed only about ten miles, three hours, eventually more west than south, to Isla Todos Santos, two tiny islands. We anchored on the east side of the north island, a bit deep, about eight fathoms. We were the only boat at the foot of some old mining ruins. The area between the two islands is a shoal.

We slept well and were underway again at dawn, with no thoughts of turning back, headed for Colnett, about forty miles southeast. Conditions were what we were learning to interpret as normal. Colnett is an unusual and distinctive landmark, unlike any other on the western Baja coast. It is highly stratified and nearly coal black. Good anchorage is available on the bight south of the cape in four to six fathoms in a sand and shell bottom. Wind can gust down from the cliffs, sometimes causing rolling, the cruising guides warn. Anyone with experience at Catalina Island wasn't going to lose any sleep over some rolling.

About thirty miles from Colnett was Isla San Martin, which, in an act of massive bad judgment, I decided to bypass. San Martin is a cone-shaped remnant of an extinct volcano. When northwest winds are strong, the anchorage can be dangerous, the cruising guides warned. There is sometimes a fish camp on the beach. Anchorage is in three-to-four fathoms. I entered, no other boats were there, but I changed my mind suddenly, deciding to continue to Cedros Island. I think a gust of wind triggered my recollection of the "dangerous northwest winds" warning in the cruising guides and ruined the anchorage for me.

I still puzzle over why I did this, because we dangerously exhausted ourselves dealing with strange sea conditions that caught us on the way to Cedros. Worse was my failure to do the simple arithmetic of travel time. It was roughly a hundred and eighty miles from San Martin to Cedro Island, approximately forty-five hours at four knots, nearly fifty hours underway, plus the eight or so hours since we'd awakened this morning. It never occurred to me that we wouldn't sleep for two days and how fatigue could cripple our ability to think and function.

I knew fatigue had killed a lot of sailors and that it was at the core of many ocean racing fatalities, such as those of the famous 1979 Fastnet Race that killed fifteen sailors off the southern coast of Ireland in a fleet of 303 racing yachts.

The weather was fair when I made my decision, but I had no recent weather forecast, and even if I had, I couldn't have guessed how *Symbiont* would be affected by changing sea conditions. A wise and experienced sailor keeps himself, his crew, and his boat prepared for the worst conditions, not the best.

Isla Cedros is a large island, almost twenty-one miles long and two-to-nine miles wide. The island is where wind, waves, fog, and other weather can combine to make navigation difficult. Its elevation, mass, and proximity to the east coast of Baja enables it to make its own weather, I suspect (as the fjords in Southeast Alaska and capes nearly anywhere are capable of doing). The island is of volcanic origin culminating in a 3950-foot mountaintop. There is a village toward the south end. Secure anchorages are available all along the east side, very close to the beach.

When I began to have second thoughts about continuing as the weather deteriorated and confused seas required continuous steering, we were beyond the point of returning to San Martin. Tempting me onward was the silhouette of our destination backlit by the setting sun.

Steering had become strenuous and Shearlean and I were taking turns over ever-shortening intervals. I was tired overall, but most alarmingly, my arms and shoulders were growing weak and I was losing my grip on the wheel. Shearlean saw what was happening to me and looked at me with alarm. She repeatedly offered to steer, but she was no match for the wheel. Had I been a better sailor, I might have known how to adjust the sails to shift the center of effort on the hull to balance the forces on the rudder to ease the steering—but I wasn't that sailor.

What was happening, it began to dawn on me, was that Cedros Island was affecting the area's winds and currents in the channel between it and the west coast of the peninsula, creating chaotic sea conditions.

I began fearing I might collapse and from her expression, Shearlean seemed to have the same thought. We looked at each other, searching for something reassuring, but neither of us had anything left to offer. We'd been underway now, working nonstop, for about twenty hours.

Then, I thought of the engine. If I started it and put it in gear, the wash from the propellor over the rudder would be like power steering, amplifying the effect of the rudder on controlling the direction of the boat. I'd still have to steer, but it would require less effort, and maybe I could endure until we got closer to the island shore where the seas might be less agitated.

Shearlean was slumped lifelessly against the companionway bulkhead and didn't respond when I started the engine. I worried whether she was unconscious.

I realized my vision was blurred by tears of exhaustion as I slumped against the steering pedestal, but I was able to maintain my grip on the wheel.

I altered course sharply, directly toward the island, praying to find calmer waters.

Shearlean stirred and stared at me, trying to make sense of my apparent revival. That I was gripping the wheel was answer enough and she lay back and closed her eyes, surrendering to a toxic mixture of fear and exhaustion.

I didn't know a person could get so tired and weak, on the verge of physical collapse, without dying as a result.

As soon I sensed the first signs of calm seas, I changed course to parallel the island and we ran that way until morning. With the steering easier, I could sit and rest while steering, and after a time of inactivity, Shearlean revived enough to go below to find some Chips Ahoy cookies and make coffee.

At first light, we sighted our anchorage. My last reserves were depleted, and I couldn't think clearly. I stared at the cruising guide's diagram of the anchorage with no comprehension. All I wanted to do was stop and no longer be shackled to the wheel.

I released the halyards to drop the headsail onto the deck and then the main onto the boom gallows, and let sails lie where they fell as I crawled forward to the anchor windlass, too weak to stand. The bottom was ninety feet down, but we were well within the anchorage, though still far from the other boats anchored there. I freed the anchor to plunge overboard with a roar of rattling chain, and then the hiss of rope rode as we were carried forward on the incoming tide. The five hundred foot marker appeared, as *Symbiont* lost all of her momentum. I cleated the rope rode and watched wearily as it gradually stiffened, indicating the anchor had set. I did no more. I couldn't move. I thought of just curling up in the stiff folds of the collapsed headsail and going to sleep.

"Sweetie," Shearlean called. "Sweetie?"

I rolled onto my hands and knees and crawled back to the cockpit.

Wordlessly, we went below and shed our clothes, down to our long underwear, and slid beneath the bedding.

We slept the entire day and awakened after dark, sore all over and famished. While Shearlean put out snacks and drinks, I went on deck to look around and to check the anchor rode. The air and water were still, but I lacked any motivation to do anything to tidy up the deck or lash the sails in place.

We ate and drank silently, and went back to bed and slept through the remaining night.

The cruising guides state Turtle Bay is the best all-weather anchorage on this part of the coast—midway down Baja's west coast, south of Pt. Eugene. The entrance is described as wider than it looks, which doesn't change how it looks. The southern point extends about one mile into the entrance with some visible rocks, so you must favor Punta Sargasso, to port. We anchored in four fathoms, in sand, near the pier at the back of the bay.

The wind was blowing hard as we entered Turtle Bay under only a reefed main, but we were still heeled over. Inside the bay, we righted immediately, and felt the dry warmth of the desert wind that prevails inside the bay. We spent three days there, resting, getting warm, and working on the steering gear and vane.

Fuel was available in Turtle Bay at a pier that was falling down in places and needed repairs everywhere. Big boats (or anyone wanting more fuel than they want to carry in jerry jugs) had to drop an anchor and then backdown stern to the pier and tie off. Fuel is pumped through a hose from a large storage tank ashore. Smaller quantities of fuel are siphoned from fifty-five-gallon drums up on the pier. To get up on the pier, you must tie off your dinghy at the foot of a rusted, twenty-foot piece of steel ladder and climb to the top, get your jerry jugs up from your dinghy, find someone to fill them, and then get the heavy jugs back into the dinghy and back to your boat. All very challenging while dealing with the surge throughout the bay. Our way of doing it, which drew a lot of local attention, was to bring along a fifty-foot rope (a spare jib sheet is good), tie the jugs to the line, climb to the top of the ladder, let the other person in the dinghy toss the line up, then hoist the jugs while the second person climbs the rickety ladder using both hands. When the jugs were full, we tied off one end of the line to the dock, ran the free end through a jug, lowered it to within a few feet of the dinghy, swung it in rhythm with the surging dinghy, then let it drop at the right moment. Then we pulled the free end through the jug handle, back up to the dock, and lowered another one. Soon the locals wanted to try their hand at swinging the jugs into the dinghy and make it a contest, but I wasn't interested in playing games in that heat. We used the same method to load provisions into the dinghy. Since the stores ashore had no bags or boxes, we took a sail bag with us to load everything into (including a case of beer) and lowered it into the dinghy. Other yachties were standing around the ladder with dozens of small packages, watching their dinghies dancing in the surge, and wondering how they were going to climb the ladder several times carrying packages, including fragile eggs, without killing themselves or losing everything. I wondered, too.

 We finally met some misfortune. The surge was especially bad, and the tide was very low. As I waited for Shearlean to come down the ladder, a swell carried our inflatable dinghy under the jagged bottom of the disintegrating ladder and then lifted it up, causing a ragged puncture in the forward of three inflation chambers. Shearlean pinched the tear closed and we motored back to *Symbiont*. The only thing I could find to repair it with was wet-suit cement, which lasted until we got to La Paz.

Two American yachtsmen were murdered in Turtle Bay on June 2, 1984, weeks after our visit. We wrote a short news story about the incident for *Cruising World* magazine and interviewed an eyewitness. The full account of it appeared in the mid-June edition of San Diego's *The Log* newspaper, which was quite thorough and accurate, we found. To us and those we talked to it did not seem surprising that if something like that were to happen, it would happen in Turtle Bay. We found it was peculiarly isolated, with an unnatural flow of outsiders passing steadily through by truck and boat. It only required a spark.

Though still four miles east of Cabo San Lucas, cruisers are inclined to celebrate their arrival at their destination on sighting Cabo Falso, when, as we discovered, weather can make Cabo days away from Cabo Falso. With no suitable anchorage for a hundred and fifty miles from Bahia Magdalena, sailing to Cabo must be done in one step. For us, we were heading for Cabo from even farther, from Turtle Bay, three hundred and forty-nine miles distant. Cabo Falso is a high hill and clearly marked with high, white sand dunes. The true end of the Baja peninsula is marked by a cluster of rocks, including the picturesque arch, where you must turn north and then east to sight the Cabo San Lucas harbor entrance, a further four miles. As with all capes, winds can be fickle.

At dawn, after five days at sea when we sighted Cabo Falso, it was surprisingly a couple of miles north of us (I had overstood it in my caution), and we talked excitedly of how nice it would be to be back in familiar Cabo San Lucas. We looked forward to a restaurant meal and some solid rest.

In our excitement, we had failed to pay attention to the increasing frequency and growing height of the swells as we approached Cabo. The wind was building along with the seas, the closer we got.

It had been a moderately hard night, fairly cold, and the steering was becoming difficult. We checked our speed (about five-and-a-half knots under single-reefed main and staysail) around 1:00 p.m.

We had to make some northing, because we had overstood the cape by about five miles, and it was becoming hard to head north-northeast. Checking the chart against the seas and wind conditions showed we couldn't expect any lee before entering the harbor. Hopefully, though, we thought that the wind we were getting might be a local condition and produced by the Cape, and that if we headed due north for a while, or even a little east of north, beyond the cape, we might pick up a different wind and some moderation of the swells.

The swells, though, were getting steeper and were occasionally gigantic, coming from the stern quarter. Once in a while, we got caught by one breaking, sending green water into the cockpit. It soon became imperative that we watch for these swells and turn to run with them, or we stood a good chance of losing control of the boat and broaching. By now, the wind was blowing a steady thirty knots, and the seas were forcing us to steer east-southeast, away from our destination, toward the open sea and the mainland of Mexico, hundreds of miles away.

We were beginning to realize the futility of hoping to make Cabo and decided we'd better concern ourselves with coping with the increasingly treacherous seas.

We had never hove-to in such heavy weather, but according to books and advice of friends, it shouldn't have been any problem. We had no lee shore to worry about: the wind was from offshore, northerly, and the seas were from the north-northwest. I gave Shearlean the helm and went forward to quickly put a second reef in the main and then we turned directly into the wind.

We took a couple of good wallops on the port bow quarter before *Symbiont* settled into the relative tranquility of the slick she was creating to windward. We weren't sure she would remain hove-to with just the main, and so I tried desperately to winch in the staysail, so it would be backwinded and help hold us in place. Even with the big winches, I couldn't force the staysail across and gave up for fear of tearing it and losing my most useful headsail. We lowered the staysail and held our breath, watching the compass and landmarks waiting for the wind and seas to assault us again, but we stayed right there. We finally relaxed and felt a wave of exhaustion wash over us.

We went below and struggled out of our foul-weather gear. Shearlean lay on the leeward settee and I pulled the cushions off the starboard settee and lay down on the cabin sole facing forward, where I could watch the crazily dancing telltale compass above our berth. We were heeled over ten or twelve degrees. We watched and waited, listening to the mainsail slap and snap wickedly. Finally, we were convinced we would remain hove-to. The windspeed hovered between thirty and thirty-five knots.

I looked out through the companionway hatch one more time at the landmarks and saw a huge white ship coming our way. It had been dallying around the entrance to Cabo, probably trying to decide whether to put passengers ashore, then decided not. I got on the VHF, channel 16, and called them, hoping to get some weather information, but they never answered as they passed about five hundred feet to our starboard. I suspected they may have feared I would ask for assistance and did not want to acknowledge my call. They passed on by us, little affected by the seas, probably wondering if we were having fun.

We hailed any vessel in Cabo, and someone came on promptly, a woman on a cruising boat. We told her where we were and asked her what was going on with the weather. We said we had been at sea five days, and the Baja net's weather report had made no mention of these conditions. She said we were having a Norther—a common condition in the cape area. This one had been blowing for two days already and could be expected to last at least another twenty-four hours. That wasn't especially good news, we thought. We went to a cruising guide for more information. The guide said Northers were common here at this time of year, typically producing winds from thirty-to-sixty knots and lasting from three days to a week. We tried to guess where we might drift to if it lasted four more days.

Since it looked like we could be hove-to for a while, I decided to go back up on deck and retie our reefs, secure the sails better, and generally straighten up the boat and make it ready for the coming night, and, perhaps, increased winds.

The quiet and security of the cabin was shattered as soon as I went on deck, and I had to sit for a moment and readapt myself to the pitching deck, crashing seas, and roaring wind. I gathered my courage and went forward to lash down the headsails. Just as I stepped onto the bow pulpit, *Symbiont* plunged deep into a huge swell, immersing me to the knees and making me feel momentarily buoyant.

Next, I climbed atop the lashed-down dinghy and methodically re-tied the main luff and clew, re-lashed the intermediate reef, and paid little attention to the wind and seas. Becoming casual and relaxed, I looked up from my work and looked straight at the oncoming bow of a speeding Mexican freighter. From where I sat, it was headed right for our beam. In the fading light, in these seas and in our small white boat, I wondered whether we were visible. We had a good radar reflector hoisted on the backstay, but if no one was looking at their radar, that would do us no good. I watched, trying to decide if it was just the angle. It was only about a quarter mile away. I jumped into the cockpit, ripped the companionway hatch open, and yelled to Shearlean to hand me our portable strobe and a flare gun. Frightened and dumbfounded, she just stared at me. "Now," I screamed. She ran to fetch what I wanted. I hung the strobe on the stern pulpit, and it started to flash. I loaded the flare gun with the intention of firing directly at the ship's bridge. I never could perceive that the ship had altered course, but it began to appear it would miss us. It passed about two hundred feet astern and threw a wake I feared might upset the balance of our hove-to position. We remained in place.

That was a hazard we hadn't counted on this close to the tip of Baja. We were lying hove-to in the shipping lanes between the Mexican mainland and the northern ports. Back below, we talked about the shipping hazard and decided there really wasn't much we could do about it. I decided to leave the strobe flashing all night and hoped no one would interpret it as the distress signal it properly is. We didn't want to be rescued. We opened a can of stew and ate, then fell asleep.

Sometime around midnight, we awoke to find the wind was moderating a little, gusts were still up around thirty-five knots, but at times, it was dropping to twenty-five. I looked out and saw the lights of San Jose del Cabo visible off to port. The knot meter was indicating a half knot or so, and the log showed we'd moved about five miles up the coast. The shore looked a little nearer, but it didn't appear we were forereaching excessively. We should be fine until dawn, we decided. Just in case we needed it, I decided to start the engine. I pushed the start switch and there was only a dull click. Impossible, I thought. In three years, there had never been a starting problem. I switched all batteries to the starter and got the same dead click. It looked like we'd have to sail back to Cabo.

About 4:00 a.m., *Symbiont* lost her hove-to position and we woke immediately. By the time I got on deck she was back, hove-to, again. The wind was dying, gusting only occasionally to about fifteen knots. It would be dawn soon, so we began preparations to get under way for Cabo. I thought, what do we have to lose, I tried the engine one more time. It started right up. We laughed and jumped for joy. We'd be in Cabo in little over an hour.

We motored through the stillness of anchored and moored boats in the outer harbor. The sea and sky were the matching tarnished silver of early dawn.

We circled around a huge tuna boat anchored near the breakwater at the inner harbor. A seaman, a cigarette and coffee mug in his hand, looked down at us from the bridge deck and offered us a big smile and a thumbs-up sign. He knew where we'd been and what we'd been through.

"Well done," he'd said, silently.

We looked at each other in our bulky, yellow foul-weather gear, pride shining through our tiredness, and wordlessly agreed with the appraisal.

"Dear Mom and Dad," I began a long overdue letter I owed my parents about our departure to Baja. "It seems like a long time ago, but it has only been three months since we began our cruise to Mexico. We're still getting settled here in La Paz and trying to get everyone caught up on what's been happening to us and what we've been doing. I hope this won't be too intimidating because of its length."

The letter dated August 8, 1984, and mailed for me by an American tourist returning to the U.S., recounted the foregoing ordeal of getting to Cabo and our ultimate arrival in La Paz and our immersion in the cruising life.[6]

---

[6] See https://oceanoftime.robertaduke.com/letter-home for the complete text.

Cruiser's Baja

At Cabo San Lucas, the cape is a spectacular extension of eastward running rocky hills and pinnacles, surrounded by small, outlying rocks. Opposite is a long, white, sandy beach forming the outer harbor, with moorings and available for anchoring. The beach is entirely open to southeast weather.

The inner harbor is enclosed by the town, ferry terminal, and marinas. Space to anchor in the inner harbor is limited. Most cruisers anchored in the outer harbor, which was inconvenient and uncomfortable, because it was exposed to weather. Most cruisers were only visitors to Cabo and chose to head up the Sea of Cortez for La Paz and the safety of its huge bay. The prime cruising area of Baja's east coast was from La Paz north to Santa Rosalia.

I'd been to Cabo a couple of times earlier, on yacht club junkets with groups and with Baja Bob on our peninsula drive. Cabo was a tourist mecca, sometimes referred to as Newport Beach-South, though many visitors were from elsewhere. Its boating reputation was founded on sportfishing, mainly for marlin. While the length of Baja abounded with fishing resorts, Cabo was homeport to big private and charter sportfishing boats with full-time professional crews. When not fishing, it was time to party and indulge in excesses that would be taboo at home (in Newport Beach or Hollywood). Many second homes, time shares, and condos had been constructed, effectively walling off the harbor and the scenic cape from public view. From Cabo to San Jose del Cabo, a few miles east, it was all golf courses, resorts, and condos: Fonatur's, the government tourism developer's huge success, which it was trying to duplicate elsewhere on the peninsula.

La Paz was the capital of Baja Sur, and a "working" Mexican town, with a commercial fishing fleet, and populated with indigenous residents raising families, with modest means and modest aspirations. I felt it was an authentic population, whereas Cabo's population was contrived. Of course, La Paz had its aspirational element, but it was a minority. I noticed, too, La Paz was preferred by European and mainland Mexican tourists.

Baja offers the unique experience of cruising in the desert. It can be likened to hot air ballooning along the Grand Canyon's rim—skimming along silently under sail among cactuses.

The Sonoran Desert covers a hundred thousand square miles, including all of Baja. It takes time and patience to discover the beauty of the flooded desert that is the Sea of Cortez, a colorful wonderland of fish and marine mammals. Summer's water temperature can equal the desert's air temperature. I recall when scuba diving, experiencing no chilling sensation on entering the water, until diving twenty or thirty feet to where there was a thermocline. In the winter, the sea is the same temperature as the Pacific Ocean, around fifty-five degrees. Though coral reefs are rare, there are hours of good snorkeling in the sparkling waters with rays, sea turtles, and dense, billowing clouds of silvery fish and colorful geology, a bit like swimming through a Jacques Cousteau special, but not everyone sees it the same way.

"There's not much to see here. The place is desolate," a Long Beach couple explained to me aboard their boat in La Paz, one day. "We've been here three weeks. Sailed up to Loreto and back and saw it all. We're ready to leave."

Occasionally, in a marina slip, we were the object of interest of American tourists, usually day-trippers from Cabo. They would pause on the dock to look at us sitting in *Symbiont's* cockpit and ask, "What do you do here all day?" This was followed by a mildly apologetic expression and weak smile.

"We watch the sun set and the pelicans returning from their day of fishing. Read. Nap." Shearlean would most often answer contentedly.

The beauty of Baja is rarely gaudy, and it has its seasons and moods. I saw some of the most beautiful sights of my life in Baja's Sea of Cortez. Most often they were subtle, transient sights that required an investment of time to fully appreciate it, but well worth the effort. The sights made a deeper impression on me than the bolder, more striking beauty of Tahiti or Hawaii. Eventually, I would spend twenty-five years seeing Baja by land and sea, and was never disappointed, and always craved another visit.[7]

From La Paz, cruisers have easy access to the length and breadth of the Sea of Cortez, with many easy-to-reach destinations offering safe, secure anchorages. The heart of the cruising area, though, is the hundred and twenty miles between La Paz and Loreto, and all of the islands in between.

About thirty miles north of La Paz is Isla San Francisquito, with a beautiful anchorage at the south end that I think could justify being named Valentine Cove. Startling shades of red continuously evolve there through the day as the sun crosses the sky and the whole cove dramatically changes its appearance from hour to hour. The entire northern cliff's red face is transmuted from plum to raspberry to brick by the sun's passage.

---

[7] See https://oceanoftime.robertaduke.com/baja/ for more information on Baja.

In La Paz, cruisers distribute themselves pretty evenly throughout the waterfront, roughly the length of the *malecón*, in three primary areas.

Main Beach, Downtown

Mooring and anchoring off the expansive beach in downtown La Paz was the most popular location, lively and convenient. You could dinghy into the beach, where it was safe to leave the dinghy, and walk anywhere you needed to go. Municipal water faucets dotted the beach for replenishing your boat's fresh water supply. Moorings were available for rent in case you didn't trust your ground tackle or planned not to move again for a while.

South Central, Downtown

There were slips available with the conveniences of a marina (water, electricity, and bathrooms) where cruisers could step ashore any time. Shroyer's full-service American-style Marina de La Paz and Abaroa's Mexican boatyard, were two.

Back Bay

Farther into the bay, on the fringe of downtown, was the Marina Gran Baja where Alberto Alvarez-Morphy's National Operations Company (NOA) offered facilities adjacent to the twelve story Hotel Gran Baja. Alberto offered moorings (then under development) and a crude pier constructed of a welded oil drilling pipe framework paved with concrete slabs, with slips on two sides. The ruins of an abandoned motel dominated the site, but at the head of the pier, Alberto had constructed an office and restrooms, with showers, and the rudiments of an outdoor bar he often talked of completing "*mañana*." Alberto was rumored to be the exiled, black-sheep son of an oil-rich Mexican family. A brother we met and dined with, without Alberto, lived part-time in La Paz. Alberto was hospitable and helpful, but inevitably vague and superficial. The single best word to describe Alberto was courteous. He was probably in his mid-forties and most of what we knew about him came from others, including two Americans who worked for him, Brett Helton and Jeff Fisher, and his English-speaking Mexican staff, Ernesto and Maria.

Marina Gran Baja was associated with Stevens Yachts of Annapolis in a joint venture to develop a bareboat charter business in La Paz. Currently, there was one boat available for charter, *Sun Dance*, a forty-foot Steven's cutter.

We made sure Alberto knew we were writing for yachting magazines read by Americans he hoped to attract to his charter business, in particular *Sail Magazine* and *Cruising World* magazine on the U.S. east coast and *Sea Magazine* on the U.S. west coast.

Anchoring was free throughout La Paz bay, but I believe few cruisers trusted their ground tackle, so those staying in La Paz for long rented a mooring or got a slip. Though I was a ground tackle fanatic, I was convinced a mooring was better than the best I could do that would endure the surging "La Paz waltz," caused by the daily tide, and rented one of Alberto's moorings.

I had watched the moorings being fabricated on the beach and put in place in the mooring field.

In a grassy palm-shaded area on the beach side of the abandoned motel, a squad of Alberto's laborers was fabricating two metric-ton mooring blocks from hand-mixed buckets of concrete. They had only the simplest hand tools, and I marveled at their tenacity in manually moving a twenty-two hundred pound cube of concrete, all sharp corners and edges, across the grass, through the beach sand, and into the water until it was submerged. Next, they positioned the twin hulls of a derelict Hobie catamaran over the block and raised it a few inches off the sea bottom with a rusty, manual come along winch, and paddled or swam the Hobie to the mooring area, and lowered the block to the bottom, twenty-to-thirty feet deep. Back on shore, they briefly celebrated, and then set to work building the next one.

Saga of Jerry and Gayle

There were a handful of cruisers who found solitary anchorages for themselves in niches along the shore, suitable for just one boat. One couple was Jerry and Gayle Smith from Tennessee—Shearlean's home state. We got to know them well. They discovered, thanks to the seasonal Mexican monsoons, that their niche was actually the outfall for the main La Paz city storm sewer. When the monsoon overwhelmed the sanitation sewer system, which happened with every monsoon, the overflow was diverted to the storm sewer system, causing a real stink. The Smiths didn't move, though, because all of La Paz bay was affected, only slightly less than them. Besides, they asked rhetorically, how many monsoons like that will there be?

Jerry and Gayle had purchased their twenty-two-foot Falmouth cutter and took delivery of it in Newport Beach and sailed to La Paz. They spent the 1984/85 season in La Paz and shipped the boat back to Tennessee from Mexico by rail. Jerry was a Nashville recording studio musician. Gayle, with her heavy southern accent, taught La Paz school children English. I wondered what kind of accented English her students learned.

On their way south from Newport Beach, Jerry and Gayle mistook Isla Cedros for Isla Guadalupe a hundred and sixty-five miles away and sailed east for two days into Scammon's Lagoon, where their engine failed. They had to beat northwest for three days to clear Punta Eugenia before they could turn to run south again, which added five days to their passage to Cabo.

Other Cruisers

Some Baja cruisers had overstayed their original intentions, having apparently caught a severe case of Mexico's *"mañana* fever." Les and Joyce Fryer arrived in 1979, intending to spend a few weeks before sailing for Tahiti aboard their twenty-eight-foot sloop *Cygnus*. By 1984, they didn't talk about Tahiti anymore.

Other mature, retired couples found the strain of sailing and the stress of confined living aboard a boat, in a foreign country, were more than their relationships could endure—a common situation, varying only in degree. The most frequently cited confrontation was (He) "I'm going; are you coming?" and (She) "No way," when questioned about sailing for Tahiti. The distances were great, and the destinations varied, but the principle was often the same. Few women were enthusiastic about long-distance cruising (as Reanne Hemingway-Douglass' book title exemplified, *One Man's Dream, One Woman's Nightmare*, about sailing around Cape Horn).

Brett and Deborah Helton now had unexpected crew onboard, baby Derek. Birth control pills don't work if they're vomited overboard by seasickness, and who even thought about that when the stormy Pacific was at its worst. Safe and sound, anchored in La Paz, Deborah was appalled to discover she was going to give birth within the Mexican medical system. Upset and resentful, cruising wasn't going to be what she and Brett had anticipated. There was now an infant's swing permanently mounted in their boat's rigging, and Brett had had to find a job to cover new "cruising" expenses, so he was working part time for NAO yachts, for Alberto.

Some men were faking it, just keeping the dream alive, counting on their partners to save them from themselves, from facing up to something they now had serious doubts about doing. She'd had enough just getting to Baja and was yearning for the comforts and conveniences of life ashore, and was wishing he'd come to his senses. Some women jumped ship permanently, others made frequent trips home, and a handful, who liked La Paz and Mexican ways, moved ashore, as did Venus.

Venus

Venus, maybe around fifty, was Marguerite's marine VHF radio handle. She had had all she could take of living aboard with husband, Carl. She jumped ship, and found a waterfront apartment downtown, just off the Malecón, where she hosted a weekly open house for cruisers and others. Besides befriending cruisers and adding life to the La Paz maritime radio net, she involved herself in the community by founding the Children of La Paz foundation, offering a lunch program for children and scholarships for low-income students. For me, when my chronic back problem became painful, she gave me helpful acupressure treatments, and revealed that "chiropractor" in Spanish is spelled with a "Q."

On June 28, 2004, nineteen years after we'd returned from La Paz, we learned, in a letter from her daughter, Juliet, that Venus had died. She'd loved living in Mexico, the letter said, and the family scattered her ashes in the Sea of Cortez.

The Net

Venus was just one of the many regulars who participated every morning on the radio network open to anyone who had a marine VHF radio and was interested in news and rumors, or was looking for information or had advice to offer. The biggest net issue I recall was how, when, and whether the city would figure out how to charge cruisers for the water they got from the public faucets along the downtown beach. I often listened to the net, but never participated. To me, it was just rumors and rumors of rumors, and many participants were either know-it-alls or know-nothings, though occasionally, someone was helped.

Our Visitors

A trio of our favorite newspaper people came to see firsthand what had become of their former editor. Randy Lewis, music critic for the *Times*, his wife, Debbie, and Benjamin Epstein, a general assignment reporter, accepted our invitation to visit us in La Paz in October. They took a taxi up from the airport near Cabo to the Hotel Gran Baja where they spent the night. The next day, we took them on the boat for an overnight trip.

Shearlean greeted them with a lot of feeling, instantly turning tearful and speechless, and hugging everyone twice. Over drinks, there was news of others and the never-ending "buzz" of what was going on in Orange County editorial, and "Downtown," where all the big decisions came from. I sat back, silent, and enjoyed seeing Shearlean so animated and in her former element.

Shearlean had sacrificed her dream for mine, much, I'm ashamed to say, beyond my comprehension for too long, but which I eventually came to fully appreciate. It had been Shearlean's dream to be a journalist for one of the nation's top two newspapers: the *New York Times* or the *Los Angeles Times*. At age twenty-six, with just two years of experience, she had landed a staff writer's job with the Orange County edition of the *Los Angeles Times* and then resigned after twelve years, in 1984, to go cruising. The *Times* was referred to by its staff and within the profession as the velvet coffin. The pay and prestige were terrific, and in print journalism, there was no place up to go from there. Some people struggled their whole career to get in the door of such publications, and here was thirty-eight-year-old Shearlean Duke walking away from it. And Shearlean was still in a bit of shock herself, realizing what she'd done and fearing her professional life might be over. Somehow, Shearlean and I never actually talked about it face-to-face. I think because I was genuinely oblivious (it was just a job) and she was so loving as to not want to blame me. Rather, it slowly sunk into my consciousness, and I eventually read her journal entries when writing this memoir, and heard conversations, such as she was having now with former colleagues.

Ironically, the position Shearlean filled had been vacated by a reporter named Lael Morgan, who had taken a leave of absence to go on a yacht with her husband, Dodge Morgan, on an extended cruise. She elected not to return from her leave of absence, and the *Times* replaced her with Shearlean.

Randy and Benjamin had hosted Shearlean's going-away party at the *Times*. With no room on a boat for anything unnecessary, they wisely asked Shearlean what would be a useful going-away gift. She told them we could use a twenty-two-pound Danforth anchor, as we had no stern anchor in case one was needed. This had apparently caused hilarity and confusion, as neither man had ever before purchased an anchor. Further, gift-wrapping it disintegrated into laughing hysteria, until they decided to just present it to her in a large brown grocery bag. The actual occasion was, I'd heard, a somber affair with so many of her well-wishers genuinely concerned about why she would do this.

Three-to-four hours outside of La Paz were two islands, Espiritu Santo and Partida. At the north end of Partida were Los Islotes, home to a colony of friendly sea lions, and there were several good anchorages nearby for a visit to the beach and an overnight stay. (*Symbiont* had space for three overnight guests on two settees and in the quarter berth.) We arrived before noon and were greeted by a dozen sea lions frisking among the rocks and around the boat. I offered our guests the use of our snorkeling gear so they could swim with the sea lions, but all declined, so we floated there for half an hour and then headed back the way we came, a short distance to Caleta Partida, a volcanic crater and good overnight anchorage. I anchored and put the dinghy in the water, and after lunch, we paddled ashore and roamed around the deserted island. I expected our night to be uneventful, but long after dark, the boat began surging in response to freak winds shearing off the cliffs. We were anchored in thirty feet over a good sand bottom, on all chain, but I was concerned our friends might be apprehensive. Instead, they found the commotion exciting, and went on deck to get the full effect of the wind.

Later in October, Shearlean's nephew, nine-year-old Jeff Bain, spent three days with us at the nearby islands.

Most Baja cruisers were from the west coast of North America (except Jerry and Gayle who came to Baja from Tennessee and returned to Tennessee from Baja) and included many Canadians, mainly from British Columbia, but from as far east as Alberta, Canada. A handful of international sailors arrived through the Panama Canal or a few laying over here while circumnavigating the globe.

It was a crossroads and a world-class destination. Cruising in the desert versus palm-fringed coral lagoons was an attraction, as was the friendly host nation, Mexico. A few crossed the Sea of Cortez to Guaymas, in Sonora, Mexico, to what was often referred to as the mainland, because many thought of Baja as though it were an island, which in many ways it was. Some of those who crossed continued down Mexico's west coast to Acapulco and on to Costa Rica, the Panama Canal, and the Caribbean.

Hurricane Season

Baja Sur was vulnerable to hurricanes from June 1 to October 15. Because *Symbiont* was financed, it had to be insured, and marine insurance dictated that we had to be in La Paz by May 15, where there was acceptable sheltered anchorage available.

There are no half-measures in preparing for a hurricane. Even if the ultimate storm never comes, its threat dictates real preparation. If we're going to ride out the storm on our boat, we've got more than our boat at stake, we're risking our lives. There's only one way to do it.[8]

Regalo! Writing Our Own Baja Cruising Guide

We had arrived in Baja with our own boat, but were temporarily restricted by insurance to La Paz. In June, Alberto offered us the gift of his single charter boat, the forty-foot Steven's cutter, *Sundance*, with a crew consisting of resident charter skipper Jeff Fisher and first mate Joyce Johnston. Alberto wanted Shearlean and me to draft a cruising guide for his burgeoning bareboat charter business. With Jeff's in-depth local knowledge, I would gain the best possible information about anchorages, attractions, and hazards between La Paz and Loreto.[9]

---

[8] See https://oceanoftime.robertaduke.com/baja/ to read "Almost A Hurricane," an article I published about real hurricane preparations for a hurricane false alarm.
[9] See https://oceanoftime.robertaduke.com/baja/ to read "The Sea of Cortez is a Savage Beauty," the article I published as a guide to cruising in Baja.

My Personal Baja

By creating my own Baja cruising guide, thanks to Alberto and Jeff, Shearlean and I visited nearly every anchorage and destination between La Paz and Loreto in just two weeks. This allowed us to focus on spending most of our personal time in the places we liked best without worrying we'd overlooked anything. As a bonus, we got to know a lot more Mexican people and to intimately experience life outside of La Paz. The cruisers, too, beyond La Paz were of a different ilk.

My two favorite anchorages were Puerto Escondido and Honeymoon Cove, which we returned to many times and where we stayed for extended periods. Just sailing anywhere in the area was a pleasurable pastime and with plenty of good anchorages throughout the area. We wandered along without worrying about reaching any particular destination.

On our own, we would come and go from La Paz as whim and necessity dictated, never with any schedule. The essence of cruising was never having a schedule. The places we returned to most often were these:

Near Puerto Escondido was the first of Spain's California missions, founded in 1567, in nearby Loreto. It was the largest city on the west coast of North America by 1752.

A true hurricane hole, secure from all bad weather, Escondido means "hidden," and it is literally true. You can be almost in it and not able to see the bay from the deck of a boat. The anchorage was secure enough so that cruisers who had to temporarily leave their boats unattended in Baja (strictly against Mexican law, then), left them here.

Nearby was an administrative military post, with a half-dozen soldiers, and up the access road toward Highway 1 was Tripui RV Park, with a small store whose shelves were nearly bare all summer when rains turned riverbeds that the bridgeless highway spanned into raging, impassable torrents.

This was also the point where the Sierra de la Giganta mountain chain came down to the sea, leaving only a narrow ledge for Highway 1 to cling to on its route to La Paz. Across the highway, within walking distance of the anchorage, was Trabor Canyon, a trail through a cleft in the rock face that led to a shaded shallow pool which attracted cruisers seeking relief from the intense heat. Swarms of white butterflies always dotted the muddy brown banks of the pool, disappearing in the dazzling sunlight and rematerializing in the shade.

Loreto/Nopolo area was a happening place in 1984, undergoing the Fonatur tourist development regimen, with a new hotel offering world-class championship tennis courts. Some of Loreto's dirt streets got paved, and private investment arrived to open restaurants and shops, and more convenient airline flights now served Loreto International Airport.

During one of our visits to Puerto Escondido, I took the bus back to La Paz and brought back our truck so we could explore the remote areas between Nopolo and Mulegé.

Though not in the genre we wrote for, such tennis and golf developments were bound to impact cruisers and other marine recreation audiences. We'd heard from Sr. Soto at the tourism office that the official opening of the center was scheduled for when we would be there. Carmaker Ford of Mexico was the sponsor, and the arrangements were expected to be grand and glamorous.

At the El Presidente Hotel tennis center, the day of the event, we found actor Robert Loggia vacationing after the filming of *The Jagged Edge,* dawdling over a poolside breakfast in relaxed conversation with tennis master Ilie Năstase. Academy award winner Tatum O'Neal and boyfriend/tennis champ John McEnroe were joined for dinner by actor Ben Vereen, causing the film crew from *Lifestyles of The Rich and Famous* to hastily reorganize their videotaping plans.

The place was buzzing with Ford executives, professional tennis stars, Fonatur executives, PR staff, and local officials and dignitaries—a most unlikely crowd for the desolate east coast of Baja near Loreto. It was surreal. There were three days of intense activity as the program played out. On the fourth day, everyone had departed, creating an eerie silence and self-doubt about whether the previous three days had been real. The hotel and tennis courts were deserted.

I was to learn that such events were an infrequent but constant occurrence throughout Baja over the twenty-five years I traveled there. Some developments took root and bore fruit, but many others withered and took a severe financial toll on local residents who gambled on their success.

With our truck, we were immediately welcomed by cruisers and locals, but not taxi drivers, for transportation between Puerto Escondido and Loreto. The military post soldiers had no form of transportation, and often depended on cruisers to shop for groceries for them. With more than seventy boats anchored in the bay, there was always a cruiser looking for a ride to or from Loreto.

Honeymoon Cove

Close to Puerto Escondido was Isla Danzante with an anchorage designated Honeymoon Cove, the antithesis of Escondido's population of seventy anchored boats, with space for only one boat. We anchored there a half-dozen times, for two days to a week at a time, luxuriating in the exclusivity and contentment afforded by the picture-book cove. The cove was walled on two sides by fifty-foot stone cliffs and closed at the back by a rounded, sloping hill rising about a hundred feet. At the foot of the hill was a perfect little fine sand beach that was continually manicured back to perfection by each high tide. Yellow-green grass covered the beach above high tide, and cactus and tiny shrubs dotted the rising backdrop of cliffs and hills.

The water was alive with clouds of fish, drifting just under the surface. These schools were under attack from dawn till dusk by predatory fish from below and hungry pelicans from above. Pelicans sat on rock ledges against the face of the cliff watching with great seriousness for their feeding opportunities. Those sitting on the low rocks at the water's edge needed only to fall forward, headfirst and mouth agape, to land in the midst of a passing meal.

Early every morning, at first light, the stillness of the cove was shattered by splashing water. Until you hear it, you won't believe that there are so many variations on a single, basic sound. The tiniest fish makes a rustling on the water like a breeze through a leafy tree; the bigger fish make a sound like stones skipping across a pond as they break the surface in pursuit of the swirling schools. Individual pelicans make huge *kersplashes* like a bucket of water being dumped into the sea. Then, as pelicans take off, their feet and wings make little splashes like a happy child frolicking in a bath. Occasionally, squadrons of fifteen or more pelicans fly in a ragged line of staggered altitudes until the lead bird sights fish and dives headlong into the water, followed rapidly by the others. This sounds like a bunch of rowdy boys chasing each other in a swimming hole, and doing belly flops and cannonballs as they hit the water.

Because of the commotion, most mornings it was impossible to stay in bed more than five minutes beyond first light. Stepping out on deck into the brilliant sunlight, immersed in the sounds of nature, stretching, there's no urge to leave.

Agua Verde

We visited Agua Verde several times, but it was never a purposeful destination, yet each visit was memorable and enjoyable. For some reason, the water there was vivid green and plagued by swarms of hornets (also green), as soon as the boat was anchored. The hornets never attacked, but you had to always be careful where you rested your hand or sat down, or you might receive a painful sting. The villagers were friendly, but never intrusive—no kids swimming out to the boat asking for candy or offering trinkets for sale and no fishermen coming alongside, unbidden, offering the day's catch.

This was a genuinely remote village. Twice, on highway trips, I was determined to drive the forty kilometers of dirt road from Highway 1 to the village, but after fifteen minutes or so, I turned back at the prospect of the jarring, dusty return trip. I would try again some other time.

I guess we stopped there often because the snorkeling was good, the anchorage was secure, and its distance from Puerto Escondido made it a convenient place to rest. Agua Verde was thirty miles by water from Loreto, the nearest town.

Then, on one visit we became aware of the desperation that shrouded everyday life lived at the end of a long, rugged road. A *panga* bearing a man and child startled us when it bumped against *Symbiont's* hull, and the man timidly began speaking and pointing at the child. Shearlean wrote an article about what transpired that was published in *Sail Magazine*. [10]

The Sea of Cortez cruising guide we relied on was *Charlie's Charts: Western Coast of Mexico and Baja* by Charles E. Wood. It consisted of heavily annotated, hand-drawn charts. I confess it took me a long time to get used to using it, probably my fault. I had difficulty identifying distant landmarks in time for them to guide me to my destination. For some perverse reason, they didn't become obvious to me until I was so close I no longer needed them.

---

[10] See https://oceanoftime.robertaduke.com/baja/ to read "A Gift for Agua Verde."

Going Home

Writing was a highly portable profession, and Shearlean and I had applied ourselves diligently, but all we'd been able to earn was $14,000[11] over the past year. On balance, we had worked more than we played, though it had all been fun and interesting. But it was clearly over and it was time to sail back to Newport Beach—before boat insurance trapped us in La Paz again until October 1. We'd maxed out our credit cards, had no health insurance, and had only Mexican auto insurance.

We could go home, but we couldn't go back to what we had left. We were no longer who we had been and what we now wanted wasn't what we previously had. In cruising, we had found something we wanted, but being unable to embrace it in the form that we found it, we were confused about what to do next. How could we prevent going back from undoing everything we had achieved?

We had to start over again in order to remedy our mistakes (like a boat with a loan against it) and to come up with a more sustainable plan.

---

[11] Sample 1985 magazine paid invoices: "Going South" *Sea* $300, "Baja is Different" *Sea* $225, "How to Snorkel" *Waterfront* $200, "Cygnus V" *Waterfront* $200, "Emergency Procedures" *Cruising World* $600, "Baja Facilities Update" *Sea* $225.

A good thing about Baja was that it wasn't half a world away (like Tahiti) from where we'd come from. In fact, we now saw it as sort of an extension of our home port, handily attached physically to the bottom of what the Spanish had christened "Upper California," our home state, and connected by a highway and airports. Thanks to having the luxury of a year to explore Baja Sur by highway and sea, we met Mark Walters, third-generation owner of Rancho Buena Vista, a sportfishing resort in the east cape area of Baja Sur, roughly midway between La Paz and San Jose del Cabo. I wrote a feature article about Mark and his resort for *Motor Boating & Sailing Magazine*, which the magazine titled, "The King Of Marlin." In the process of writing about Mark and Rancho Buena Vista (RBV), I learned that fishing in the east cape was too poor from late July through mid-September to attract resort guests, so Mark closed the resort and went to property he owned in Oregon each summer. He liked having someone in his house on the resort property while he was gone, but two months in the Sonoran Desert, even beside the sea, was unappealing to even his best of friends. For Shearlean and I, it was a wonderful opportunity—far more appealing than the same time spent there on a boat. We offered to house-sit Mark's home from July 22 to September 15, starting that summer of 1985.

Though we were taking *Symbiont* back to Newport Beach, we weren't done with Baja. That chapter in our life wouldn't be over until 2007, when we parked our RV on the cliff beside Mark's house, overlooking the resort and beach at Rancho Buena Vista in Los Barriles for a final visit.

Leaving La Paz for the U.S. was nothing like leaving the U.S. for Mexico. We had been cruising all day, every day, for a year, and departure day was like any other day, just sailing in a different direction. Arriving and departing was the natural flow of cruising. I knew I'd be back in just a couple of weeks to pick up the truck, and Shearlean and I would be back in a couple of months to house-sit Mark's place about an hour south of La Paz off Highway 286. I was pleased to not be grieving over being forced to return to California.

We did tell the La Paz port captain we were taking *Symbiont* back to the U.S., and we looked in on Sr. Soto at the tourism office to let him know we would be returning, and we bid *adios* to Alberto and his staff at Marina Grand Baja. I made sure he understood I would return in a few weeks to pick up my truck parked on his property.

Getting Underway

With just a touch of sadness, we motored out of La Paz harbor for what we realized was the last time, and scanned the waterfront to capture a lasting impression. Last-minute chores and getting *Symbiont* ready for sea had been tiring, so we planned to anchor early and arrived at Ensenada de los Muertos in the late afternoon. Its white sand beach was deserted, but the fish camp near the ruins of a pier was occupied. We anchored in four fathoms and noticed the slight Pacific roll reaching us from around the cape. Los Muertos, the cruising guide notes, has always been an active anchorage because of its road to La Paz.

Arriving at Cabo the following evening, we found room to anchor in the inner harbor for easy dinghy access to replenish the diesel fuel we had consumed coming from La Paz, for shopping Shearlean needed to do, and for a bon voyage dinner we felt we owed ourselves. Back at *Symbiont*, I pulled the dinghy onboard and tied it securely to the trunk cabin and padlocked the outboard on the stern rail to frustrate any opportunistic thief.

We hadn't been in the open ocean for more than a year and needed to prepare ourselves for big swells and sailing out of sight of land and being underway all night *en route* to Bahia Magdalena, the first available anchorage, a hundred and sixty miles north of Cabo. Our cruising between La Paz and Loreto had basically been in sheltered waters, always in sight of land with secure anchorages seldom more than an hour away.

Apprehensive as I was, I was unprepared for the ease with which we rounded Cabo Falso and headed out to sea, away from rocks and current, and the treacherous lee shore. We intended to follow our practice of sailing offshore at night and sailing back on shore during daylight. We'd done all of this before and we were retracing a familiar route in a tried-and-true vessel, with home ultimately over the horizon.

To document our voyage home and update my parents about our travels, Shearlean began a letter to my parents in her computer journal, starting April 12, 1985, when we anchored in Bahia Santa Maria (Mag Bay), the second day after departing Cabo.

Dear Bud and Martha,

We traveled a hundred and sixty miles from Cabo San Lucas up the Pacific side of Baja and to our great pleasure (and relief) the weather has been outstanding. Our trip from Cabo to here was forty hours, nonstop, of course. There are no safe anchorages between here and there.

So far, the weather is better than it was on the way down the coast! It has been so calm that for two days running, we were able to play backgammon on a non-magnetic board on the cockpit table while underway with the autopilot steering.

We are laying over a day here in Mag Bay to rest. And what a day this has been. Our lucky day. Wish you were here. All you'd have to bring is the white wine and we'd have a feast. Let me explain:

Bahia Santa Maria is a ten-mile long, beautiful, wind-swept bay, not frequented by many yachts. Today we are the only boat here. Imagine Newport Harbor with only one lone sailboat at anchor and you get the picture. Around noon, a local Mexican panga went zooming by, loaded with his catch of the day. Since we are out of fresh meat and fish, except for one chicken, we flagged him down. He turned out to be an abalone diver. As we have learned before, on this side of the coast, fishermen prefer to trade for their goods. Money here is fairly useless to them. There is nothing to spend it on. Favorite trade items are whiskey, cigarettes, and .22 caliber bullets (for hunting rabbits) and sports team T-shirts.

Knowing this from our trip down last April, we stocked up; so we traded a carton of Marlboros and two Lakers #32 (Magic Johnson) T-shirts for eight big abalones. Eight abalones, to give you some idea, pounded out and sliced for serving, equals about three pounds.

We were ecstatic. Abalone for dinner. Our mouths watered as we continued our boat chores in preparation for our departure tomorrow.

Then, at 3:00 p.m., a big Mexican shrimp boat entered the bay. It seemed to be headed straight toward us. In this huge harbor, why would they want to anchor so close, we wondered. We got a little sweaty-palmed as they steered for our stern, closing in and only fifty feet away. Bob kept waving them away; they kept coming. I thought maybe it was a Mexican game of chicken.

Then, as they were right on our stern, one seaman shouted in English, "Cigarettes?" All I could think of was: "I'll give them the damned carton to keep them from ramming us." Funny, but it never occurred to me that they wanted to trade. I ran below, picked up six packs of Marlboros and ran topsides, holding the Marlboros high so they could see them. The seaman nodded and yelled: "Camarones?"

They wanted to trade shrimp for cigarettes. I couldn't believe our good fortune. What a deal. But you ain't heard nothing yet. Neither the shrimper nor we had a dinghy ready to launch so we had to figure out a way to transfer our trade goods. Bob stuffed the Marlboros in a plastic bag, packed the bag in a plastic toolbox, ran a rope through the handle of the toolbox and threw it overboard. The box drifted toward the shrimper and a seaman hooked it and hauled it aboard. Then, the seaman put some shrimp into the toolbox and Bob hauled it back. We couldn't see what he put in and didn't really expect much.

Well . . . have you ever seen shrimp the size of a Buick? We have a whole toolbox full of them. I swear. Biggest shrimp I have ever seen. What can I say? Wish you were here . . . with a bottle of Chardonnay. Our big decision now is: Do we eat the shrimp or the abalone for dinner? Pigs that we are, we decided to compromise, shrimp cocktail for appetizer, abalone for dinner. I imagine we'll be eating shrimp and abalone three times a day for a week. But who's complaining?

Anchored at Isla Asuncion, we had a very sobering, interesting, reflective experience yesterday involving another cruiser—a terrified fifty-ish former Hollywood stuntman. It began when I answered a call on the VHF radio from a man hailing anyone near Asunción. He sounded nervous, upset, desperate for human contact. He began by asking if we had any crew aboard who would help him take his boat north to Turtle Bay (our next stop) only forty-eight miles away. From Asunción, Turtle is an easy one-day trip, not even an over-nighter. Turns out the man and his wife were anchored in nearby Asunción Bay, but we couldn't see them because of the fog. We told them we were planning to come in there when the fog lifted and explained that we were anchored nearby off the island, only half a mile away. They sounded relieved when we volunteered to come visit and talk to him. Bob and I both detected fear and desperation in his voice. He vaguely mentioned an accident off Cedros Island and admitted that he was scared and ready to give up cruising and return home to the U.S. When we got to Bahia Asunción, he called again and asked to come over to "ask about an engine problem." Well, to make a long story short, he arrived two hours later and within the first five minutes, poured his heart out—his terror, his dread, his panic at facing the ocean again. I was truly moved by his pain and his personal courage in admitting his fear. He is terrified to even go back forty-eight short miles to Turtle Bay. Eventually, we learned that he and his wife panicked off Cedros Island and had to be towed in when their engine failed. Their boat hit a mooring buoy bigger than their boat at Cedros, breaking several port lights and suffered other minor damage.

This was the same area that gave us so much trouble coming south, where we exhausted ourselves by being unprepared for turbulent sea conditions that made steering difficult.

For a month, they sat in Turtle Bay, a secure anchorage near Cedros, while the man (whose name is Joe) made repairs—very *slowly*—to his boat. Dee, his wife, wondered why he was so slow to get the boat repaired. Joe never confessed his fear to Dee, but merely procrastinated until he could procrastinate no longer. Finally, last Thursday, they set out heading south to Cabo. Joe said he was terrified as soon as they left the harbor, but hoped he'd get over it. He didn't. (He never once mentioned his fear to his wife, who thought he was a bit tense, but nothing more.) Now, here they sit. Afraid to go back, afraid to go forward. But at last, Joe admitted his fear to his wife. Stereotypes aside, he is a macho Italian, black-haired black-bearded, with twenty-six years behind him as a stuntman, taking all sorts of risks, jumping off buildings, smashing up cars in chase scenes, etc. He and his wife have been living on their boat and preparing for this trip for six years. Joe now realizes he is not cut out for this way of life. He is truly surprised to learn this about himself. He seemed grateful to have someone to talk to and, I think, knowing we were total strangers he'd never see again, helped. Anyway, Bob and I figured, we just happened to be in the right place at the right time as far as he was concerned. We felt we did our good deed for the year, listening to him and reassuring him. Bob was especially sensitive and helpful. (I think it means more coming from another man.) The whole thing sure made me think a lot. Also, made me not so ashamed of my own fears. Perhaps the truly brave man (or woman) is the one who admits he is afraid.

Out of Shearlean's hearing, Joe had asked me whether he and Dee could sail in company with us to Bahia Tortuga, explaining that there was a highway there into Bahia Tortuga and friends from San Diego could drive there to help them sail back to the U.S. I shook my head before he was done speaking, explaining I couldn't prevent him from following me, but I wouldn't commit to assisting—at the risk of my boat, myself, and Shearlean—by promising to come to his aid underway. I pointed out he was safe where he was, and I believed he would find the courage to get back to Turtle Bay on his own. As an afterthought, I offered him passage on *Symbiont* to Turtle Bay, but he didn't respond. He reached out and gripped my shoulder, sagging momentarily, then straightened and said, "Out here, there's no one to yell 'cut,' you know? All those years in Hollywood, there was always somebody to yell 'cut' if things got bad." Then he turned away. I watched, sad, as he headed his dinghy back to his anchored boat.

With the prevailing wind from the northwest, the voyage back from Cabo was supposed to be a miserable slog to windward. Instead, we were enjoying fair, warm days and gentle seas, and had too little wind for consistent sailing. We were motoring most of the time, the autopilot steering and Shearlean and I relaxing, with Beethoven wafting around the boat. Except for the fog, caused by a sudden chill about two hours out of Asunción, every day had been uneventful.

Fair conditions returned for our passage from Asunción to Turtle Bay where we planned to spend a second night so I could recuperate from refueling the boat for the final leg to Ensenada. We arrived at Turtle Bay with just five gallons of diesel fuel remaining. Using jerry jugs, I had to make three trips between the boat and the pier to ferry eighty-five gallons of fuel to the boat, heavy work in the hot desert stillness of the bay. I congratulated myself again on converting the sanitation tank to a fuel tank, giving me the range under power to take advantage of these mild conditions.

A cruiser came alongside in his dinghy asking if we had any kerosene, which we did, for a couple of oil lamps in the cabin. He offered a bottle of Chenin Blanc wine in exchange for our quart of kerosene, which he needed for his galley range, so I traded with him. We were now prepared for another seafood feast if we could score more shrimp, abalone, or lobster.

Departing Turtle Bay for Isla Cedros, conditions remained good, but late in the day, as we approached our Cedros anchorage, it was obvious the height and frequency of the swells was increasing, signaling a change was coming.

Thinking this front would be short-lived, we departed Cedros late the next morning for Bahia San Carlos. Our Cedros anchorage had been pretty miserable and I judged it wouldn't be much worse underway, but conditions became more severe, and our trip north was suddenly reminding us of our difficult trip south. We decided to stop fighting it and hove-to, to ride out a storm, for the first time in a year. But being old hands at this now, and confident in *Symbiont's* capabilities, we tuned in the KNX radio drama hour at 9:00 p.m. and enjoyed a Sherlock Holmes mystery. Afterward, we fell asleep, usually for ten-to-fifteen minutes at time, until dawn, when conditions began to moderate, and we decided to get underway.

Bahia San Carlos doesn't look like much on the chart, but the cruising guide says it has been a popular anchorage for commercial and pleasure boats for many years. We anchored in four fathoms in sand, bow to the western most *arroyo* closest to the big rock off the point. A sheer plateau rises almost from the water's edge, about two thousand feet. Calm and still, we immediately went to sleep and didn't wake until noon to a bright sun and the call of sea birds. A fisherman anchored in close to shore saw me on deck and waved a lobster in the air. I waved back, gesturing him to come over. He came alongside and offered to exchange four nice-sized lobsters for our last bottle of Jim Beam. We hadn't eaten much in the past twenty-four hours and were starved. We ate all four lobsters and washed them down with the bottle of Chenin Blanc we traded for in Turtle Bay, and took a long nap until early evening. We listened to music, played backgammon and read, then slept.

At 11:00 a.m. the next day, we were both on deck, preparing to depart San Carlos for Ensenada, when we heard a whale blow nearby, then a second, and then a third. A trio of gray whales, each about the size of *Symbiont*, were gliding toward us, submerging just behind the boat and reappearing seconds later a couple hundred feet off our bow; a simultaneous shiver of fear and admiration tingled up my spine as I began to bring the anchor onboard. "That's about as close as I ever care to see whales," Shearlean remarked.

The sea was calm and the weather mild as we motored north, the main was sheeted in tight to reduce rolling. Shearlean came on watch at 5:00 a.m., bringing her journal and pen to continue her ongoing letter to my mother and dad about this trip from Cabo. I went below and lay down on the settee and went immediately to sleep.

I awakened to Shearlean's shouting, "Come look, come look, come look!" Groggily, I slid the companionway hatch back and raised myself to see what the uproar was about. We were surrounded by dolphins in every direction, as far as I could see. Shearlean was carrying on like an eight-year-old, pointing excitedly at what was totally obvious—an ocean full of dolphins, babies, tail walkers, jumpers, speedsters. I think it took five minutes for them to pass us and another five minutes to completely disappear.

Without the excitement of the dolphins to distract us, I noticed *Symbiont's* motion. The swells we were among were huge, instead of cutting through them we were climbing their backs and surfing down their faces. I could make out the skyline of Ensenada in the pall to the east.

1985—Newport Beach to Ensenada Yacht Race

I don't recall exactly when it was that it dawned on me there was a chance we would be arriving in Ensenada at the same time as the 1985 Newport Beach to Ensenada Yacht Race. Nothing about planning our 1985 voyage home had taken that coincidence into account. It must have happened when our progress up the west coast of Baja made our arrival in Ensenada predictable, that I finally put two and two together. The 1985 race would take place the weekend of April 27 and 28, and I sure didn't want to arrive during the finish of the race.

With our anchor down in the familiar surroundings of Ensenada, April 25, 1985, Shearlean opened her journal to write the end of her letter to my parents:

Here we are at anchor in Ensenada, two days short of one year from the day we departed Newport Beach, April 27, 1984.

I'll be quick before I pass out. Bob and I are tired. At sea thirty-two hours to get here. Encountered gigantic swells about twenty miles from here. Biggest swells I ever saw. Like mountains. Anchored here at 7:30 p.m. To celebrate, all we had left was a little vodka, no ice, some apricot juice. Had three stiff drinks. A tub of popcorn. Canned tuna sandwiches and French fries. Good night.

Love,
Bob and Shearlean

The afternoon the race started, Shearlean and I went to the hotel suite Bob and Mary reserved annually for the race (they never stayed, only hosted the race party there). They were only mildly surprised when we walked in and their reaction was typical of others who knew us, just matter-of-fact greetings, and we blended in pretty seamlessly, as though we'd never been gone, which was fine by us.

We experienced a bit of déjà vu when, as in 1984, we were the only yacht remaining in Ensenada after all the race participants departed for home. We didn't want to be part of the fleet returning to Newport Beach, so we didn't depart Ensenada until May 2, though we had grown restless and eager to get underway. We checked out with Ensenada immigration and the port captain on a warm and overcast Thursday, and departed at 6:00 p.m.

The wind was still and the sea flat as we motored all night toward the glow of San Diego. We arrived at Pt. Loma off San Diego at 4:00 a.m. and tied up at Shelter Island Harbor Police dock at 5:30 a.m. We used a public phone on the dock to report to Customs and Border Protection, and then motored over to the Harbor Island fuel dock, where all we had to do was stick a fuel pump's nozzle into our fuel tank and wait until the tank was full and the pump turned itself off. Wow, how easy was that?

From the fuel dock, we motored over to the Coronado Yacht Club's guest dock, where we were offered three nights free dockage, including electricity and water, and clean restrooms with hot showers. We were nearly overcome with joy and gratitude.

After long naps and unlimited hot showers, early that afternoon we walked a block or two from the yacht club to a pizza place where I began ordering our pizza in Spanish, not having ordered anything in a restaurant in English for a year. The cashier gave me a strange look, wondering—no doubt—why I was practicing my fumbling Spanish. Thankfully, Shearlean interrupted in English to complete our order. I laughed at myself as I tuned in to English being spoken all around me.

With pay phones convenient everywhere, we called our yacht club, BCYC, in Newport Beach to ask about a guest slip there and to put our name on the waiting list for a permanent slip for *Symbiont*. I called the rental agent for our condo and told her she could give our tenants notice to be out by October 1. I called Bill Eisenlohr to ask him to bring the car we stored at his place to the yacht club. When I drove him back home, he agreed to fly with me to Cabo to bring our truck back to the U.S. Shearlean called a couple of people at the *Times, Orange County* and invited Randy and Debbie, who visited us in La Paz, to dinner at the yacht club. We were getting the word out that we were back, but wouldn't be back for good until September, because of our resort house-sitting gig in Baja.

A week later, Bill and I landed at Cabo airport, got a taxi to Marina Grand Baja in La Paz, and picked up the Ford Ranchero truck and drove back to the U.S. in two days with no problems.

On May 25, 1985, I turned forty-seven years old, and on June 21, 1985, Shearlean turned thirty-nine years old.

Now what?

Boating Writer

I had lots of help taking my boat someplace I'd never been before in the form of many navigation publications, such as cruising guides, coast pilots, nautical charts, light lists, and other documents describing what I might encounter. Even ancient mariners, such as Magellan, Cook, and Columbus had rutters—seamen's guides carried by early navigators. Getting to Baja and back was a straightforward process, requiring only diligence and requisite skills.

Changing the course of one's life was far more difficult, I was learning, than going cruising. Life-changing guidance was scarce and vague, and the risks seemed greater. For giving up one professional life for another, there were no guides.

Listing pros and cons of life-changing problems and solutions hadn't worked, it had gotten me nowhere—as I should have known. Back in the U.S. permanently, I was tempted to take the easiest course and look back to what was familiar—finding a job. But I worried about losing my determination to find a path to continuing this sailing life I discovered I liked so much. Could I sustain my faith that something would turn up if I kept myself open to chance long enough for something to materialize?

I was worried and depressed being back onboard *Symbiont* at BCYC. All the exhilaration of cruising for a year had evaporated. I felt as though I had run my ship-of-life aground on this shoal called Newport Beach and was stranded. I began thinking I could only be rescued by a King Tide—an exceptionally high tide occurring only during new and full moons when the Earth, moon, and sun are aligned just right—that could float my *job*-boat back into navigable water.

Back in Newport Beach was being back in the rat race, but I didn't want to give up seeing the world from the deck of a boat just because my first attempt had failed. Nevertheless, when in the rat race one must do as the rats do: get a paycheck and pay the bills. There is no time to lose, because the pace of debt is merciless.

I'd decided to walk away from surveying, though I'd surveyed a few boats in Baja for cruisers whose insurance had expired or been canceled because they took their boats to Mexico. Rebuilding my surveying business wasn't a practical option, because it would be slow and ultimately an inflexible, full-time business. Freelance writing hadn't paid the bills in Baja, so it wasn't going to cover the cost of living in Newport Beach.

There was some equity in our condo to borrow against, rent from the condo slightly exceeded our mortgage payment (but that would disappear when the renters departed), and there were paltry receivables due from magazine articles, but I couldn't afford even our slip rent at the yacht club out-of-pocket.

"Now what?" was a nearly existential question. How far dare I retreat to proven security versus how big do I dare gamble on something speculative? Could I accept that things would probably work themselves out and rely on my innate competence and adaptability, and just go for it?

One morning in the yacht club bar on my third cup of coffee—surrounded by affluent and established fellow members—I found a classified ad in the remnants of a fat *Los Angeles Times* Sunday edition for a computer technical writer, wanted by the newly formed Unisys Corporation in south Orange County to write online computer user documentation. I applied and was hired, despite the substantial gap in my resume. Suddenly, effortlessly, I had a hefty paycheck, health insurance, and retirement benefits. Ignoring my dislike of such work, I lasted almost a year and resigned in time for my 1986 housesitting stay at RBV.

Shearlean had visited the *Times, Orange County* editorial office looking for freelance writing assignments and had come away with some general assignments plus the gifts of a weekly column ("A-Plus" about secondary education in Orange County) and a monthly column ("On the Waterfront" about marine activities along the shoreline of Orange County). She felt redeemed. This arrangement ultimately turned her journalistic career with the *Times, Orange County* into a twenty-five-year association.

She wouldn't have to resign to go housesitting because she could take this sort of work with her to RBV.

Moving back into our condo October 1, I was able to offer *Symbiont* for sale and listed her with a brokerage in Long Beach that specialized in serious cruising boats. I made no money off the sale but the boat payments, slip rent, and other costs went away, enabling me to pay off credit card balances.

I remember vividly the instant I decided to sell *Symbiont*. Shearlean and I were sitting on the port settee, the boat swinging about as the tide changed. Bright sunlight swept slowly across the interior wood trim through the open companionway and there I saw it . . . raw wood showing through the satin varnish finish.

The "warm and wood-filled cabin" of gorgeous ribbon-grained mahogany and fine-grained teak, elaborately carved, featured in Fuji's brochures and ads, needed refinishing. The boat was nine years old, and the years and sun had taken their toll.

"I can't do it," I told myself then and there. I had put so much into *Symbiont* already, I didn't feel capable of doing any more. In fact, I felt resentful. Without the glare of the sun, the interior still looked good, but the reality had been revealed to me. Refinishing the interior would be a thankless, extremely difficult job of tedious surface preparation and massive cleanup when done. It wouldn't add one cent of value to the boat.

Advertised as "a Baja vet, owned by a marine surveyor" *Symbiont* sold quickly at a fair price. I never met the buyer because, I think, the boat and my improvements spoke effectively for themselves.

We sold our condo in Laguna Niguel to extract our equity, and on the strength of my job with Unisys, bought a condo in Newport Beach, where we would live for the next ten years.

We were back. But had we swallowed the anchor and sold out to the rat race?

We continued rearranging our lives, still hoping that by persevering with believing in ourselves and consistently making choices that reflected our long-term goals, we would achieve the independent life we wanted. We banked and invested surplus funds, and put the crisis-mode of returning from cruising behind us.

Back from our 1986 RBV house-sitting and freed from the rat-race peril of Unisys corporate employment, I was rejuvenated. I had recovered from the doldrums. With a fixed address and dependable telephone, fax machine, and postal service, I was able to improve my writing productivity over Baja to the degree that my freelance writing income was approaching my Unisys paycheck. I was able to be on a boat on the water more than when I owned a boat. As long as we were frugal and careful with money, we could afford to live in Newport Beach despite not having typical "jobs" or consistent paychecks. Again, we had no health insurance or employer contributions to a retirement plan. I would be hitting the big five-o in 1988 and was beginning to think seriously about needing something more secure than freelance writing about boats. (Shearlean had already run head-on into forty). Meanwhile, writing about boats and nautical life was a terrific way to live. Maybe I wasn't seeing the world from the deck of my own boat, but I was seeing daily life from the deck of *a* boat—which could be construed as seeing the world. I was satisfied to redefine my dream to conform to reality.

In 1980, I had started writing about boating on a whim and on the chance that it might help promote my surveying business. Coming from a technical writing background, journalism—particularly feature writing for national and regional newspapers and magazines—was foreign to me. I was used to writing about Polaris submarines, atomic weapons, spacecraft, ballistic missile computer systems, and main-frame computer business software. Fortunately for me, Shearlean had a degree in journalism and was an award-winning feature writer. She was my writing tutor and the anonymous editor of my freelance features until I mastered the craft.

Freelance writing is a precarious profession. It offers priceless opportunities, but a writer would starve depending on it exclusively. Nearly every article is speculative: will a reader be interested in the subject, will an editor recognize its value, will it need revision, when will it be published, how much will be paid for it? Payment, for example, depends on where it appears in the publication (feature, column, side-bar), and when payment is made can depend upon acceptance or publication, and be subject to when the accounting department authorizes the check.

With Shearlean's employment providing us with stability, I could afford the risks and rewards of being a middle-aged freelance writer. Some might say it was a form of active retirement, and I wouldn't dispute it.

Not all freelance writing compensation is monetary. Because of our lifestyle, Shearlean and I had the time to do things others didn't. As a result, we occasionally received all-expense paid trips to exotic locations and the use of a charter boat in exchange for writing an article about the location and charter business. State or national tourism departments, sometimes individual companies, wanted to appeal to a particular demographic readership and would choose to advertise in an appropriate publication. The advertiser would offer the publication an all-expense paid trip in exchange for advertising and publishing a feature story, but few magazines had staff with the time or skills to accept such offers. But the magazines knew Shearlean and I, and offered us the trip so the publication could get the display advertising dollars it coveted. Some of these trips, if purchased, would have cost thousands of dollars (which Shearlean and I couldn't afford), but all we had to do was show up and write about our experience.

While this arrangement may sound ideal, it was a mixed blessing. On the one hand, we always wanted more such trips, but on the other hand, there were inevitably out-of-pocket costs that would have made too many "free" trips too expensive for us.

Writing what were generically known throughout the boating press as "Boat Reports" was the bread and butter of boating magazines and boating writers, and the most rewarding in every way for me and my technical writing approach to freelance writing.

In exchange for advertising dollars, boating magazines published feature articles about manufacturers' newest model boats. A boat would be provided, usually from a local dealer, and I would take it out for a superficial sea trial, similar to the sea trials I did as a marine surveyor for boaters seeking insurance. For the benefit of the report reader, I would do a bow-to-stern narrative walk-thru of the boat, describing the layout of the accommodations and commenting on the decor, fit, and finish of the vessel's interior. There was a measured nautical mile off the ocean beach of Newport Beach where we could run the boat at its rated cruising RPM and at maximum RMP to calculate its speed. I operated the boat myself to get a feel for its handling and performance, while someone from the dealership operated it the rest of the time while I roamed around the boat underway. A sea trial took about two hours (dock to dock) and the balance of the inspection required an additional two hours.

I casually inspected and commented on inconspicuous, but typically ignored features, such as fit and finish of screws and bolts, presence or absence of backing plates for through-deck hardware, such as mooring cleats, and protection of exposed electrical connections for a practical aspect to my boat reports.

I wrote a lot of reports about sportfishing boats, for which there was then a big market. These boats ranged from forty-six to sixty feet and ranged in price, as tested, $350,000 to $1.2 million in 1990 U.S. dollars. I also reported on cruising sailboats, high-performance waterskiing boats, inflatable dinghies, trailerable fishing boats, and high-tech, ultralight ocean-racing boats.

I wrote profiles about boating personalities and/or their boats, including American surf-and-sailing entrepreneur and pioneer Hobie Alter, creator of the *Hobie Cat* catamarans, actor Peter Fonda, TV personality John Davidson, and John Wayne, Groucho Marx, Roy Disney (sailing nephew of Walt), the Beverly Hillbillies' Buddy Ebsen, and others who frequented Newport Beach. I wrote about obscure, wealthy guys who could afford to indulge their boating whims, such as a wealthy marlin fisherman who roamed the world on his converted oil platform service vessel that he turned into a mothership to transport his sixty-two-foot sportfishing boat to marlin fishing tournaments around the world. The mother ship also served as a traveling dry dock and shipyard for the fishing boat. He wasn't the only guy doing this.

Dame Fortune hadn't forgotten Shearlean and I (alternatively, I could say we continued to trust her). In 1988, through her *Times* network, a colleague nominated Shearlean to replace himself upon retiring from his part-time position teaching English composition at the nearby University of California-Irvine (UCI), which offered a small salary, but provided full benefits (including healthcare coverage for a spouse). Shearlean was accepted and was able to continue with her *Times* columns (and she would have summers off). Another benefit of this fortunate circumstance was that Shearlean brought home to me one day a letter from Calavo Growers of California (an avocado growers cooperative in nearby Tustin, California) seeking a part-time UCI student to write employee newsletters and other business communications.

If my price were right, I thought the co-op might hire a fifty-year-old freelance writer instead of a student. I could do the work of two or three students, in less time, and of higher quality, without supervision, and do it as a contractor, at an hourly rate, with no benefits or other overhead detrimental to Calavo's bottom line. That would be my pitch, anyway, when I applied.

I feared I would get laughed out of my application interview, because my terms of employment might be a deal-breaker. I proposed to work part-time, twenty-five hours per week, for twenty-five dollars an hour, have all summer off, July through September, and I wanted to be able to take off for up to a week if a special opportunity presented itself. I would hire, train, and provide telephone support to a journalism student from one of the local universities to produce the newsletters and other routine publications using the support of printing and graphics vendors I would establish. I required no benefits as I was on Shearlean's UCI health insurance.

The CEO who hired me was about my age and I suspect he saw something in my quixotic goal that he sympathized with. When he accepted my proposal, he may have kept his fingers crossed, but it all worked out as I intended (better, I bet, than he dreamed). My corporate communications results made him look very good to the board of directors, co-op members, and employees, and I never appeared as a line item in his budget. It was rather as though I didn't exist.

I never dreamed I would be working in agriculture—more unlikely even than owning a boat, considering my roots. Calavo renewed my original contract with no changes (I didn't ask for any) for ten years. When the CEO who hired me retired in 1997, I resigned. The new CEO eliminated my job and turned corporate communications over to the manager of human resources, who resigned shortly thereafter. Consequently, I resumed doing Calavo's corporate communications (now at my PR consulting rate) for another six months from my home office while Calavo got things squared away under the new CEO.

By the early 1990s, while working part-time for Calavo, I was writing for an impressive list of fourteen or more boating and marine industry publications.[12] Away from boating, I was writing features for the nationally circulated "Home Office Magazine," and writing a monthly home office column for the *Times, Orange County*. (I'd been working from my home office—back when it was called a "den"—since 1976.)

Now, everything Shearlean and I did was boating-oriented, one way or another, by force of habit or serendipitously. We were invited to do a magazine article about Christmas in Rio de Janeiro, Brazil, and brought along one of our yacht club's burgees to exchange with the Rio yacht club—which had nothing to do with Christmas in Rio, but everything to do with gaining entry to the club and seeing its fleet of yachts.

---

[12] *UCI Journal, Professional Boat Builder, Pacific Yachting, Latitude 38, Sea, Motor Boating & Sailing, Sail, Cruising World, PassageMaker, Waterfront, Sport Fishing, Hot Boat, Marine Business Journal,* et al.

Having qualified for an International Food Wine and Travel Writers Association membership, we were invited to be guests of the city of Halifax, Nova Scotia, Canada, where we spent all of our free time exploring the province's maritime history and learning about its famous Blue Nose schooners and boatbuilding legacy.

When we traveled privately, I planned an itinerary for each trip so I could visit as many harbors, boatbuilders, yachting venues, and marinas as possible. Shearlean insisted we should display a bumper sticker to warn other drivers—THIS VEHICLE STOPS AT ALL BOAT YARDS. (She was incredibly patient to often wait in the car while I toured sail lofts, ships' chandleries, marine hardware foundries, and yacht production lines.)

There was hardly a recreational boating subject I didn't write about, eventually including much about the business side of boating from retail sales to professional boatbuilding and repair, continuously, for twenty-six years. It was sometimes a turbulent and tenuous experience battling with publications, editors, and art directors, but one I thoroughly enjoyed, and, in hindsight, felt fortunate to have accomplished. The last published boating article I wrote appeared in *PassageMaker Magazine* in March 2007.

From her UCI experience, Shearlean discovered she enjoyed teaching, and around her fiftieth birthday, she decided to get a master's degree to qualify for a tenured university position teaching journalism. I was growing anxious about keeping up with the cost of living in Newport Beach and the pace of life in Orange County. We found ourselves frequently discussing where to escape to, and we concluded that finding a college town to retire to would be a good idea. I had arrived in California in 1962, and after thirty-five years, getting out of California was my top priority. For Shearlean, who arrived with me on my return to the state in 1970, California was still the "golden state," and she had a sister and nephew here, but she gave in to me.

When she got her degree, we drew a line across a map of the U.S. to mark the snow line, and she applied for her first full-time teaching job at universities south of that line. She accepted a position at East Carolina University (ECU), in Greenville, North Carolina, and we moved there in the fall of 1997. A big part of the appeal of ECU was that Shearlean was from east Tennessee, on the border with North Carolina, and living there might be a bit like returning home and be some compensation for giving up California. We soon agreed that culturally and academically ECU was a disaster (we were both too California-ized to adapt), and were immediately convinced we had become westerners with our decades on the west coast. We wanted to see snow-capped mountains and the far Pacific horizon again, and to return to the west. We'd previously considered moving to Washington, and that became our new goal. After two years at ECU, Shearlean found two journalism openings at Western Washington University (WWU) and applied for both of them, feeling certain she would get one—and she did.

Shearlean suffered the brunt of our unfortunate North Carolina move, but I was more fortunate. I brought with me both some boating writing work and some Calavo work resulting from the co-op's unsettled executive situation, and Greenville was the home of Overton's Boat Supplies, a large boating retail and catalog business. I had met Parker Overton on a hotel shuttle bus taking me to a Chicago boat show a couple of years earlier, and he remarked that I should look him up if I were ever in Greenville, so I did. He offered me freelance work writing product, marketing, and catalog copy for his company. Though reduced, my boating writing income was uninterrupted by moving to North Carolina.

Moving to North Carolina demonstrated how ubiquitous the boating life could be. Not only was Overton's headquartered in Greenville and several national boat manufacturers were located within a few miles (offering boating editorial opportunities), but we quickly discovered a pair of visitors to our yacht club in Newport Beach, Katy Burke and Taz Waller, who lived in Oriental, North Carolina, not far from Greenville. Katy was well-known boating writer and author, and Taz was a boatbuilder. We became fast friends over our two years there, and maintained our friendship long afterwards. It was the personal highlight of living in North Carolina.

Oriental, named after a civil war shipwreck on the Outer Banks, was a tiny waterfront town that billed itself as North Carolina's sailing capital. Area sailing clubs held races there throughout the year and it was a convenient base for cruising sailors and charterers.

I did own a boat again, from 1997 to 1999, and enjoyed a unique form of North Carolina (and southeastern Virginia) boating, exploring the state's approximately two hundred miles of the Intracoastal Waterway, whose waters are sheltered by barrier islands that extend three thousand miles along America's Atlantic and Gulf coasts. North Carolina's main bodies of coastal water are Currituck Sound, Albemarle Sound, and Pamlico Sound. My boat was a 1985 eighteen-foot Four Winns I/O-drive runabout, never dignified with a name.

In 1999, we moved again, returning west, but decided to make a great expedition of it. We had three months to get to Bellingham, Washington, near the Canadian border south of Vancouver, British Columbia. I bought a small travel trailer and planned a leisurely camping trip across Canada to make the very most of the trip. We took our time driving and camping northward in the U.S. to the Canadian border. In Canada, we turned east and took a ferry to Newfoundland, where we got onto the beginning of the 4,860-mile Trans-Canada Highway in order to start west from the farthest east possible. We spent three months crossing Canada, with occasional detours, mostly dry camping (no facilities), sometimes stopping for up to a week, and arriving in Vancouver, B.C., a few days before classes started at WWU.

Cheyenne Summer – Panama Canal

The Panama Canal is a crossroads of the world and an engineering marvel, connecting the Pacific and Atlantic oceans, previously separated by two continents. Fellow boaters (Baja) Bob and Mary, his wife, first saw it from the lofty deck of a cruise ship and resolved to touch it and see it from the depths of the one-hundred-ten-foot-wide by one-thousand-foot-long locks. They would do it from the deck of their own boat, working their own mooring lines and maneuvering their vessel themselves. They would need some help, though, and asked whether I would like to go along as crew.

The very idea of passing between two continents now separated by only a hundred and ten feet, leaving one ocean and entering another after crossing a small lake, and experiencing the workings of a maritime wonder of the world fired my imagination and enthusiasm. It was July, and I was on my annual summer break from Calavo. I answered with an emphatic "yes" to guarantee that they could count on me. To prepare for the trip, I read David McCullough's *Path Between the Seas*.

Taking a small boat through the Panama Canal ranked high on my boating bucket list, which included such unlikely wishes as transiting the Suez Canal, rounding the great capes, including Cape Horn and the Cape of Good Hope, cruising the Red Sea, and cruising Antarctica. I had been on a small cruise ship in the Mediterranean and Aegean Seas in 1975, and I had made it to other bucket-list destinations, including Baja, Tahiti, and the Great Barrier Reef. Not on my list, but what should have been, was a decade of transiting Alaska's Inside Passage in the twenty-first century.

In 1993, Bob and Mary owned *Cheyenne Summer*, a sixty-eight-foot (seventy-three-feet overall) Irwin ketch. Designed for cruising shoal waters, such as the Bahamas, it had a centerboard keel, featured a spacious center cockpit, and offered four staterooms, each with a private head. Not the sort of boat a couple would choose to sail themselves, no matter how capable they were. *Cheyenne Summer* had a full-time professional crew of three, a captain, deckhand, and cook, who shared quarters in the fo'c'sle (forecastle). Additional guest crew included another friend, Dale, also looking for adventure. I don't remember whether Shearlean was invited and couldn't accept, but we both traveled a lot separately, for both business and pleasure, so traveling without her wasn't unusual.

Earlier, Bob had his crew deliver *Cheyenne Summer* to Golfito on the west coast of Costa Rica near the border with Panama. It is a large, well-protected bay, surrounded by evergreen rain forests, an area that receives up to two hundred inches of rain annually. We left the capital, San Jose, the next day on a charter flight to Golfito where we spent two days on *Cheyenne Summer* before departing for Balboa, Panama.

While I like adventurous travel, I prefer it on land or water than in the air. Four of us with luggage caused our small plane to struggle to gain and maintain altitude as we approached the San Jose mountains that rim the west coast of Costa Rica. I felt myself straining in my seat in an effort to help the laboring single engine. At times, I sensed all of us holding our breath until the pilot found a pass between the peaks to ease the plane through. I'd never been so glad to be back at sea level as when we landed in Golfito.

The canal was about three hundred and sixty nautical miles away—about sixty hours at six knots. We reported our arrival at the canal by radio to Flamenco Island control at 8:34 a.m., and received permission to proceed to the Balboa Yacht Club. The approaches to the canal have to be among the busiest patches of ocean in the world, with ships and boats of every size continuously arriving and departing. All seven of us were busy with tasks during our two-hour approach to the canal until we docked at the yacht club.

Bob, the thorough master planner of many expeditions, had retained the services of a canal agent to handle the voluminous paperwork and to lead us on our rounds of canal and government offices in Panama City. We were scheduled for an early transit Tuesday morning.

We handlined ourselves in the first lock up into Gatun Lake without difficulty. We were told bad weather had closed the Atlantic canal anchorage to shipping and there were severe civil disturbances (violent riots), so we were permitted to stay in Gatun Lake for two days (normally not allowed). A raucous population of howler monkeys made sure we knew we were anchored in their jungle and flights of colorful macaws added to the chorus.

We had again requested a center chamber position in the next lock and use of our own handlines again for locking down to Colon, but when we arrived at the locks, we found we were going into the lock ahead of a car carrier (a ginormous vessel for which the word *huge* is too small). Instead of tying to the lock wall and managing our own raising and lowering, we were ordered to tie alongside a canal tug that would tie off to the canal wall. As we feared, we had several scary moments getting alongside and staying alongside the tug. The tug's crew was inattentive to our efforts to tie to them and to their own mooring lines as the water level changed, and were tardy in adjusting their lines. The tug began to tip toward us as the water level dropped. Some arguments broke out with the canal pilot on our boat about handling and maneuvering. We were all very experienced sailors and knew better about our vessel than the pilot did, and were assertive about our decisions and actions. We got through unscathed.

At Colon, we saw no signs of riots, but didn't hang around. We took a taxi back to Panama City and flew back to Orange County the next day. The crew took *Cheyenne Summer* to Fort Lauderdale, Florida, for service and access to the Bahamas, where Shearlean and I later joined owner Mary and other guests for a cruise.

It is possible to transit the fifty-mile-long canal in one day. And in retrospect, transiting was a breeze, thanks, especially, to our efficient and competent agent. Agent or not, though, we possessed every possible piece of paper pertaining to the crew and the boat, and plenty of copies of each. To handline ourselves through, we had to be able to heave a line fifty feet. That's easier said than done if there is wind or the line is wet, or you have thrown it several times already. If we had been willing to wait (such as for a center lock position) we could have probably gotten whatever position we wanted. Otherwise, we had to take what came along (like tying to a tug).

If you don't have a yacht of your own to take through the canal, but want the experience, hang around the Balboa Yacht Club and let it be known than you are available to handline on a boat going through and you will probably be recruited.[13]

---

[13] See https://oceanoftime.robertaduke.com/boating-life/ to read my feature stories "Panama Passage" and "Cheyenne Summer's Canal Transit Step by Step."

Lilli Sohex, Cook Islands to Tonga

From 1988 to 1992, elderly-but-fit fellow yacht club members and lifetime boaters, Jack and Charlene Johnson, circumnavigated the South Pacific Ocean in their Valiant 40, *Lilli Sohex*. They were too old, and it was too risky, they knew, to do their extended cruise solely as younger cruisers often did, so they arranged to be joined along the way by boating friends and family to crew for a segment of their voyage.

In the Cook Islands, one of the remotest regions of the Pacific, their crew failed to arrive. They were stranded at Rarotonga, the capital, nearly nine hundred nautical miles west of the Kingdom of Tonga, where their next volunteer crew was scheduled to meet them. If they didn't get to Tonga on schedule, the Tonga volunteer crew would have to abort, and they could be stranded again.

I hadn't seen Jack and Charlene since they left the U.S., and knew nothing of their voyage as it progressed, so Jack's phone call was a surprise: "Could you come to Rarotonga (*where?*) to help us sail to the Kingdom of Tonga (*where?*) in two days?" Jack said he would send me a round-trip airline ticket, with an open return date, and said the voyage might take about ten days (*sailing being an unpredictable way to get somewhere*).

Working part-time, then, as manager of corporate communications for Calavo, where my employment contract entitled me to take time off on short notice, I went to my boss, Al, and told him a special opportunity had arisen. I explained that I needed to go to the Cook Islands for ten-to-fourteen days to rescue a stranded friend who needed my help to get his boat to Tonga, adding that I had no Calavo work pending that couldn't wait until I got back. He said okay, so I called Jack to tell him I was coming.

I flew from Los Angeles to Honolulu and then to Avarua, Rarotonga, and it was a luau all the way. The Honolulu flight, direct to Rarotonga, was only half-full. Many of the passengers were islanders traveling with their musical instruments and baskets and coolers of food. The Hawaiian word, *luau*, is the perfect word to describe our in-flight party. The islanders played nonstop music, danced in the aisles, and passed around food to the passengers for the entire flight.

We set sail for Tonga's capital, Nuku'alofa, the day after I arrived and enjoyed smooth seas and steady mild winds, except for one day's brief squall that brought us a rare spiritual visit by St. Erasmus of Formia, patron saint of sailors.

Squalls are common at sea, with a train of them sometimes visible throughout the day. One afternoon, after intersecting the path of a squall, we saw a green, luminous glow at the top of the mast and I went below to the electrical panel thinking we'd accidentally turned on the masthead anchor light, but we hadn't. I returned to the cockpit and Jack and I continued to stare at the glow atop the mast.

"That's St. Elmo's fire[14]," Jack declared.

---

[14] St. Elmo's fire, named for St. Erasmus, is a weather phenomenon in which luminous plasma is created by a corona discharge from a pointed object (such as a ship's mast) in a strong electric field in the atmosphere, such as thunderstorm lightning. (Wikipedia)

We'd both heard tales of it but had never experienced it, but it matched our conditions. We were impressed that it lingered for about twenty minutes after the squall passed.

Our otherwise unremarkable passage to Tonga took a little over eight days, averaging a hundred and twenty-six miles per day. My most vivid memories of Tonga were a Sunday morning I spent strolling through town, hearing hymns sung by church congregations, accompanied by the rustle of a boisterous sea breeze stirring the palm trees, and being confronted at the restroom area of the public market by an impressive display of AIDS prevention posters. All four walls of the restroom building, the walls of surrounding buildings, and most other surfaces were covered by anti-AIDS graffiti, government-sponsored signs, and international medical organization posters.

I later heard from Jack that he'd found extensive damage to the boat's electrical and electronic systems, similar to a lightning strike, which Jack attributed to our St. Elmo's fire event.

Jack, a retired aerospace electronics engineer, summarized his and Charlene's voyage in these words: "In 1988, Charlene and I sailed away across the Pacific in our forty-foot sailboat, a Valiant 40.[15] We sailed from Newport Beach to the Marquesas Islands, Tuamotus, French Polynesia, Cook Islands, Tonga, Fiji, Vanuatu, New Caledonia, Australia, Indonesia, Singapore, Malaysia, and Phuket, Thailand. After four years in the tropics (1988-92) we were worn out, sold our boat in Singapore, and came home to Corona del Mar [California]. An incredible life experience of four years."

For the next decade, when Jack introduced me to anybody, he included that I was the guy who rescued him and Charlene in the Cook Islands, making it sound way more heroic than it was.

---

[15] More than two hundred Valiant 40 cutters, designed by Robert Perry, were built by Uniflite and Valiant from 1973 to 1992. It was a double-ended, aft cockpit design, with a cutaway keel and skeg-mounted rudder.

Gang's All Here, A Group Charter

A two-week yacht charter in the French West Indies, equivalent to a year's vacation for the typical jobs of so many Americans, was our reward for making time instead of money a priority since our Baja adventure. We were with a like-minded gang from the Bahia Corinthian Yacht Club (BCYC), who put a high priority on leisure time. Yes, some were wealthy, and some were retired, but most were entrepreneurs who were able to organize their businesses or professions around leisure opportunities.

This was one fantastic opportunity, I felt.

Lew Spruance, our organizer, was a good example of an opportunist. I found it hard to understand exactly what Lew did for a living. I knew he was a salesman. I knew he traveled a lot. I knew he was high up in the yacht club hierarchy and had been organizing trips like this for twelve years. I could only be certain, though, that he sold women's lingerie. I found that out one evening walking with him from the yacht club bar to the men's restroom, when two women coming out of the women's restroom simultaneously raised their full skirts to show their panties and said simultaneously, "Thanks Lew, for the free samples." Shearlean and other female sailors had received free "samples" of very feminine long underwear to keep them warm in their sailing gear.

We were a veritable armada, comprising fourteen charter sailboats, consisting of Morgan 46s, and Endeavour 40s and 37s. Twelve of the boats were skippered by the charterers and two had professional skippers provided by the Bahama Yachting Services in Philipsburg, Sint Maarten island.

Sint Maarten was the Dutch half of an island shared with St. Martin, the French half of the island.

The French West Indies and Dutch Antilles are a chain of islands that informally divide the Caribbean Sea from the Atlantic Ocean, more or less off the southeast coast of South America, a thousand miles east of Miami, Florida. The French first occupied Martinique in 1635, but a complicated history of French, Dutch, and British exploration and settlement ensued.

Our group flew from Los Angeles to New Orleans and from New Orleans to Philipsburg for our charter.

To me, this was Europe in the ocean in the "new world," as it was once called. Here France and Holland had their chance to interpret tropical America according to their cultures. It proved to be a fascinating blend of recognizable and alien influences.

Sailing here reminded me mostly of sailing in Southern California, but with much milder weather, warm water, and balmy trade winds. This was blue water, open-ocean sailing, with deep water right up the coast of the islands, and scattered, but commodious, anchorages. Unlike California's Channel Islands (except Catalina), many resorts and other amenities populated these islands, frequently attracting us ashore more often than other charter destinations.

Bob Longpre was the skipper of record for our Morgan 46, which was fine with me, giving me a break from skippering a charter boat for a change. Our Morgan 46 was a center cockpit ketch with a fin keel and spade rudder designed for Charley Morgan by Henry Scheel. The vessel's overall length was forty-six feet, six inches, with a beam of thirteen feet, six inches, and a draft of six feet. Displacement was thirty thousand pounds. The engine was a Perkins 4-154 diesel.

It was the first time I had sailed a boat with a mizzen mast (a second mast near the aft end of the boat). A mizzen mast sail distributes some of the force of the sails to the aft end of the boat to better balance the sail propulsion. It made no noticeable difference to me in sailing the boat, and skipper Bob made no particular use of the mizzen sail.

With six feet and four inches of head room, and just two couples onboard, it was a very roomy and comfortable boat in every way, and the cockpit layout made sailing and handling the boat effortless.

As Lew pointed out, a group charter as large as ours enabled big economies in airfare, hotels, and charter rates, but given the large area of this charter, everyone could go their own way. Though we formed a large group of fifty-six individuals (four people times fourteen boats), we seldom crossed paths with others of our group, unless it was pre-arranged.

Shearlean and I had a fine time and enjoyed chance encounters with others of our charter group, but I decided that it was all too civilized for me. It was what I supposed a Mediterranean charter would be like. I would prefer something more basic with more roughing it and making do with whatever is at hand—more Baja-like. Nevertheless, an occasional taste of luxury shouldn't be missed.

I wrote an article about this charter that appeared in the July 1986 issue of *Cruising World* magazine about how to organize a large group charter and about the location. [16]

---

[16] See https://oceanoftime.robertaduke.com/ to read "Gang's All Here."

Lake Powell, Colorado River

The Colorado, the great river of the American southwest, is a silt-chocked trickle where it oozes into Baja, Mexico's Sea of Cortez, having spent its might carving the Grand Canyon and plunging over mega dams at Lake Powell and Lake Mead in its death spiral to the ocean.

Lake Powell sprawls across the heart of the splendid "four-corners" area, comprising the junction of Utah, Colorado, Arizona, and New Mexico, which Shearlean and I had thoroughly explored by car in both winter and summer. It was never a place I thought of as a boating destination, though millions of annual visitors recognized its two thousand miles of shoreline as such.

When boating friends, Bill and Mary Eisenlohr, invited us to join them with their neighbors, Jim and Marj Smerber, on a Lake Powell houseboat the summer of 1990, we discovered this vast inland sea. I knew Jim and Marj slightly as long-time neighbors of Bill and Mary, with adjoining acreage in rural Riverside County, California. Jim was a trucker and entrepreneur, sometimes owning one big-rig truck and sometimes several, occasionally with partners. He enjoyed the peculiar hobby of collecting classic farm tractors he would spy on long-haul trucking jobs. He would buy these and bring them home in his truck to restore and resell them. Maybe six feet tall, slender, tanned, in his mid-fifties, Jim never looked well to me. He smoked heavily and had diabetes, which he stubbornly neglected to care for. He was notoriously short-tempered with his adult children, but he loved donning his host's hat for his peers. Marj was a small, curly-haired blond with an ever-cheerful expression, a born peacemaker, who (some said) was responsible for Jim living as long as he had.

The houseboat was a late model fifty-footer docked at Wahweap Marina in Page, Arizona, and strangely named *Chicken Ship*. When Jim and some partners had a lucrative contract hauling eggs for a huge chicken ranch in Utah, they had jointly purchased the boat and christened it in honor of the largesse that paid for it.

Though Bill and Mary had to cancel, Jim and Marj said Shearlean and I were welcome anyway, and so began three consecutive *Chicken Ship* summers on Lake Powell, which I tend to remember as one big, extended cruise. Bill and Mary never shared any of our trips.

Jim and Marj had been doing this long enough to have mastered the logistics of houseboating: they knew which marinas were least busy and best stocked with provisions, and which anchorages guaranteed the best shade or scenery. The *Chicken Ship* towed a fast runabout to scout anchorages and claim a spot for the *Chicken Ship* when it eventually arrived at its sedate displacement speed. The runabout could quickly ferry us to nearby attractions, run errands for more ice, or take us fishing, while *Chicken Ship* remained snug in her choice anchorage.

Lake Powell, named for western explorer John Wesley Powell, lies in a geological area of 3,500- to 5,000-foot rocky plateaus, encircled by 7,000- to 9,000-foot mountain peaks, eroded by wind and water with endless networks of major and minor canyons, and rock sculptures. Whether in total or piecemeal, it deserves the appellation "awesome." Three major rivers feed the lake: Colorado, Escalante, and San Juan.

Few boaters come to Lake Powell to explore, most are neophytes who come for a few days for the sun and water sports, and stay near the marina. An unfortunate few needed to stay within range of support services.

Probably the most common question asked of a boat of any sort is: "How many does it sleep?" Even conventional hundred-foot yachts rarely sleep more than six guests comfortably (along with three crew bunked in the fo'c'sle). Houseboats, often shared by two or three families, were often crammed with fifteen or more adults and children. The more relevant question in this case is: "How many will it toilet?" The first toilet crisis sometimes strikes before the houseboat leaves its slip. With no marine sanitation engineer onboard, a radio distress call is made to the rental agency for help, while a mutiny is threatened by the impatient vacationers. Several times Jim responded to such calls from houseboat skippers far away from support from Wahweap. Taking pity on a hapless boatload of fun-seekers, he would zoom to their location in the runabout to see what he could do.

Jim was an explorer, as was I, so during our three cruises, we made the most of our desire to see as much of the lake as possible. In July 1992, we made it as far as Dirty Devil Canyon, near where the Colorado River enters the lake, the farthest navigable point from the dam. Roughly, very roughly, that's more than a hundred and ten miles (calculated from a straight line) or about twenty-one hours of motoring at five knots. The actual time and distance of such a trip is pure conjecture because, like most rivers, the Colorado meanders, many turns double back on themselves, and there are endless tempting diversions along the way.

Looking at my annotated map of Lake Powel from that time, I see 1992 was a summer of major exploration of most of the lake by us—in fact, its entire length. We ventured up the Escalante River arm beyond Forty Mile Creek Canyon, up the twisting San Juan River Arm to an area of old oil wells in the area of Spencer Camp, and on a day trip out of Hite Marina, we went up the Colorado River as far as Steel Arch Bridge, where Jim felt the amount of debris in the river made it too risky to continue.

We spent two days there gathering driftwood until we had a pile on the lake shore perhaps eight feet high. On the second night, cocktails in hand, we dragged our folding lawn chairs upwind of our pyre, put a match to it and sat back and watched it burn for hours. It was extremely satisfying having cleared debris from the river and shoreline, and we got plenty of exercise stacking the pyre and experienced the hugest campfire any of us ever saw.

Lake boating may be considered benign by many, but the fiercest wind I ever encountered was on Lake Powell, and it came with no warning. We were docked at Hall's Crossing. The day was clear, normal by any measure. This late morning in July, the marina was full when the wind hit as though it were an explosion. We later heard over the marine radio from Wahweap that the gust measured sixty miles per hour and was isolated to the Bull Frog Bay area north of and opposite Hall's Crossing.

The wind hit suddenly and lasted one or two minutes, but it ripped, swept, and tore every loose or poorly secured item off a hundred houseboats—hats, coolers, dogs, chairs, canvas covers, towels, food, paper plates, napkins, paper towels, Coke cans, plastic cups, flip-flops, drying bathing suits, sunglasses—and deposited it all in a heap along the fuel dock and storefront of Hall's Crossing Marina, instantly creating the appearance of a landfill site. Small dogs (I'm unsure about small children) were rolled and skidded along decks and docks, and some into the lake. I was on the roof of *Chicken Ship* and felt I was about to take flight and distinctly felt wind flogging my face. In the moment of silence that followed, everyone looked about, searching other faces to see if what just happened really happened. And then a clamor began and built until it became an uproar, as people took inventory of their companions and boats. As far as we could tell, we hadn't lost anything worth recovering. Real damage, as far as others were concerned, was limited to torn and lost awnings and storage covers, and missing chairs and tables.

Was it a microburst—a violent, short-lived, localized downdraft that creates extreme wind shears at low altitudes and is usually associated with thunderstorms? Or was it clear-air turbulence—the turbulent movement of air masses in the absence of any visual clues, such as clouds, which is caused when bodies of air moving at widely different speeds meet? I never heard anything official.

Another unforgettable weather phenomenon, one year, was a magnificent lightning storm that may have lasted an hour while ominous weather stalled over the area. We had gone to a marina for milkshakes and we were feeding bits of bread to carp at the dock. The early afternoon sky began to darken, and the wind quickened with occasional gusts. We ignored it until we noticed that it was growing so dark that we would have needed a light to read a book. Then thunder began and increased in intensity and frequency, so we left the marina and anchored out of the wind in the lee of the point that formed one side of the marina. Lightning bolts appeared in rapid succession all around, but some distance away. Thunder and lightning intensified as day turned nearly to night. Thunder was so loud and seemed so near it caused me to cower as I felt its impact. Long brilliant bolts with multiple branches—looking like a vast river-tributary system of light—exploded above us. Flashes of sheet- and ball-lightning traversed the clouds perpendicular to the ground. We were surrounded by it, and eventually our fear subsided. Finally, I felt at ease and awed with a demonstration that negated the spectacle of any fireworks show I'd ever seen. Several times, it seemed the storm was about to end when it renewed itself, and grew more powerful. It went on longer than seemed possible, maybe an hour. No rain ever fell. The wind never became savage; it was weird, spooky, and mesmerizing.

Jim's son, Boyd, and his dog were once guests for a couple of days, as Boyd wanted to use the runabout to go fishing. His dog was an ill-tempered Rottweiler, which made threatening growls when anyone came near it or made a sudden move. The *Chicken Ship* was filled with tension, and I felt like I was in a cage with an unpredictable beast. Shearlean and I spent a comfortable night on the boat's roof, under the starry heavens, finding it easier to ignore the swarming bats than the Rottweiler patrolling the boat's interior. The next day, Jim banished the dog to the runabout. In protest, Boyd slept in the open runabout with the dog the following night. Boyd was a very successful fisherman and we shared a generous, but stressful, fish dinner together, with the marooned dog whining throughout. It wasn't clear to me whether Jim's issue was with the dog, his son, or both. I knew there were family problems and thought I should ask before the next trip who would be onboard.

Marj's old and nearly blind toy poodle fared better than the Rottweiler, but was about as useless around the houseboat as a Rottweiler was for fishing. Fortunately, it didn't demand much attention, but unexpectedly it earned my total admiration; it did have a use. Either a stowaway from the dock or brought aboard *Chicken Ship* with provisions, a rat got onboard. We heard it under the floorboards, in the galley, and around the range. The poodle noticed, too, and was keenly interested in the source of the sounds. Jim and I started removing floorboards and cabinet drawers and emptying surrounding cupboards thinking if we were lucky, we might catch and kill the rat. The poodle was right with us in the thick of our hunt and when the final floorboard came up, the poodle was on the rat in a flash and had it clinched, squirming and squealing between her teeth. She dropped it, disabled and bleeding, and trotted over to her cushion with an air about her, as if saying, "That's how it's done." I had a high opinion of that dog ever afterward.

Shortly after dark, soon after dinner, while we were still picking up and cleaning up, we all four paused, simultaneously, and looked at each other. We all stood still listening for something no one seemed able to name. We went back to what we were doing, when Marj said, "Hear that?"

Shearlean said it sounded like, "Help."

We all went out onto the aft deck. There was a light breeze, and the moon hadn't risen yet. All was silent. Then we heard it loud and clear. "Help!" But we couldn't tell what direction it came from, as though the sound was wafted by the breeze. But we knew from the urgency it conveyed that it was real. Jim and I got into the runabout and Jim steered in the direction he thought the sound came from and then we stopped the engine to listen. "Help!" We restarted the engine and turned a few degrees then stopped the engine again. "Help!" It was louder and closer. I called, "Hello."

"Help, help! Over here!" came a reply.

In the beam of Jim's flashlight, we saw a man wearing swimming trunks and a life jacket sitting on a bobbing jet ski. He was visibly shivering, but managed an ear-to-ear grin. We motored over, got him onboard the runabout, and tied a towline to the jet ski. *Chicken Ship* was visible maybe a quarter-mile away, and we motored back and took him into the warmth of the cabin. He was in his early twenties, extremely pale, and still shivering. He said he had run out of fuel about three hours earlier and our lights were the first sign of life he'd seen in that time.

He had been with a large group that had rented two houseboats. He believed he hadn't been missed because each group assumed he was on the other boat. We radioed the sheriff's office and reported our find and said we would put Roger up for the night. After breakfast the next morning, the sheriff's cruiser came by to pick up Roger to return him to his group. He hadn't been reported missing.

Though I still have a photo of me in swimming trunks and beer in my hand, sitting in the shade under a large, clock-faced thermometer, its pointer resting on a hundred-twenty, had skinny Roger fallen off the jet ski, he might not have survived being immersed in the lake water all night. A summer water temperature of seventy-seven degrees Fahrenheit is still twenty-one degrees cooler than the human body. The experience was a sobering reminder that hypothermia is a deadly danger to boaters in any body of water.

During the same period, Shearlean and I had the opportunity for a radically different outing, this one on Lake Mead, behind Hoover Dam at the southern end of the Grand Canyon. An inflatable boat[17] dealer in Newport Beach promoted his business by sponsoring and organizing large outings for owners of inflatable boats and potential customers. The utilization and characteristics of Lake Mead are far different from Lake Powell, offering less recreational facilities, and being more lake-like than river-like.

This outing was to launch on Lake Mead and to proceed up the Colorado River under the south rim of the Grand Canyon where we were to camp overnight on a beach near an area of rapids, which the more daring inflatable owners could run for fun and excitement. It was an area where visitors were required to pack-in-and-pack-out—including all human waste, trash, and signs of human trespass. It was a valuable training exercise for anyone anticipating adventures into sensitive wilderness areas of any kind.

Though the rapids were genuine and challenging, no one was injured or killed. A few costly outboard motors and inflatable boats were severely damaged, but none lost, and everyone had a great and formative experience.

---

[17] An inflatable boat consists of a fabric hull attached to a rigid fiberglass bottom and propelled by a powerful outboard motor.

An earlier sponsored inflatable boat outing in which I also participated was with an armada of inflatable boats crossing the thirty miles of open ocean to Catalina Island from Newport Beach for an overnight camping trip. I took along my nephew, who had visited me on *Symbiont* in Baja, now a teenager. We discovered that, at night, a dozen or more feral pigs had scoured the campground we'd chosen and forced us all to move our sleeping bags onto the picnic tables to avoid aggressively hungry animals.

Bay Islands, Honduras

I learned more about boating from this charter vacation than any of a dozen other charter vacations, because it was my first time sailing in shoals. Shoal sailing was also called "cruising with one foot on the beach," by mariner Don Douglass, who recommended it, "Because that's where all the scenery is," verses blue-water sailing, or off soundings, which is "water . . . water everywhere."

Since I'd learned to sail only a few years earlier, I had sailed only in waters "off soundings," the opposite of shoals. In Southern California, my home waters, a sailor was immediately off soundings as soon as he was out of the harbor in waters too deep to measure, free of concern with running aground.

Our yacht club group traveled to the Bay Islands of Honduras, the Central American nation wedged between Caribbean neighbors Belize and Guatemala, for a tropical bareboat charter. In 1979, this area was suffering political turmoil, including the disappearance of political opponents, economic upheaval, and interference by the United States, which backed Contra rebels against Sandinista Marxists. It was also an active malaria area, so we had been advised to take a prophylactic course of antimalarial drugs a week before departure.

We flew to San Pedro Sula, Honduras, one of eighteen political districts where we spent the night (advised not to leave the area of the hotel) and the next day flew to Roatan, the main Bay Island, which we'd been assured was immune from the general unrest of Honduras. Two vans took us to Oak Ridge harbor, where we picked up our Caribbean Sailing Yacht (CSY) 44, a cutter-rigged, shoal draft (four feet, eleven inches) center cockpit sailboat, designed and built explicitly (as the name implies) for cruising the shoals of the Caribbean. The CSY hull was constructed with up to one-and-a-half inches of solid fiberglass-reinforced plastic resin, consisting of fourteen dual layers of fiberglass mat and sheet. What this meant in practical terms (as I witnessed), was that the boat could survive running aground on rocks or reefs, or being blown ashore by high winds, and could be hauled back into deep water, unscathed.

We were sharing our boat with Shearlean's colleague, Pete Donovan, a *Times, Orange County* sports reporter, and his wife, Jill. They were in their mid-thirties, athletic, energetic, and enthusiastic. They weren't the least intimidated that they had zero knowledge or experience with what we were doing. What they were so jazzed about was that this was their first vacation without their three children, and it was the most far-out thing they could think of doing. Their excitement never waned. This all worked in all of our favors, because they would instantly do whatever boating thing they were told to do, without questions or discussion.

The Bay Islands, of which Roatan is the largest, are described as the jewels of Honduras, some of the most beautiful islands in the Caribbean. They offer fantastic fishing, snorkeling, scuba-diving, white sand beaches, and a unique, diverse blend of Central American and Caribbean culture. Roatan Island is the ancient spine of a coral reef from a time when the sea level was much higher.[18]

---

[18] Today's coral reef is part of the world's second largest coral reef system and is known as the Meso-American Barrier Reef, exceeded in area only by the Australian Great Barrier Reef. (Wikipedia)

The day we arrived, we were tired from travel and the charter briefing, and preoccupied with getting the boat squared away, so we were motoring to a nearby bay for the night, when I realized the scenery around us hadn't changed. The binnacle compass wasn't moving. The boat wasn't moving. I looked over the side and there was no wake. The engine was running normally and the boat was level. Shearlean, Pete, and Jill were going about their chores, unconcerned. I pulled the engine throttle to idle and shifted the gear to neutral, and my three crew looked at me simultaneously.

"We've run aground," I said. All three stared at me, uncomprehending. "The boat's not moving," I added.

The forward end of the keel of the CSY 44 forms a short ramp to minimize the impact of hitting a submerged obstacle, allowing us to run aground so gently we'd never noticed. And me, I had not been piloting the boat through shoal waters as I should have, but was incompetently driving the boat as though I were on a water highway. I wasn't in California anymore, operating a boat off soundings, I was in barrier reef country, among many islands, where I could see the sea bottom if I looked.

I put the engine in reverse and gave it some throttle, but we didn't budge. Impatient and eager to extricate myself for this humiliating circumstance, I was unwilling to wait for the tide to float us off. In my nautical books, I'd read about kedging as a means of getting an aground boat afloat again, but I'd never kedged in real life. Still, I understood the principle: Take the boat's anchor out into deeper water the length of the anchor rode (typically two hundred to three hundred feet) and drop it to the bottom. Bring the bitter end of the anchor rode back to one of the powerful sheet winches (used to operate the headsails), and start cranking. Pulling on the anchor will cause it to set itself in the sea bottom, and continued cranking will pull the grounded vessel off the obstacle it's stuck on and into deep water where the anchor lies.

I had Pete bring the dinghy we were towing around to the bow and lowered the anchor to him, instructing him to put it in the center of the dinghy, where it wouldn't foul the rode, which I would lower to him, and to coil the rode in the stern of the dinghy. He followed my instructions to motor away from our boat about twenty degrees off the bow until all the rode was laid out and to then drop the anchor. I had retained enough of the anchor rode to lead it back to the cockpit sheet winch, took a couple of wraps around the drum, and asked Shearlean to tail the winch for me, and began to crank. Eventually, the rode went taut as the anchor set in the sea bottom and I kept cranking, which began pulling the bow around in the direction of the anchor, and with a few more cranks, the rode went slack as our boat was afloat again.

Looking at the nautical chart I had been given but hadn't bothered to check, I saw where the local channel was that would lead us to our anchorage for the night. We got there with no further piloting mistakes, but problems of a different sort awaited us.

After cocktails and discussion of the next day's itinerary, dinner, and a few beers, we were ready for bed.

It was only an instant after we turned out the lights that we heard the frenetic *tic-tic-tic* of tiny claws running through the bilge of our boat.

"What's that?" Shearlean and Jill asked simultaneously.

"Rat," I said, disgustedly, and added, "there's nothing we can do about it tonight. Get some sleep."

Tic-tic-tic went on for a while, then either the rat went to sleep, or we did.

In the tropics, in particular, boaters are warned to never bring anything onboard the boat that has not first been unpacked and inspected on the dock. Rats and cockroaches are two critters likely to be packed with the groceries delivered to you at the dock. Even if the critters didn't come from the grocer, they were likely to arrive from the dock or surrounding jungle.

The next morning, I took the dinghy back to the charter dock to tell the manager about our rat. He handed me a rat trap, a lot bigger than I was expecting, and said I would need to find some bait. He suggested peanut butter. On the way back to the dinghy, thinking about rat bait, I passed a local fisherman cleaning his early morning catch. I held out the trap and said, "Bait?"

He whacked the large fillet in front of him in two and handed me the slab of barracuda he had just gutted. "*Muy bueno*," he said.

I offered him a dollar, which he refused, pointing to the barracuda dismissively, saying, "*comida.*"

I thanked him again.

Back at the boat, everyone eyed the size of the trap, reflecting, I thought, the expression I must have had when I received the trap. Breakfast was being prepared, but was put on hold as I armed the trap and baited it with a piece of fish.

A boat's bilge runs the length of the boat and is open the full length to let water freely drain into the sump, the lowest part of the bilge, where it can be pumped overboard. In the bilge, rats and cockroaches have access to every part of the boat, but are relatively inaccessible for extermination. If the trap didn't work, the rat might be with us for the entire charter.

I lifted up the nearest cabin sole hatch and set the trap in the bilge and replaced the hatch. I was washing my hands at the galley sink, and the others had turned back to breakfast preparations, when we were all startled by a snap, and peered at the hatch that covered the trap. I wiped my hands on my jeans and lifted the hatch, and there was our rat, about the same size as the trap, quivering in its death throes. No wonder the fisherman had offered me fish for bait; it had attracted the rat in an instant. I threw the rat overboard and stored the trap in a deck locker.

At orientation, we had been warned not to eat any fish caught in the area of the reef because they could be toxic. Especially, we were warned, not to eat barracuda, which was a common predator on reef species.

Being always eager to try local food everywhere I travel, and never having eaten barracuda before, I was reluctant to discard the big barracuda fillet I'd been gifted. If the fisherman could eat it, I figured I could, too. Besides, it was probably caught in the open sea, away from the reef, by a native person with local knowledge. I put the remaining fish in a plastic bag and said, "Dinner," as I placed it in the refrigerator, despite the incredulous looks on the faces of all three witnesses.

We got the boat underway for a distant anchorage in a protected bay near a waterfall. I was planning basic fish stew with fresh baked bread provided by the charter company. Being freshly provisioned, we had everything we needed: olive oil, onion, celery, garlic, canned crushed tomatoes, and, some white wine.

Shearlean was used to this, but our friends sitting at the dinette, arms folded protectively across their chests, were both studying me intently, trying decide whether I was kidding.

"C'mon guys," I said, "rat bait chowder. Where else are you going to get a barracuda dinner around here?"

I cut up the barracuda, combined the ingredients in a pot I filled with sea water, which evoked a disgusted look from everyone. "Sea water's fine for cooking," I said, defensively. "It saves the limited fresh water in our boat's tank, and it's going to be boiled. They always say boiled water is safe." No one agreed, but no one tried to stop me.

Shearlean set the table and when the chowder was done, I dished up a bowl and extended it to someone to take, but no one reached for it. Three pairs of eyes stared at me, demanding an explanation.

"Okay," I said, setting the bowl on the dinette table and sliding onto a seat. "I'll eat it and if I survive, will you try it?" Three heads nodded slowly, and I dug in.

I've never been so scrutinized while eating. Finally, Shearlean said, "Well?"

"I feel fine, it's good," I said, but there were still no takers.

Minutes passed and I stood up from the dinette, intending to refill my bowl (and proving I could stand), when the tension broke, and in unison, my crew agreed to taste Bob's rat bait fish chowder.

As soon as I read that the Cayos Cochinos (Hog Islands) were "a remote destination, accessible from Roatan only by motorized canoe," I knew I had to go there. They are two main islands, close together, that are part of a large marine preserve featuring spectacular coral reefs. We anchored in a tiny bay only a few hundred feet from a white sand beach in a shallow opening in the reef.

When I checked the marine weather on the radio, it mentioned a front with high winds, but I gave it no thought. The wind arrived the next morning as forecast and much to my alarm it was blowing straight into our anchorage and stretching our anchor rode taut, setting us disturbingly close to the beach. The wind was building and gusting, and white caps were accumulating right at the entrance to our tiny bay, causing the boat to pitch and jerk on the taut anchor rode. If the anchor failed, we'd be on the beach in seconds. If we could get to the other side of the islands, we'd be protected from the wind and the building seas, but I had no information about the channel between the two islands that would lead to the other side.

I radioed the charter center and told them where we were and about our situation. Calmly, matter-of-factly, the voice over the radio told me to watch for a man they were sending to help us, who could show us the way through the channel to the other side. We no sooner stopped talking than a small brown man wearing a dirty, drab, olive tank top and red swimming trunks four sizes too big for him was paddling a tiny dugout canoe, using only his hand, to the stern of our boat. He climbed into our dinghy, lifted his peanut-shell of a canoe into the dinghy, and then, hoisted himself over our transom and into the cockpit, offering each of us, in turn, his hand. He raised his left arm and waved in the direction of the channel, nodding vigorously.

I quickly realized talk was useless, maybe impossible, so I nodded and smiled, indicating agreement with his gestures. I sent Pete to the bow to oversee the anchor windlass and started the engine. With some careful maneuvering and cautious use of the throttle, I crept up on where the anchor lay, while Pete retrieved the rode by hand from what slack I provided him by moving up on the anchor. I had instructed Pete to let me know when we were directly over the anchor and to secure the rode. If the boat's pitching didn't break loose the anchor, I would run over the spot to break it loose, and he should immediately haul in the rest of the rode. My job was to turn hard to port and use a lot of throttle to get into the channel before the wind knocked us out of position.

The anchor broke loose on its own and I executed the turn, instantly finding shelter from the wrath of the wind and waves. Our guide gestured this way and that, and I tried to steer in proportion to his movements. Sometimes he would pull on the wheel, because I was oversteering, and other times he pushed on the wheel because I was understeering, but we worked our way through the labyrinth of rock and coral to the peaceful lee side of the island, and anchored in calm water without incident. Our rescuer seemed happier than we four at arriving at our destination. He turned away from the helm toward the transom, obviously intending to leave, while I desperately tried to thank and reward him. I had a good folding knife in my pocket, something I thought would be a valuable tool for him, and I handed it to him as he was about to lower himself into our dinghy. He accepted the knife with a broad smile and stepped into the dinghy, put his canoe in the water, got in and hand-paddled himself to shallow water, where he walked into the brush, dragging his canoe. The front moved on through by evening, and by the following morning, you'd never have known anything had happened here yesterday.

Roatan was the site of infamous Port Royal, which, during the seventeenth century, was home to over two thousand pirates, with some five hundred houses, even a church, and was the scourge of early European explorers and merchants. That heritage, it seemed to me, had been preserved in the modern population as some kind of swagger or buccaneer attitude of the people we met. Nothing malignant, more a free spirit, devil-may-care approach to life. For instance, we took our dinghy over to nearby Guanaja, a densely populated cay, home to about six thousand people, and described as the "Venice of Honduras," because of the network of waterways that ran through it. No streets, it was all boardwalks, everyone we saw was poorly dressed, there was no sign of commerce, and there were many bars. All were busy on a midweek afternoon. We went into a bar for a beer and to get out of the sun, and were immediately set upon by young men asking—no, demanding—that we buy them beer. Quickly, a few became many, and they pressed tightly around us. I didn't know what to make of it, whether it was a prank played on tourists or a genuine threat, so we left. But my image of Guanaja has stuck with me all these years as what a modern Pirates of the Caribbean lair would feel and look like.

More typical of ordinary Bay Islanders that I met was Calvin Bodden, owner of the Happy Landing waterfront bar in Oak Ridge. Whether locals or tourists, most patrons arrived at Happy Landing by boat, tying up conveniently placed pilings, reminiscent of the American West, where cowboys rode into town on horses and tied them to hitching posts in front of the saloon.

Somewhere in his mid-forties, speaking English with a British accent, I saw Calvin as a cheerful, benign hustler eager to entertain bar patrons with local stories about area attractions and Bay Islands' history. We visited Calvin three or four times and lingered over drinks he served, whether we ordered them or not. When business was slow, he joined guests at their table and kept up a constant stream of chatter that inevitably resulted in laughs. Though he tried, he never convinced me he was the discoverer of Calvin's Crack (a noteworthy cleft in the barrier reef surrounding Roatan), a local scuba-diving attraction. He didn't talk about scuba diving as though he ever did it, and was incredibly vague about the site and the circumstances of his discovery. I remained skeptical, but never challenged him, but neither was I able to determine that this Calvin was the one for whom the crack was named.

The Happy Landing bar was within sight of the difficult dog-leg harbor entrance at Oak Ridge. When I brought our boat back to the charter center to service the refrigeration system, I bumped into the rock wall of the entrance and was having trouble recognizing the channel, when Calvin's voice came over the radio, offering me encouragement and advice about how to maneuver. He didn't know it was me, but he could see a boat in some difficulty from his bar and wanted to help.

Much to my shame and aggravation, I never successfully navigated that channel, coming or going, after four attempts. The only thing, to my credit, was that I was a prudent enough skipper to have done no damage to the boat, which is the best you can do if you're going to bump into a rock in the water.

I wasn't writing for boating magazines then, so I published nothing about my first experience in shoal waters, but Shearlean wrote a feature about our trip for the November 27, 1979, *Times*, about American expatriates living in the Bay Islands, titled "Cheerful Captives of the Caribbean."

Her story was about former Southern Californians Anne and Paul Hemmers, who had moved to Roatan six years earlier and lived on a leased, twenty-acre hillside farm. They had quit taking antimalarial drugs, ignored the fist-sized tarantulas and swarming mosquitos, and dismissed the unstable government. Instead, they focused on the simple lifestyle, low cost of living, and natural wonders of the Bay Islands, declaring they couldn't be happier with their choice.

Their story made me think about settling in such a place, an alternative to seeing the world from the deck of my own boat, but Shearlean and I lacked the resources that would guarantee real independence, such as the Hemmers enjoyed.

Bob and Shearlean with *Elusive Lady*

Elusive Lady's sister ship, *Mañana*

Bob and Shearlean on the eve of the Baja Departure

Bob Duke on writing assignment at Bora Bora, Tahiti

Sweetie Pie sister-ship underway, Gulf Islands

Shearlean at *Sweetie Pie's* helm in an Alaskan fjord

Captain Jim Kyle, *Home Shore*

Home Shore, coastal Alaska

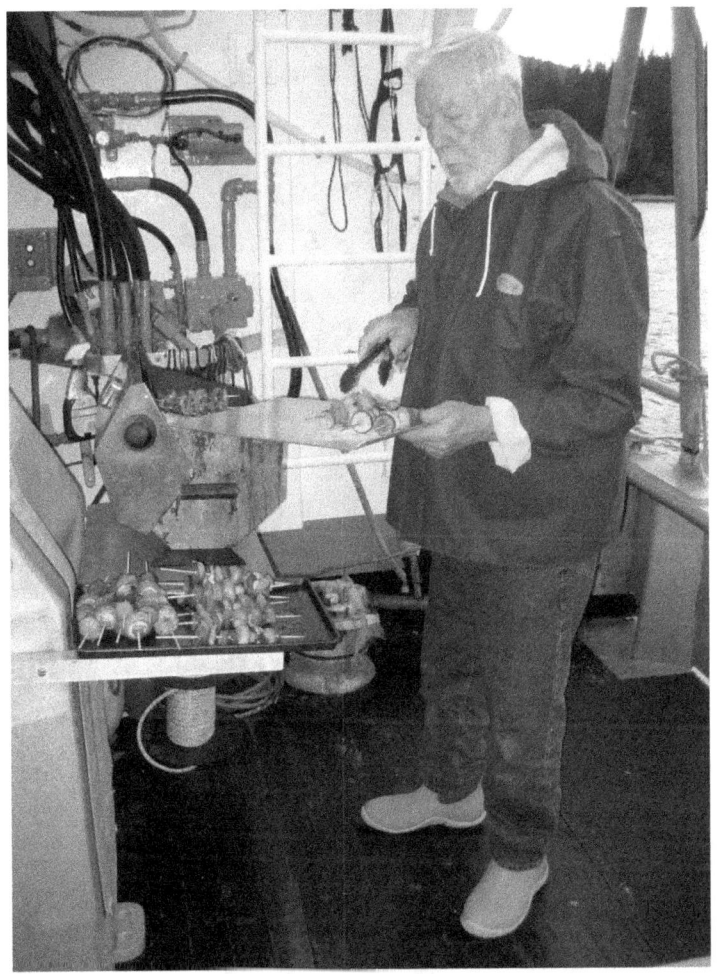

Bob Duke grilling kabobs aboard *Home Shore*

End of the training cruise on *Home Shore*

Bob Duke at *Home Shore*'s helm, Alaska

Sea Change, 2015

Symbiont

Whitsunday Islands and the Great Barrier Reef

Australia is both a country and a continent, so seeing all or just a lot of it in one visit, even for two weeks, would be a feat. I learned more about the inhabitants and culture than the geography, thanks to a head start from my Australian friend, Bob Steel, who managed Maritime Outfitters in Newport Beach. Bob was something of a magnet for Aussie sailors visiting Southern California at a time when Australian boatbuilders were building custom sailing yachts, and sailing them to the U.S. to sell on the American market. It hadn't been too many years earlier that Australia became the first challenger in a hundred and thirty-two years to win the 1983 America's Cup, resulting in all of U.S. *yachtdom* being inundated with everything yachting about Australia. So, I was fully primed for immersion in Australia.

Cairns (pronounced "kenz") is a coastal city in far northern Queensland, founded in 1876 to serve Hodgkinson River gold miners. Its tropical climate, rainforest, and access to the Great Barrier Reef (GBR) make it attractive to tourists. Of special interest to boaters are the nearby Whitsunday Islands, misnamed by explorer Captain James Cook, who failed to account for the International Dateline on the day of his discovery—it was actually "Whitmonday."

Once again, Shearlean and I were beneficiaries of a magazine with a tourism promotion junket its staff couldn't accept, albeit desperately wanting the display advertising package bundled with publishing a feature article on tourism, this time about the Whitsunday Islands of Queensland. Could we go to Australia for two weeks? an editor asked.

There are seventy-four islands centered around namesake Whitsunday Island, and the area is one of the most popular yachting destinations in the Southern Hemisphere. It is a sheltered, tropical area, protected by the Great Barrier Reef, which is ranked as one of the seven natural wonders of the world. The islands are forested and many are uninhabited. Even ones that are developed are otherwise uninhabited, except for the developer. The climate is mild, comparable to Southern California, and the Aussie inhabitants seem to have an affinity for *Yanks*.

This was a perfect example of the sort of world-class destination a sailor is unlikely to reach cruising his own boat, a destination that makes bareboat chartering such a great way of reaching exotic destinations without the grueling experience of circumnavigating the world, though, getting here for a bareboat charter was a jet-age sort of grueling—a nineteen-hour flight from Los Angeles (but with reclining seats).

(Contrary to what I just said, Jack and Charlene managed to cruise the Whitsundays on their own boat, the forty-foot Valiant, *Lilli Sohex*, as described earlier in my account of my passage with them from the Cook Islands to Tonga. They sailed for four years until they couldn't sail anymore and sold *Lillie Sohex* in Singapore and flew home to Los Angeles—an alternative cruising strategy I once considered on a smaller scale.)

We were gifted the use of a thirty-one-foot bareboat charter sloop for three days to cruise the islands according to our own itinerary. The sheltered islands offer numerous coves and sandy beaches, and no weather or other challenges to contend with. In nearly every way possible, it a very forgiving area suitable for the most lubberly of beginning boaters.

While the Whitsundays were some of the best sailing I've experienced, an included crewed two-night sailing tour was the worst, so bad that Shearlean and I jumped ship, mid-cruise, at a destination hotel, where I pleaded to be accommodated a day earlier than we were scheduled to arrive. I won't say we feared for our lives, but such wouldn't be out of the question, given all that could have potentially gone wrong. I worried about the six others—paying guests—who remained onboard.

This boat, I think it was named *Romance*, was a sixty-foot gaff-rigged brigantine ketch, with four staterooms, outfitted to resemble its nineteenth-century cousin. The moment I stepped on deck, all of my boating alarms went off. There were two massive 8D lead-acid batteries (weighing a hundred and thirty-two pounds each) sitting unsecured on the deck next to the electric anchor windlass. I saw no anchor but supposed it must be at the end of the chain, hanging straight into the water from the windlass (though *Romance* was tied to the dock). Something was seriously wrong.

The passageway to our cabin was so narrow I had to walk with my duffle bag clutched to my chest in front of me. Opening the cabin door, I found the berth filled the cabin except for a small space between the foot of the berth and the door. To enter the cabin, we had to crawl across the berth. That little bit of effort proved the ventilation was inadequate. Later, we discovered there was one head and shower for eight guests. The captain and crew slept in the main cabin and used the head on deck.

"We've got to get off of here," I whispered to Shearlean, who didn't disagree, but how? Our next host wasn't expecting us until two days from now. If we jumped ship, where would we go?

To my amazement, we got underway with the anchor still in the water and motored to a nearby cove, where the captain released the windlass brake and the anchor chain rattled overboard until it hit bottom. We had dinner ashore at a resort restaurant, which picked us up in its courtesy skiff.

After an uncomfortable night on *Romance,* a cold breakfast was laid out on deck (at least the coffee was hot) and we sat around in the fresh morning breeze and bright sun, getting acquainted with fellow guests. Then a loud, gurgling discharge caused us all to look over the side at what someone had just flushed overboard and was now floating alongside the hull. We all quit eating, put our food back on the buffet or took it with us to the other side of the boat and pretended nothing had just happened.

I knew from the *Romance* brochure map that we were near Hayward Island, a five-star resort that was to be our next host. I explained to *Romance's* captain that Shearlean and I needed to phone the Queensland tourist board about issues with our itinerary. I reasoned that having already enjoyed *Romance's* hospitality, we might as well move on to Hayward Island instead of journeying back to it tomorrow. We hadn't unpacked our bags, so we were ready to leave. The captain laboriously hand-cranked the anchor windlass until *Romance* signaled the anchor was off the bottom when she began drifting with the tide. We motored along until Hayward Island came into sight and we were taken ashore in *Romance's* dinghy. The gracious resort welcomed us as though we weren't early, and we were immensely relieved to be off *Romance.*

I wrote nothing about our *Romance* misadventure and said nothing to the tourist board. The other *Romance* guests didn't seem as put off by its condition as I was, and its operator was among my official hosts. There was too much *too right* about Queensland to feature comments about one bad apple. Maybe younger guests saw the romance in *Romance* that was lost on a fifty-three-year-old former marine surveyor.

We spent two weeks as guests in Queensland, the longest junket we ever experienced and one of the best organized and managed. Every event, and there were many, went off without a hitch, always on time and, except for *Romance*, exactly as represented. I went scuba diving on the Great Barrier Reef, where everyone on the dive boat became a certified scuba diver in one afternoon. We toured the jungle in an Australian-style safari wagon, with a flora and a fauna guide explaining everything we saw. A night in a twenty-one-story Hamilton Island casino hotel introduced us to wild cockatoos that fought for perching space on our balcony railing. (We were warned that the bird made famous by a '70s American TV detective program, *Baretta*, could take off your finger in one bite.)

The one thing I counted on seeing most on my trip to Australia I was denied: there are no kangaroos in Queensland. I was offered a ride to the zoo to see one, but it seemed outrageous to me to go to a zoo in Australia to see a kangaroo, and I declined the invitation. Still bothered by my failure to see a kangaroo, I mentioned it to everyone when I got home and learned that I was in good company in my disappointment. It seems the popular writer Mark Twain also failed to see a kangaroo during his 1895 Australia visit and had feelings similar to mine.

Known more for their casual dress than are Americans, Australia delighted me with what it calls "Queensland casual," which I mistook as to be the uniform of some mature men's scouting organization, because I saw so many men my age dressed similarly. They all wore walking shorts, collared shirts, calf-length socks, and leather shoes, but had no insignia or badge. A bit timidly, I asked one of our hosts why those men were dressed like that and received the answer "Queensland casual." The women accompanying these men were dressed in ordinary fashion. I stuck with my jeans, pullover knit shirt, and deck shoes (which I favored at the time).

I saw something similarly puzzling years later when I moved to Bellingham, Washington, where I noticed mainly men there wearing wool socks with open sandals, even on rainy days. Older and wiser then, I didn't ask anyone about it.

Bahamas: Cheyenne Summer and Bareboating

Cheyenne Summer's passage from strife-torn Colon, Panama, to Fort Lauderdale, Florida, was uneventful, I was told. After her 1993 haul out and servicing, following her transit from the West Coast of the U.S. to the East Coast, through the canal, Bob and Mary planned to use the boat for what it was designed for—cruising the Bahamas.

Mary hosted a Bahama cruise for her all-female yacht racing crew, from Newport Beach, which included Shearlean (and her lucky spouse) to join her for the cruise. For years, Mary and her women-only crew had been actively racing her Schock sloop *Valentine*. Mary was born on February 14, thus the boat's name. I was curious to see how *Cheyenne Summer*'s professional skipper would hold up under the scrutiny of so many experienced sailors, and whether those experienced sailors could contain their views on sail-trimming and such, and really make it a vacation.

Christopher Columbus made his first landfall in the Bahamas in 1492. There are seven hundred islands and over two thousand rocks and cays, sprinkled over a hundred thousand square miles of ocean off Florida's southeast coast. The archipelago is an ecological oasis, boasting the clearest water on the planet. Bimini is just fifty-three miles, about eight hours at six knots, from Fort Lauderdale, just a day's voyage even for a sailboat. Freeport, on Grand Bahama Island, is an overnight sail of about fifteen hours, ninety-four miles at six knots.

Bimini was our first landfall, because it is closest to Fort Lauderdale. It consisted of three tiny islands with a year-round population under two thousand. Famed explorer Juan Ponce de León was allegedly lured here in the early 1500s in search of the "Fountain of Youth," and a site still bears that name.

While Bimini has had more than its share of celebrity visitors, author Ernest Hemingway is probably most responsible for making it known to the public. He lived on Bimini from 1935 to 1937, staying at the Compleat Angler Hotel. He worked on *To Have and Have Not* and wrote a few articles, but mostly he fished aboard his boat *Pilar*, trolling the deep blue offshore waters for marlin, tuna, and swordfish. Hemingway was attracted to Bimini by tales of the incredible fishing available in the Gulf Stream, the legendary "river" of warm water that rushes north past the Bahamas. An Atlantic blue marlin weighing five hundred pounds, caught off Bimini, allegedly inspired Hemingway to write *The Old Man and the Sea* and *Islands in the Stream*.

We spent the night in a marina there. I was thrilled to be there, having read so many articles, including Hemingway's, about fishing and adventuring, but no one else was interested; shopping and dining were higher priorities. We enjoyed a couple of remote anchorages, some snorkeling and swimming in gin-clear water lapping at snow white beaches. Our destinations were Freeport and Nassau.

The city of Freeport emerged from a land grant comprising fifty thousand acres of swamp and scrub to become a cosmopolitan city and free-trade zone. It is the capital of Grand Bahama Island and was founded in 1955 as a center of tourism, offering every amenity an island visitor could hope for: pristine beaches, golf, water sports, diving, gambling, duty-free shopping, boating, nightclubs, and fishing.

Nassau, on New Providence Island, is the capital and largest city of The Bahamas. With a population of 274,400 as of 2016, or just over 70 percent of the entire population of The Bahamas, Nassau dwarfs all other towns in the country. It is the center of commerce, education, law, administration, and media of the country.

The town that would eventually be called Nassau was founded in 1670 and began as a fort and was named Charles Town in honor of England's King Charles II. During this time, there were frequent wars with the Spanish, and Charles Town was used as a base for privateering against them. In 1684, the town was burned to the ground during a raid. It was rebuilt in 1695, and renamed Nassau in honor of William of Orange, who belonged to a branch of The House of Nassau, an aristocratic European dynasty. He would become William III, King of England, Scotland, and Ireland. The name Nassau derives from the town of Nassau in Germany.

It was interesting and distracting to see these cities, but having a nice yacht and surrounded by all of The Bahamas, they were of little interest to me and made no lasting impression, except that they offered what cities offer everywhere.

Witnessing a shootout between the police and bank robbers was my most vivid memory. My first thought at the time was asking myself, why would anyone choose to rob a bank on an island? How do you make your getaway? But the robber was caught in the act and taken into custody, so getting away didn't become an issue.

When it happened, we were shopping. I felt like the designated male escort for the ladies of the cruise, being the only male guest. There were five or six of us browsing the merchandise in some boutique when we all heard the distinctive *pop, pop, pop* of gunshots nearby. We all rushed to a large window at the back end of the store, where we watched in stunned amazement as a uniformed police officer and another man exchanged gunshots on the sidewalk in front of the bank, two doors away. The policeman was wounded but didn't go down, and the robber threw down his gun and raised his hands as police cars arrived almost instantaneously.

We retreated from our ringside window, too excited and alarmed to continue shopping, finally acknowledging our group folly to watch a gun battle standing in front of a large window. We had no desire to go out onto the street because of all we had witnessed. We finally decided we should go directly back to the boat, which was in the opposite direction from the crime scene.

We decided to return to Fort Lauderdale, traveling overnight, so we would arrive in the early morning, giving us plenty of time before our flight home. It turned into a memorable night for me, because I imagined myself sailing across the Milky Way in a festive sea of starlight and accompanied by distant brightly lit cruise ships, looking like Hubble-telescope images of cosmic galaxies. I chose the 2:00 a.m. watch, with the engine running only a little over idle RPM and the mainsail up and flat to minimize rolling. I steered through a magnificent light show of overhead stars reflected in the sea and cruise ships idling the night away to arrive at their next port-of-call at dawn.

There was only the gentlest breeze, the sea was flat, but our wake cradled the boat in phosphorescent splendor, and the vibration and hum of the engine was soothing; I could have steered all night.

I had been to The Bahamas a few years earlier when Shearlean and I did a bareboat charter in the Abacos, on the eastern perimeter of the islands. It was another shoal water, Pirates of the Caribbean-themed charter inspired by Honduras' Bay Islands charter. The Bahamas was not nearly as interesting or as challenging as the Bay Islands, but loads of fun and as storied a nautical destination as I could ask for. It would have remained on my cruising bucket list if I hadn't done this charter. The Bahamas is so vast and so varied that I'm certain there is something there for everybody.

The era of piracy in the Caribbean began in the 1500s, and phased out in the 1830s, after the navies of the nations of Western Europe and North America with colonies in the Caribbean began combating pirates. The period during which pirates were most successful was from the 1660s to 1730s. Piracy flourished in the Caribbean because of the existence of many pirate seaports throughout the area. Piracy in the Caribbean was part of a larger, historical phenomenon of piracy, as it existed close to major trade and exploration routes in nearly all the five oceans of the world.

I was glad we chose the Abacos, because its fringe location gave it a sort of rural or off-the-beaten-path feel that came across to me in the people we met, facilities we dealt with, and marine features we enjoyed. It was certainly uncrowded.

The Abacos, as we experienced them, were a giant sea-and-sand playground for adults. We gradually began spending most of each day in the water, swimming and diving, and hiking in the shallows towing our dinghy behind us by its painter by hand. It was an irresistible temptation to return to our evolutionary aquatic origins. Dressed in big-brimmed hats, T-shirts, reef-walking sandals, and bathing suits, only our arms and legs required sunscreen.

Hiking through the shallows of a shorefront town, I spied an ice cream shop at the boardwalk, paralleling the beach. We beached the dinghy and walked over and each ordered a chocolate milkshake that we consumed while continuing our hike. It was so intensely good that we stopped on the way back down the beach and bought another.

This was the first time we chartered a powerboat for a bareboat tropical charter. We began our charter with a sailboat, a CSY 37, a sloop-rigged, aft cockpit cousin of the CSY 44 we had in the Bay Islands. It was entirely satisfactory and had all the desirable feature CSYs were noted for. Though The Bahamas has its share of rocks, it is not as "rocky" as the Bay Islands, and the odds are that if you go aground in The Bahamas, it will be a soft grounding that you can probably free your boat from without kedging; just be patient and the tide may float you off or get off the boat to lighten it, and no harm is done. Also, the incredibly clear water and reflective sea bottom of The Bahamas lets you pilot your way around visually with someone at the bow telling you what lies ahead.

Our powerboat charter was a different story. It was a thirty-five-foot fiberglass Taiwan-built trawler, single diesel, aft-cabin boat. It wasn't designed and built for tropical chartering. I suspected it had been put into charter by the owner as a way of earning some income to cover expenses. The biggest problem was inadequate ventilation, and it was a major inconvenience to climb over the transom safety rail to get to the swim step and the dinghy. Ventilation to the aft master stateroom was obstructed by the main cabin, so we used the bow cabin with its big open deck hatch that funneled the breeze in over the berths. The main cabin windows had no blinds or curtains to block the sun, so we sat on the shaded side of the weather deck much of the time. These were early days for power bareboat chartering and purpose-built and outfitted power boats of various kinds (including multihulls) soon came along, but we were convinced to stick with proven sailboats that had pioneered tropical bareboat chartering.

A particularly fond memory I have of the Abacos was that it was the first place I ever ate grits that I actually enjoyed and asked for more. Shearlean was from Tennessee, definitely grits country, and I had lived in Alabama and East Texas, also grits country, where I suffered just having grits on my breakfast plate. But I had breakfast one morning in a Marsh Harbor restaurant run buy a local lady who looked very old, but moved like she was very young. She was putting together what appeared to be a takeout order, which I asked her about. She said she also cooked for the jail prisoners, and pointed across the street to a rundown-looking pink building.

"Lucky jailbirds," I remarked, thinking of my tasty breakfast, including the grits.

Writing Myself to Tahiti

I first fell under the spell of what I call "Tahiti of the Mind" in the early '70s when Shearlean and I vacationed at the now defunct Club Med at Moorea. Club Med (as it was commonly known) was a French travel and tourism operator specializing in all-inclusive holidays. It attracted mainly young singles and couples to resort villages around the world, including French Polynesia. We liked it enough to do other Club Med vacations, including Cancun, Mexico, and Hanalei Bay, Hawaii (which I revisited when delivering *Aorangi* after the 1983 Transpac race).

Though not being able to sail *Symbiont* to Tahiti from Baja was a big letdown, writing about boating got me to Tahiti twice more, stranding me once, much to my delight.

My second Tahiti trip was arranged by Shearlean, though we both had to work to pay for it. An editorial friend of Shearlean's at a slick Orange County lifestyle magazine had received one of those free trip offers that no one at the magazine had the time or desire to accept, and offered it to Shearlean. And, she selected me to accompany her as the assignment photographer. I was able to accept, because this was obviously one of those special opportunities for time off which I had negotiated in my Calavo contract.

We were headed for what was then a novel hotel of palm-thatched bungalows built on pilings over Bora Bora's Mauna Beach lagoon. We could go snorkeling right off of our bungalow's deck and watch fish through the glass coffee table built into the bungalow's floor. We spent five days bicycling around the island, attending entertainments at the Hotel Bora Bora as invited guests, dining at Bloody Mary's, and daily enjoying French cuisine, bread, and pastries. We flew on UTA French Airlines to Tahiti's capital, Pape'ete, and then took a local flight a hundred and forty miles to Bora Bora. Distressingly, we learned that our "free" seats on UTA were the ones that didn't recline (for ten hours) and that the government airline was perpetually threatening to strike, putting our time and date of departure continually in doubt. But we learned from our experience cruising on *Symbiont* that traveling can be fraught with far more and worse difficulties, so we weren't much bothered by these conditions. After cruising, when anything would go wrong while traveling, Shearlean or I would remind ourselves audibly with the remark, "Well, at least we can't sink."

My third Tahiti trip I did as a dual writing assignment in partnership with a friend, Larry Dunmire, a Newport Beach freelance photographer, to cover an International Billfish Tournament for *Sport Fishing Magazine*. Larry had wangled a Tahiti photo assignment from an annual Australian boating publication, but needed someone to write the article to accompany his photos. He agreed to split his fee with me in exchange for the article. I then asked the magazine editor if he had any interest in an article about Tahiti fishing. My timing couldn't have been better, because the third International Billfish Tournament was planned for Tahiti at a time compatible with Larry's schedule. Larry could recoup the part of his fee he was paying me by providing the magazine with photos to complement my tournament article. Larry's client got us both round-trip airline tickets on UTA (this time with reclining seats), and I, with a letter of assignment from *Sport Fishing Magazine*, persuaded the Tahiti tourist board to comp me a hotel room for the duration of the tournament, which I would share with Larry. As things would turn out, *duration of the tournament* was a key condition.

With Larry as my photographer, I was able to get him onboard some billfishing boats, where he could get fishing photos for me and also get his client's offshore photos of Tahiti. All the information I had to gather was the same as Larry's article required, it just had to be presented differently for two different audiences. It worked out as a win-win situation for everybody involved, until the tournament ended before our UTA ticket return date.

With the tournament over, I was kicked out of my accommodations and suddenly Larry and I were on the street. Next, we had confirmation that UTA was definitely going to strike before our return flight, and we could end up living out-of-pocket in very pricey Pape'ete.

We knew no one in Pape'ete, but resourceful Larry knew the manager of the Hotel Bora Bora and telephoned him about our plight, and he said he could put us up until UTA settled its strike. Intra-island flights were cheap, so we flew to Bora Bora and were given a room usually used by employees and friends of the hotel.

After shutting down Tahiti tourism for three days, UTA felt it had made its point with the loud assistance of stranded tourists and began flying again.

I haven't been back to Tahiti or Bora Bora since 1990, but the internet says the Hotel Bora Bora closed in 2008 for reconstruction and hasn't reopened. Designed in traditional Tahitian style, with sixty-five luxury rooms, it first opened in 1961.

Larry took a prized photo of me at the hotel, sitting in a beached outrigger canoe, a flower behind my ear, a mai tai in one hand, pecking with one finger at the keyboard of my laptop computer with the other, writing happily, though stranded—in paradise.

Yacht Club History Project

Boating trips into the past are rare, but Shearlean and I were able to travel back in time when we were hired to tell the story of the seventy-five-year history of the Newport Harbor Yacht Club (NHYC).

In the late nineteenth century, a pile of sand known then as East Newport Town Company was established on the shore of the Pacific Ocean, at thirty-three degrees, thirty-six hours and two minutes north, and a hundred and seventeen degrees, fifty-three hours west, where Orange County would one day share forty miles of scenic California coastline.

Thanks to its harbor, Newport Beach has a long-and-storied yachting history, a getaway for Hollywood denizens preferring beach sands to Palm Spring's desert sands and choosing yachting over golfing. Newport Beach has become home to wealthy boat owners, the location of numerous waterfront businesses, and a vacation destination for many from the western U.S. and Canada.

Our writing job was to prepare the draft of the club's history, which would consist of gathering, organizing, and writing the information that would ultimately be the text of a four-hundred-sixty-nine-page book, to be published in 1991. Others would be hired to design the entire book, gather photographs, prepare graphics for reproduction, edit the whole contents, and print and bind the book.

As a former *Times, Orange County* editor, and now columnist writing "On The Waterfront" monthly, and other *Times* freelance features, Shearlean was well-known throughout the county from her *Times* byline, which had been appearing there for nearly twenty years.

I'm uncertain what was known about me. I'd had a regular byline in *Sea Magazine* for a while and was read, I'm sure, by many club members. Plus, I'd become nearly a fixture on the waterfront since I'd taken up surveying with Pike Putnak.

We felt privileged to have been selected and were enthusiastic about delving into the history of the area we had called home: twenty-one years for Shearlean and nearly thirty years for me.

From conception to planning to implementation to fulfilment, the history book took somewhere between fifty years, with Dr. Albert Soiland's brief first history in 1936, and two years with this seventy-fifth anniversary version, depending on your frame of reference. My time writing the draft took about four months in 1990.

I had written a couple of other histories for clients' significant corporate anniversaries, but nothing on this scale. Given a chronology and list of milestone events for any organization, writing a history is a pretty straightforward process. This being a yachting history and incorporating a significant chunk of Newport Beach history, the subject matter was of intense interest to me, and I had to be careful not to get carried away by my own curiosity and squander my time. I made it a point to make what was of special interest to yacht club members (mostly based on interviews I did with many of them) of special interest to me.

Going to a yacht club every day to work, instead of my home office, whether the club was open to members or not, verged on luxury. It was especially appealing when the club was empty and silent and the docks were nearly deserted and I could roam around the premises and immerse myself in picturing its past when the clubhouse was little more than a barracks—a rudimentary shelter for hardy individuals and families roughing it at the beach and sailing dinghies among Lido and Balboa Islands in Newport Bay. Later, as facilities were expanded and improved, the club rented rooms to members and guests. For years, taking a big boat out of the bay into the ocean could be a harrowing experience, because continuously shifting sands could close the harbor entrance or drastically shift the channel.

A key to the NHYC's history, growth, and longevity—as with most other yacht clubs, including my own BCYC—was its emphasis on youth. Looking back seventy-five years, the contiguous thread of history is the thread of junior sailing programs that included not only members' children, but also community children. The program had the full support of older members, such as the aptly named Rocking Chair Fleet. Without a vigorous youth program, up to and including young adults, yacht clubs have no future, as some have discovered the hard way.

It was a challenge and a genuine pleasure to piece together seventy-five years of Newport Beach boating history, much of it firsthand accounts from yacht club members who had lived it. I soon learned that not everyone agreed on the "facts" of this event or "that anecdote" that was common NHYC lore. Often, someone I interviewed started out saying, "I can tell you the real story behind . . ." Or as word got around about what I was doing at the club, I was approached by individuals, who prided themselves on knowing the *real* story, to volunteer to be interviewed for the history.

Many early movies were made in Newport Beach, thus acquainting actors with the area, and the club provided the only good private boat facilities in the bay and the best on-the-water accommodations until the 1950s.

Hollywood was attracted to the club as early as 1916, with members including cowboy star Tom Mix, dramatic actor John Barrymore, and actor/producer Douglas Fairbanks, Sr. Many actors from the "golden age" of Hollywood—Humphrey Bogart, Spencer Tracy, Richard Arlen, Dick Powell, Lauren Bacall, Errol Flynn, Victor McLaglen, and John Wayne were members and guests; Wayne was a longtime Newport Beach resident with a house on Bay Shore Drive. Part of the early Hollywood attraction of Newport Beach was that it was "out-of-town" enough for the celebrities to be anonymous. Sensitive to being accused of being "starstruck," the club was quick and persistent to point out: "The (Hollywood) connection was neither sought nor avoided."

Actor Humphrey Bogart, an avid sailor of his fifty-five-foot yawl, *Santana*, and NHYC member (until his death in 1957) was the object of more lore than even colorful Bogie could have reasonably been expected to generate. It seemed everyone had a Bogie story.

"I think Bogart cried when the board summoned him to tell him he was being thrown out for living on his boat, unmarried, with Lauren Bacall. He pleaded with them and they relented. He married her soon after," according to member Henry Grandin, Jr.

Unattributable, therefore unpublished, are Bogie tales involving his third wife, Mayo Methot, nicknamed "Sluggy" for her well-known drunken combativeness, which was said to account for the frequent uproar aboard *Santana* at the yacht club's docks. In contemporary parlance, there is speculation that the off-screen, mild-mannered Bogie was a victim of domestic violence.

There are other notable yacht clubs in Newport Beach, but only one has earned the accolade *THE* Yacht Club, and that's Newport Harbor Yacht Club. But it was the first and to the irritation of the other clubs, through no effort I know of on its part, NHYC has long been the object of this sobriquet by the community and yachting public at large, and it has stuck. On entering the harbor, visiting yacht skippers have reportedly asked directions to *THE* Yacht Club and have never been asked which yacht club they meant. I assume if questioned about this, a NHYC spokesperson would reply, standing on precedent, "The connection was neither sought nor avoided."

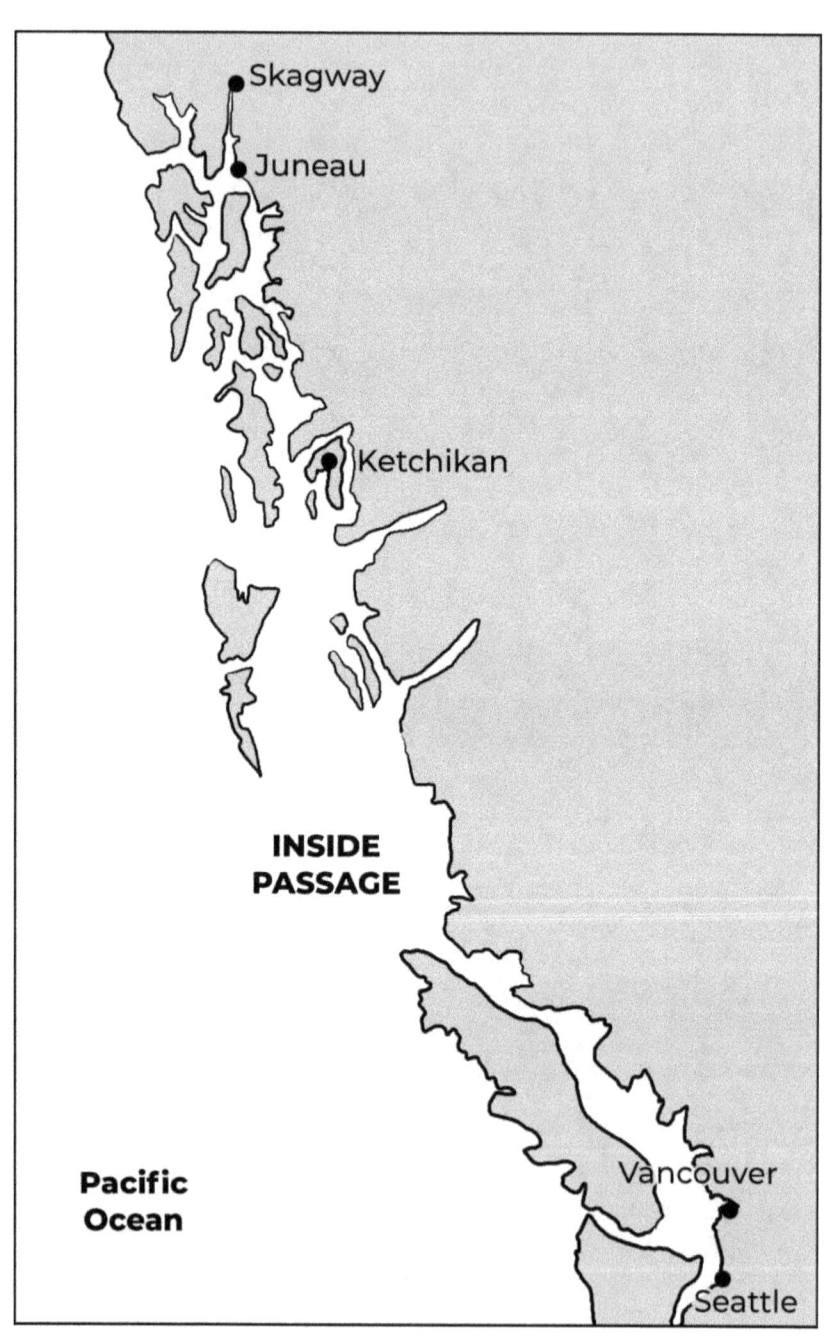

Map of the Inside Passage

Marine Highway Ferry to Alaska

It may be bending the facts to the breaking point, but I like to think of Shearlean's and my twenty-fifth wedding anniversary cruise to Southeast Alaska as a crewed boat charter. So many people were traveling all over the world in the '90s over the holidays that I was determined to find an uncrowded destination for our December 31, 1995, wedding anniversary trip. I thought, "Who goes to Alaska for Christmas? No one." I was certain there wouldn't be anyone there, and I was nearly right—almost to a fault.

Thinking the weather would be poor but not terrible, we packed our foul-weather gear. Knowing that Southeast Alaska weather is moderated by the proximity of the Pacific Ocean, we discounted the threat of freezing conditions.

The State of Alaska Marine Highway Ferry System provides year-round ferry service from Bellingham, Washington, to Alaska's coastal communities. The ferries make up a large part of Alaska's highway system, covering thirty-five hundred miles of coastline and thirty-five communities stretching from Bellingham to Dutch Harbor in the Aleutian chain.

The Marine Highway is a designated route through the Inside Passage, which is so named because it passes inside the protective islands off the coasts of Washington, British Columbia, and Southeast Alaska. These islands shelter recreational and commercial vessels not capable of or not desiring to operate in the open ocean. The Passage's southern terminus is Seattle, Washington, and its northern terminus is Skagway, Alaska, a nautical distance of approximately a thousand miles.

While the routes through the Inside Passage are myriad, the main route is designated the Alaska Marine Highway. The highway is the heavily traveled route from Seattle to the major cities of Southeast Alaska: Ketchikan, Wrangell, Petersburg, Juneau, and Sitka. The Alaska State Ferry follows the marine highway, as does heavy barge traffic freighting goods between Alaska and the lower forty-eight states through the Port of Seattle.

Openings in the Inside Passage barrier that can profoundly affect commercial and recreational boat travel include:
- Juan de Fuca Strait, between the north coast of Washington and the south end of Vancouver Island.
- Queen Charlotte Sound, at the north end of Vancouver Island.
- Dixon Entrance, at Cape Fox between Prince Rupert, British Columbia, and Ketchikan, Alaska.
- Milbanke Sound, between Bella Bella and Klemtu, British Columbia.

Recreational cruising boats use this same route, though often deviating from the Marine Highway, to explore areas off the beaten path.

Cruising boats avoid or minimize exposure to open sea conditions at Juan de Fuca Strait and Milbanke Sound by detouring away from the highway through passages and behind islands. But there is no avoiding Queen Charlotte Sound and Dixon Entrance, critical areas for every

Inside Passage voyage. Itineraries are planned around crossing these areas, and tales of difficulty and even danger cite both locations.

Queen Charlotte Sound and Dixon Entrance are dangerous to cruising boats because they may not be ready for the open ocean conditions that can develop here. Prudent skippers avoid bad conditions by monitoring weather reports, being alert to changing local conditions, and by seeking shelter until conditions improve.

Ferries and other commercial vessels are, for the most part, immune to the hazards faced by recreational boats, so accidents and losses are rare, yet they do occur. On March 22, 2006, British Columbia ferry *Queen of the North* sank on the Marine Highway with the loss of two lives. Commercial vessels, such as tugs and fishing boats, still encounter problems in such hazardous areas as Wrangell Narrows and Seymour Narrows, which continue to claim victims despite their long-standing notoriety.

The region of Southeast Alaska includes communities from Ketchikan, Alaska, along the Marine Highway to Yakutat at edge of the Gulf of Alaska. Most of these communities receive year-round service.

Ketchikan is the state's southeastern-most major settlement. Downtown Ketchikan is a National Historic District, consisting mainly of Creek Street, a boardwalk commercial neighborhood that was a red light district in the gold-rush days. With a 2018 population of 8,289, it is the fifth-most populous city in the state. The surrounding borough encompasses suburbs both north and south of the city, along the Tongass Highway. Incorporated on August 25, 1900, Ketchikan is the earliest extant incorporated city in Alaska and is nicknamed "First City." Revillagigedo Island, so named in 1793 by Captain George Vancouver, is where Ketchikan is located. (I've never heard the island's name pronounced the same way twice.)

Our ferry was the *Matanuska*, named for the Matanuska Glacier, in the Chugach Mountains of Alaska. It was built in 1962, and was four hundred and eight feet long, with a seventy-four-foot beam, and a draft of seventeen feet. It displaced 5,685 tons, and consisted of three passenger decks and one vehicle deck. The diesel-powered ship, still in service, has a crew of forty-eight. It can carry five hundred passengers and eighty-eight vehicles at a speed of fifteen-and-a-half knots (nineteen MPH). Accommodations consist of private and shared staterooms, reclining seats, a cafeteria and bar, and solarium. I mention the solarium because passengers with sleeping bags and tents can camp their way to Alaska—even in winter—at the lowest fare. I reserved an outboard stateroom for Shearlean and me, with upper/lower bunk beds and a bathroom, only for the longest leg of the trip, Bellingham to Ketchikan, thirty-eight hours. Our ticket allowed us to reboard the ferry to continue our trip from Ketchikan to Petersburg, eight hours, and Petersburg to Juneau, nine hours. We would fly home from Juneau on January 3, 1996.

For Christmas in Ketchikan, I reserved a suite at the Cape Fox Lodge, on a hill overlooking central Ketchikan, which was accessible by an incline railway car from the lobby to the waterfront.

For Petersburg, I reserved a waterfront B&B, with a communal kitchen, and for our anniversary, December 31, our last ferry stop was in Alaska's capital, Juneau, where I reserved a room at a spa.

The only excitement during our ferry travel was from Ketchikan to Petersburg through Wrangell Narrows, and came at night, just after we had gone to bed. The ship began rolling violently, whipping about left and right, frightening Shearlean and making me dress quickly to see what was going on. Opening the stateroom door, I was alarmed by passengers crowding the side decks on both sides of the ship, their conversation boisterous. As far as I could see ahead of and behind the ship, there was a twisting display of red-and-green lights, which—given the Christmas season—I took to be decorations, but I discarded the notion as silly. The ship turned sharply, keeping the red lights to starboard and the green to port, marking the narrow channel. As we twisted and turned, a new pair of red-and-green lights appeared ahead of the ship. We were in Wrangell Narrows, a twenty-mile-long channel about which piloting and navigation chapters have been written, and about which an entire small book has been published: *Wrangell Narrows, Alaska,* by Captain William M. Hopkins, seventy-two pages.

Arriving in Ketchikan in the early evening of December 23, we shouldered our duffel bags and walked and rode to the lobby of the hotel in the incline car and checked in. Notified that the restaurant would be closing soon, we dropped our bags in our room and went to dinner. When we returned to our room, there was a huge fruit-and-cheese basket sitting on the bench at the foot of the bed. How nice, I thought, as I unfolded the enclosed note: "Holiday greetings from the management and staff of the Cape Fox Lodge. We are closed for the holidays from December 24 through 26, so our staff can spend the holidays with their families. We will reopen December 27. In case of an emergency, hotel security can be contacted at ext. 22."

I raced to the lobby, but the reception area was abandoned and dimly lit, the restaurant was dark. Towering in the center of the lobby, a brightly lit Christmas tree twinkled and a subdued version of "Jingle Bells" wafted through the space. Images of an abandoned holiday hotel danced through my head as visions of the movie *The Shining* presented themselves. My surroundings took on a more sinister look. There was a huge fireplace blazing opposite the plush sofa on the opposite side of the lobby. I wondered whether there were any other guests. With the snacks we had in our duffle bags and the fruit basket, we wouldn't starve, but I was undecided about how I felt about this "surprise."

The silence and lack of activity were a little spooky and an endless supply of jolly and somber Christmas Muzak playing throughout the hotel had me thinking about finding the "off" switch.

Rain is ever-present in Southeast Alaska, mostly a drizzle that can be surprisingly soaking. Our bright yellow foul-weather gear and calf-length rubber boots were comfortable protection against the rain, so we ignored the weather and went walking everywhere around town.

When we learned the hotel was closed, we thought we would find an open restaurant in town, but all other businesses were closed, too. Ketchikan was a ghost town without pedestrians, and the only sign of life was the hissing of tires on wet streets.

As with most trips, we roamed the streets along the waterfront. We found our way to Thomas Basin, the downtown marina, and walked the extensive docks looking at boats, the majority of which were small, commercial boats, mostly gillnetters and long-liners, as common among residents here as were riding mowers in other parts of the U.S. Dozens of bald eagles, their feathers plumped up against the rain, sat stoically atop sailboat masts, alert to our intrusion.

Next, we headed for the Totem Pole Park, a modest walk out of town. Shearlean, feeling the call of nature, was urgently looking for a restroom or a dense clump of bushes, when I suggested she try the Coast Guard station just off to our right. She headed straight for it, as I found some steps to sit on. She disappeared inside, so I assumed she was welcome and was using the facilities. Nearly fifteen minutes passed before a bright yellow figure reappeared. She arrived a bit breathless and with a big smile on her face, saying there was a single young man on duty who was eager for some company and talked nonstop even while she was in the restroom.

We continued on to the totem park whose stylized animal images were an ominous sight in the gloom of the low, grey rain clouds, the trickling runoff and loud dripping from the surrounding firs and cedars. It was a strange walk in the park that seemed to perfectly fit the present mood of the whole city of Ketchikan.

As we started back to the hotel, an old pickup truck stopped beside us and offered us a ride. The woman driving it smiled and nodded toward the huge, uncooked turkey on the seat beside her. "Just put that in your lap," she said. We chatted on our way to the Creek Street incline.

She was from Washington State and visiting family in Ketchikan for Christmas, and guffawed at our statements of why we were here now.

We asked her to drop us at the Ketchikan Yacht Club, but found it was closed for the holidays, and rode a bus to another marina at the other end of town and walked back to the hotel. It rained off and on during our whole stay, interrupted by what the weather forecast called "occasional sun breaks."

We arrived in Petersburg after dark and were disoriented about where we had landed relative to our B&B. Someone dropping off someone or something at the ferry offered us a ride to the B&B. He was a local and interested in why we were there and had the same reaction as the woman in Ketchikan, but provided us with a quick history and orientation to Petersburg. He pointed out the prominent Sons of Norway Hall as we passed.

At the door of our B&B, there was a note saying it had been left unlocked because of our late arrival. We went in and went right to bed, without bothering to unpack. We met our hosts at breakfast. He was a fisherman and the B&B was her enterprise, an energetic couple in their mid-fifties.

We learned there was great bear-watching at the city dump and that Petersburg was open for business. There were three marinas, creatively name North, Middle, and South. We were next door to Middle Marina, which, unsurprisingly was in the middle of town. We spent the morning walking the docks and looking at boats. Because of the holidays, the marina was deserted, and we surprised wildlife camped out on the docks and unattended boats, including sea lions, ducks, geese, swans, otters, and eagles.

We worked up an appetite by noon and found a fresh seafood store across the street from the harbormaster's office that offered Styrofoam bowls of takeout salmon chowder and fresh-baked sourdough bread, so we ordered two, and took them back to the harbormaster's office and sat on the bench under the overhanging roof and watched the bald eagles coming and going, and preening on the masts and outriggers of the boats.

Though there wasn't really any place to drive, I rented a car to go to see the bears at the dump, not only because the dump was a long walk, but the car was a bear-proof shelter for watching a trio of black bears close-up. While we had the car, we picked up a chowder and sourdough lunch again, and drove to a bird sanctuary far out of town. We ate at a concrete picnic table sheltered by a cedar shake roof while we watched bald eagles squabbling over their catch on the beach and saw impressive aerial combat among the big birds trying to fly off with an oversized catch.

Another use I had for the car was my interest in seeing residential areas surrounding the town. The houses were ordinary, but most had a boat or two stored in the yard and the wreck of a truck or beat-up trailer for hauling firewood.

Because there was a tempting variety of live seafood available from tanks at the chowder market, we decided to cook a couple of meals: live Dungeness crab and shrimp, and local salmon on ice.

We visited North and South marinas and sat in bars drinking Alaskan Amber and listened to local talk. In a commercial fishing harbor such as Petersburg, our bright yellow rain-gear stood out among the common commercial gear that was muted tones of brown, green, red, and orange. Our boots, at least, were commercial grade.

We arrived in Juneau in the early morning of December 31 and took a taxi to a spa resort high up the steep mountain slope that is the city's background, about which I remember only one thing: each room had an outdoor hot tub overlooking the city lights and harbor. Twenty-five years of marriage, wow! Let's celebrate!

Juneau is stretched out along the foot of steep mountains on a narrow band of habitable land that gives the illusion that it might slide into the sea at any time. It has more marinas than even I could wish to visit, though we did visit two and looked in at the Juneau Yacht Club and had a drink at the bar.

I've never been a big fan of cities, except the most famous, such as Paris or London or New York, so I wasn't keen to tour downtown Juneau. We were there for the glaciers and as a means of flying home.

Mendenhall Glacier, though about twelve miles from downtown, is nevertheless an in-town glacier, partly because Juneau's configuration makes it one of the largest cities by area in the United States; it has the space for a glacier. For convenience, we signed up at the spa for a glacier tour and when we arrived at the glacier, I saw for the first time the distinctive and beautiful blue of glacial ice. At the parking lot at Mendenhall, you could just walk up to the glacier and onto it with crowds of other people surveying the mass and wonder of so much ice.

That night there was a light snow, enough to coat everything, and we found it irresistible to sit in our private hot tub and sip on a complimentary bottle of champagne, and gaze at the city lights while large snowflakes drifted in our view. We found we had little interest in anything other than each other and were tired of working at traveling and were in a mood to just drift along. The next day, though, we had agreed to do something spectacular and expensive to memorialize our anniversary. We were going to take a four hundred dollar (in 1995 dollars) helicopter tour of glaciers in the mountains behind Juneau, including landing on a glacier for a short hike.

"Jump in," our pilot said as the whirling blades overhead gathered speed. It was as though our seat belts were connected to the throttle of the helicopter, because it rose straight up the instant my belt buckle clicked shut. Somewhat surprising to me, all of Juneau was spread out beneath us as we pivoted and continued to gain altitude toward the wall of mountains behind the city. More and more mountains seemed to materialize, as though they were crowding forward for a look at us, rather than us speeding toward them. Then, suddenly, flat slabs of glaciers dominated our view behind the mountain ridges as we sped over the featureless white wilderness spread out below. All this time, the pilot kept chattering away about names of peaks, mountains, and glaciers surrounding us and with no prelude, we quickly descended and landed before I could tell we were near enough to the ground to land.

I'd been in helicopters and small planes before, but hadn't transitioned so quickly from one altitude to another, and one place to another, so swiftly. I felt as though I couldn't keep up with myself, that somehow my mind was lagging behind my body. Shearlean looked a little disoriented, too.

We stepped out of the helicopter and onto the glacier. The sun was severely bright, nearly blinding, the air was still and the rotor blades now mute. It was as though we had landed on another planet, just ten minutes from taking off. Since the glacier could support the helicopter, it was safe enough to walk wherever we wanted, but hiking seemed pointless, so we stood around the helicopter talking with the pilot and remarking upon the utter, barren wildness just a couple of air miles from the thickly forested ocean shore skirting the state's capital city.

I was pleased with the trip, happy we did it. I certainly remember it, and our anniversary had been wholly satisfying.

After three days in Juneau, we flew home on Alaska Airlines, directly to Orange County, California, and back to our Newport Beach condo, where it was *always* sunny (with occasional rain breaks).

Gray Whales in My Living Room

Sitting on our living room sofa behind a picture window, I watched gray whales feeding in Bellingham Bay for the third consecutive week.

We arrived in Bellingham, Washington, in mid-August 1999, after three months of camping across Canada, from Newfoundland to British Columbia, in time for Shearlean to start her job as a professor in the Journalism Department of Western Washington University (WWU).

We continued living in our camping trailer briefly until we rented a unit in a recently completed waterfront condo overlooking the bay. A large marina full of commercial fishing boats and yachts was spread out at the foot of the steep hillside the condo was built on. Beyond the harbor was the expansive bay, with Lummi Island in the distance.

Wow! Am I ever lucky to be here, I said to myself over and over, as I feasted on the visual treats, I could not have conjured better in my most fanciful dream.

For all I knew then, the appearance of whales was a routine event, but it never happened again in the twenty years I lived in Bellingham. Gray whales migrating north along the Pacific Coast, from their nursery in Scammon's Lagoon, in Baja, Mexico, was an annual event, but no one recalled the whales entering the bay until I arrived in August 1999. I learned that an El Nino event had reduced their normal source of food and desperate hunger had driven them into the bay seeking food.

I never suspected that gray whales, humpback whales, and I would become frequent companions for the next fifteen years.

When we'd traveled on the Alaska ferry from Bellingham in 1995, the city had captured my imagination, as did Southeast Alaska, but I never foresaw living here, nor had I fully appreciated all that it had to offer a dedicated boater like me.

Though I'd been in North Carolina for two years, I had continued writing generic boating articles for *Dockside* magazine. Now that I was in the Pacific Northwest, I proposed writing a northwest boating column and features for *Dockside* that would open up the northwest to advertising opportunities for the California magazine, thus continuing my employment.

Bellingham was also the last major U.S. harbor at the southern end of the thousand-mile-long Inside Passage, leading to a crown jewel of the U.S. park system, Glacier Bay, Alaska, the northern terminus of the passage. Membership in the informal fifty-nine-degree Club was a bucket list achievement for boaters who take their own boat to the face of Grand Pacific glacier at the farthest end of Glacier Bay at fifty-nine-degrees north.

Realizing where I was and what the location offered in the way of local boating among the numerous U.S. San Juan Islands, and the equally inviting nearby Canadian Gulf Islands, I decided I had to have a boat again.

Sweetie Pie was out there somewhere waiting for me to find her. Washington, which ranked seventh among boat-owning states, had thousands of boats for sale within a hundred miles of Bellingham. I was eager to start looking. I hadn't owned a serious boat since *Symbiont* and was looking forward to owning a boat again, especially where the cost of ownership was relatively low. For example, when I left California in 1997, marina slips were renting for $17/foot per month and that was for the length of the slip or boat, whichever is greater. In Bellingham, slip rent was $5/foot per month. It was no joke that in Southern California, boaters put their newborn's name on slip waiting lists so they'd have a slip when they grew up.

I joined the Squalicum Yacht Club in Bellingham, where a member invited me to go sailing with him and I was alarmed at how sore and stiff I was for days afterward. At age sixty-one, I feared my sailing days were numbered. Besides, I had a premonition that the Inside Passage wasn't sailing territory. Not that sailboats didn't travel the Inside Passage, but they had to rely on their engines to make reliable progress; the sheltered waters made the winds unreliable.

I searched for a power boat, something I'd not even thought about since *Elusive Lady*. In the twenty-plus years since then, affordable fiberglass trawler-style power boats were available. With new low-cost diesel engines, the boats were capable cruisers in sheltered and coastwise waters.

Price was important and an older, little-used trawler, well maintained, could be a great bargain. When I found her, her name was *Sangria,* and she was owned by a fussy man about my age, who kept scrupulous records of every engine hour and mile traveled in this 1977 Mainship 34, a flybridge sedan trawler, with a single diesel engine.

I got a slip in Squalicum Harbor, the main marina in Bellingham and changed her name to *Sweetie Pie*, my endearment for Shearlean.[19]

In a sedan-style boat, you can walk inside the boat from bow to transom, important in a rainy climate. There's a cockpit at the back end of

---

[19] See "Sweetie Pie's Specs and Improvements" in the Appendix.

the boat, where there is a ladder leading to the flybridge helm on the cabin top. *Sweetie Pie*'s single stateroom was in the bow. The galley and head were aft of the stateroom, and from there it was two steps up to the main cabin with the interior helm to starboard. Furnishings were a convertible sofa and two chairs, and a wall-mounted propane fireplace. A sliding glass door closed off the main cabin from the cockpit, and was the only way in and out of the cabin.

Reconnoitering with Captain Kyle

A chance meeting in Bellingham harbor at the Web Locker café coffee shop, the spring after our arrival, triggered my purposeful transition from being a full-time boating writer to becoming a professional mariner (of sorts). I always thought harbor cafes offered some of the best breakfasts available, anywhere. They usually opened at 5:00 a.m. for the fishers returning from fishing all night and for day fishers getting an early start.

Most mornings, after taking Shearlean to her office at the university, I went to the Web Locker café for breakfast. There was a boisterous group of twelve or more men at two tables pushed together every morning. Because I became a semi-regular, they invited me to join them, and that's how I met Captain Jim Kyle, owner of the salmon seiner *Home Shore*, with forty years of experience of the Inside Passage.

I learned that a large part of the fishing fleet home-ported in Bellingham fished in Southeast Alaska in the summer. I had the idea that I might be able to hitch a ride up the Inside Passage as preparation for taking *Sweetie Pie* there myself. I thought I could pay for some fuel or otherwise compensate someone, somehow for the privilege. They'd be departing soon, and if I didn't find a boat quickly, it would be another year before I could do it.

When there was a rare silence at the table, I voiced my wish to accompany someone, and the one person at the table who listened attentively, but seldom spoke said, "Why don't you come with me," smiling broadly.

"Okay," I replied and introduced myself to Captain Kyle.

He invited me to come to his boat when the coffee group broke up. I confess to being put off seeing what was obviously an older wooden boat. Though the paint looked good, I recalled how *Elusive Lady's* paint hid her problems and my surveying experience with old wooden boats reminded me of all the ills so many of them suffered.

As Jim showed me through the boat, my nose was on high alert for the distinctive smell of rotting wood, mold, and excessive humidity. When we went down the ladder into the engine room, I was thinking about the scent of lube oil and diesel fuel, and the sight of rust, and, maybe, an engine cooling system leak, but detected none of these. Overall, top to bottom, the entire boat was sweet-smelling. And I said so to Jim, knowing it was one of the highest compliments to pay a wooden boat owner: "It's a sweet-smelling boat throughout."

Home Shore was built in 1944, when few new commercial boats were built because of WWII. She was sixty-two feet long, with a seventeen-foot beam and eight-foot draft. The pilothouse was added later. She was repowered in 1965 with a Caterpillar 343 six cylinder diesel engine producing 365 horsepower. Under ideal conditions, she could cruise at nine knots economically.

When I picked up Shearlean at the university, I was still excited by the prospect of the trip and blurted out that I was going to Sitka, Alaska, in about two weeks. She wasn't as thrilled as I was, but knew it meant so much to me.

We departed for Sitka, on Baranoff Island, Alaska, at dawn on May 14, 2000, approximately a thousand miles from Bellingham.

I was totally comfortable about traveling on *Home Shore*, confident in its condition and Jim's ability. Crew berths on *Home Shore* were in the fo'c'sle, beneath the bow deck and forward of the engine room, basically in the bilge. Access to the fo'c'sle was through a floor hatch, down a six-rung steel ladder and through a soundproofed door, forward of the engine.

Shearlean dropped me off at the boat on departure day. She'd never seen the boat before, and had misgivings about its age and strangeness. I kissed her goodbye in the galley and descended into the engine room, and she lowered my duffle bag to me and left. She told me later that it felt like she was dropping her dog off at the pound. It was years later that I told Jim about her remark. I think he was miffed, but did manage a grin at the colorful image.

Beyond any expectations, this voyage changed my life, bringing benefits and accomplishments that enabled me to be the mariner I set out so long ago to be. Eventually, it provided me with the platform for a fulfilling late-life boating career. As with so much of life, this was a time, place, and circumstance impossible to anticipate. It was another demonstration, to my way of thinking, of continually seeking and staying open to opportunities, and being rich with time to take advantage of the serendipitous ways life evolves.

In 2000, I turned sixty-two years old and took social security, and in 2003, I became eligible for Medicare, both of which made me feel secure in taking risks at an advanced age. Thanks to the housing real estate market, we'd accumulated some money. With Shearlean a tenured professor at WWU, if we were careful and lucky, we were set for life.

I continued as Northwest editor for *Dockside* through 2003, but decided I'd found something better to do, in association with Jim Kyle, and my idea for an Inside Passage Training Cruise (IPTC). I also decided to write and publish a book in 2004, titled *Cruising to Alaska: Tips & Tactics from 20 Skippers*.

Jim was fifty-six years old, slender, balding, and serious, the very image of a humble college professor. He had been a high school English teacher for a time, but he found it unsatisfying. As a teen, like many other young people in this area, he had once earned college money by crewing on salmon fishing boats operating out of Bellingham. Though starting a family, he abandoned teaching and took up commercial fishing, buying a small salmon seiner and eventually upgrading to the larger *Home Shore*.[20]

Some fishers travel to Sitka nonstop, but Jim's insatiable love for the territory made him want to savor it at every opportunity. As we traveled, I followed our course on nautical charts and in a couple of cruising guides I'd brought along. We anchored every night, and every morning I awoke in a picturesque bay or cove, often with a grizzly prowling the beach looking for breakfast, bald eagles in treetops watching for prey, and the raucous call of ravens proclaiming their territory. Others of our crew included Erin Dollar, free-spirit twenty-something cook, and thirty-year-old Ben Kyle, Jim's middle son and first mate, already sensitive to his inherited receding hairline.

Where boating in Baja was an experience in cruising through the desert, traveling the Inside Passage was cruising through the mountains. All the visible land was the peaks of flooded mountains covered by dense forests and blessed with fabulous waterfalls throughout.[21]:

---

[20] "Home Shore" is a term Alaska fishers use to refer to the whole of Alaska's coastal waters as they were defined by the U.S. government in its defense of fishing rights contested by Cold-War Russian fishing trawlers.

[21] You can find a brief version of my Inside Passage experience From *Cruising to Alaska: Tips & Tactics from 20 Skippers* (Good Enough Publishing, 2004). The book is no longer available, but you can read the original chapter, titled "Destination—Southeast Alaska," at https://oceanoftime.robertaduke.com/.

John Muir, in *Travels in Alaska,* called the Alaska portion of the Inside Passage, "one of the most wonderful countries in the world." He was impressed by the sheltered ocean waters populated by myriad forested islands. He described it as a nearly endless sea of calm, lake-like waters, inviting to cruise ship passengers and solitary small boat skippers alike. David Johnson, skipper and Southeast Alaska veteran, comments, "Dent Rapids, Seymour Narrows, Octopus Islands, and Cape Caution act like turnstiles regulating the passage of cruisers to Southeast Alaska. Lots of boats won't go farther than these points. People that get beyond Seymour stop at Cape Caution. People won't go all the way because they don't have time or are afraid. They turn back."

The Inside Passage is as magical as mythical Brigadoon, Shangri-La, or Bali Hai; it so enchants those who visit, that many must return again and again.

While millions of travelers have made this voyage since tourists first arrived in the late nineteenth century, few have seen it as recreational boaters do, right at sea level.

Though it has been explored by mariners for centuries, it is not an entity on any nautical chart. It has neither latitude nor longitude. In fact, its exact route, the beginning and end, is a matter of disagreement.

The Inside Passage was known to early Spanish, Russian, English, and American explorers, and has been the route of cruising boats for about a hundred years. Though it is the path of the Alaska Marine Highway, which is routinely plied by countless cargo vessels, fishing boats, the ferries of two nations, cruise ships, and yachts, the Inside Passage retains its primeval character. In a small, lone boat venturing through the passage, the pervading silence and vast space swallows the roar of a diesel engine and even time itself, leaving the boat and its crew in a seeming limbo.

So, officially, what and where is the Inside Passage? The *Columbia Gazetteer of the World* says it is the nine hundred and fifty mile route through the Alexander Archipelago of British Columbian and Southeast

Alaska; the combined passages between islands and mainland protected from storms and conditions of the open ocean.

On and Off the Marine Highway

A glance at any Inside Passage nautical chart or planning map reveals uncountable sources of shelter all the way from Seattle to Glacier Bay. Lees of points and islands provide temporary shelter from adverse winds and seas. Numerous coves, bays, and inlets provide secure anchorage with protection from the severest conditions of the Inside Passage. With planning, shelter is seldom more than ten nautical miles or one-and-a-half hours away.

While the routes through the Inside Passage are myriad, the main route has its own designation: the Alaska Marine Highway. The highway is the heavily traveled route from Seattle to the major cities of Southeast Alaska: Ketchikan, Wrangell, Petersburg, Juneau, and Sitka. The Alaska State Ferry follows the marine highway, as does the heavy barge traffic freighting goods from the lower forty-eight states through the Port of Seattle.

Two openings in the Inside Passage barrier that can profoundly affect commercial and recreational boat travel and cannot be avoided include: 1) Queen Charlotte Sound, at the north end of Vancouver Island, and 2) Dixon Entrance, at Cape Fox between Prince Rupert, British Columbia, and Ketchikan, Alaska.

These are two critical areas for every Inside Passage voyage. Itineraries are planned around crossing these areas, and tales of difficulty and even danger cite both locations.

Queen Charlotte Sound and Dixon Entrance are dangerous to cruising boats because they may not be ready for the open ocean conditions that can develop here. Prudent skippers avoid bad conditions by monitoring weather reports and by being alert to changing local conditions.

Typical Southeast Alaska cruising boats take about four hours at seven knots to cross the sound and entrance, an easily planned and managed passage for any competent skipper. Even when conditions are not optimal, the short duration of the crossing and promise of secure shelter make them tolerable.

A Century of Cruising the Inside Passage

Exactly who started recreational cruising in Southeast Alaska, and when, may be impossible to pin down, because it is as obscure as the shore of Glacier Bay's Blue Mouse Cove on a foggy day.

Ordinary individuals have been cruising the Inside Passage and Southeast Alaska for about a century.

In 1906, W.S. Phillips, in an article titled "On the Northwest Coast" in the *Seattle Post-Intelligencer*, wrote about how the protected Inside Passage waters were an inviting destination for the newly invented, gasoline-powered boats of his day. Called "launches" then, Phillips noted how the area was protected from storms and offered unrivaled scenic beauty.

Early Inside Passage Cruisers

Muriel Wylie Blanchet proved the feasibility of early small boat cruising in the Inside Passage. Beginning in 1927, she and her five children made fifteen cruises in the Inside Passage in her twenty-five-foot powerboat, *Caprice*. Blanchet's book, *The Curve of Time*, documents her cruising adventures and has encouraged thousands of others to follow in her wake.

Later cruises became commonplace, but the voyage could still be interesting and adventurous enough to produce a book as evidenced by the 1999 best seller, *Passage to Juneau*. In the book, author Jonathan Raban interwove Vancouver's explorations with his own physical and metaphysical explorations through the Inside Passage.

Underway in The Inside Passage

Upon departing Bellingham, you are immediately within the Inside Passage among the San Juans, a compact cluster of islands between the southern end of Vancouver Island to the west and the Washington coast to the east. The islands are bordered by the Strait of Georgia that lies between Vancouver Island and the mainland, ending at about the island's midpoint at the infamous Seymour Narrows and the southern end of Discovery Passage.

Trending northwestward along the Vancouver Island coast is a second cluster of equally enchanting islands, the Canadian continuation of the American San Juans, the Gulf Islands. Boundary Pass, the international border between the United States and Canada, separates the two clusters of islands.

The Strait of Georgia is a major body of water that is difficult to cross in unfavorable weather. As a rule, northbound cruisers angle northwest, staying in the shelter of the Gulf Islands, following the coastline of Vancouver Island. Between Cape Lazo and Campbell River, as they approach Discovery Passage, cruisers must make their first major course decision. Pass through Seymour Narrows and commit to troublesome Johnstone Strait or postpone entering the strait by detouring northeast around Quadra Island through a series of rapids and whirlpools that are often easier and preferable to deal with than a long passage in Johnstone Strait.

Because Johnstone Strait is the shortest route north, it is favored by most commercial traffic, but conditions for small craft are often difficult and can cause delays. Gale and small craft warnings can last weeks.

Exiting Johnstone Strait, some shelter is available, and it is a fairly short run to Port Hardy or other anchorages at the northern end of Vancouver Island, or to Blunden Harbor or other anchorages on the mainland to await conditions for crossing Queen Charlotte Sound.

There is no alternative to crossing Queen Charlotte Sound. From Cape Caution to Cape Calvert, about thirty nautical miles, the effect of the open ocean can first be detected at Cape Caution, which increases as the sound is crossed, and then diminishes as Cape Calvert is approached. Generally, crossing the sound is enough for one day and cruisers head into Fury Cove for the night. Others continue up Fitz Hugh Sound before stopping.

Gradually, as you leave the San Juan and Gulf Islands, the number and kinds of cruising boats decline and change. North of Nanaimo, weekend and holiday boaters all but disappear. At Port Hardy, you are among cruisers headed as far as Glacier Bay and other far north destinations. These are boats and people you will likely see again in Prince Rupert, British Columbia, and Petersburg, Skagway, and Sitka, Alaska. Here, the boats and boaters are noticeably different (more substantial, with weightier ground tackle), and the country has a wilder flavor and is more remote.

Ahead for Southeast Alaska-bound cruisers is Prince Rupert through Fitz Hugh Sound, Princess Royal Channel, and Grenville Channel. From Prince Rupert, the challenge of Dixon Entrance looms along with the accomplishment of arriving in Alaska.

Dixon Entrance lies between the northern end of the Queen Charlotte Islands and the southern end of Prince of Wales Island. Conditions at Dixon Entrance may seem like a duplicate of Johnstone Strait, perpetual gales and small craft warnings. Dixon Entrance, though, consists of East Dixon and West Dixon. West Dixon, because it meets the Pacific Ocean directly, is generally worse than East Dixon.

Like Queen Charlotte Sound, there is no alternative route and the crossing is about thirty nautical miles. It is easy to cross, starting early from Prince Rupert and arriving at Foggy Bay, just north of Cape Fox, when conditions are favorable. Many boats eager to reach Ketchikan continue there the same day but others stop at Foggy Bay.

At Ketchikan, you clear customs back into the United States. Leaving Ketchikan, the usual course is up Clarence Strait, through Stikine Strait or Ernest Sound, and up Frederick Sound, via Wrangell and Petersburg if you wish, to the south end of Admiralty Island, where you must choose an east or west course. On the eastern side, Stephens Passage leads to Juneau, and on the western side, Chatham Strait leads to Icy Strait and Sitka.

Destinations Past and Present

Available time dictates cruising itineraries, more than the season, followed by the cruiser's special interests and personal preferences. (For Jim, time becomes an issue when openings for fishing quotas approach and he wants to be able to fish the first day.)

Two kinds of time affect cruising itineraries: calendar time and boat time. Calendar time is how many days the cruiser has to get to his destination, linger there, and return home. Boat time is the daily distance a boat can cover.

Depending on the vessel and how it is operated, cruising the Inside Passage can be done on almost any schedule. Typically, commercial fishing boats averaging about eight knots will travel from Bellingham to Sitka, nonstop, in ninety hours, running day and night. A more relaxed and typical commercial passage (such as I enjoyed with Jim) is done in six or seven days, with some travel after dark and with time for short side trips or brief layovers.

Sample recreational cruising itineraries include the following:

Prime Time, a Nordhavn 50, departed Bellingham's Squalicum Harbor, on April 27, 2001, and traveled 3480 miles over 134 days.

Skylark II, a Tollycraft 43, departed Bellingham on May 23, 1992, arrived in Ketchikan June 5 and Glacier Bay June 26, where it remained until June 30. It returned to Bellingham August 5, after cruising that included Sitka, a total of 75 days.

Don and Reanne-Hemingway Douglass, authors of "Exploring Southeast Alaska," list the following suggested cruising itineraries in their book:

- Ultra-Marathon requires 75 miles of travel per day for 28 days.
- Highlights requires 53 miles of travel per day for 42 days.
- Classic requires 42 miles per day for 60 days.
- Dream requires 31 miles per day for 97 days.

The Cruising Season

The usual period for cruising the Inside Passage is from May 15 through September 15. Generally, the weather has improved sufficiently by May 15 to guarantee mild weather and can be expected to remain mild until September 15. Before and after these dates, conditions tend to be unsettled and bad weather can be expected to be more severe and to last longer. More experienced cruisers often go earlier and return later, cruising from April 1 through October 1. With sufficient time, caution, and experience, the Inside Passage can be cruised year-round.

Cruisers intent on spending all their time in Alaskan waters bypass everything south of Prince Rupert, if fuel and weather permit.

Boat Companions in The Inside Passage

While you are never traveling the Inside Passage alone, its vastness can make you feel alone when you only glimpse distant vessels during a whole day's run and share a large anchorage with only a couple of other boats.

Many commercial boats in Southeast Alaska are seasonal visitors, just like cruising yachts. Fishers from as far south as California journey to Southeast Alaska, according to the opening and closing dates for various fisheries such as salmon, halibut, crab, and herring. These boats, typically thirty-five to sixty-five feet long, are operated by crews of one-to-three persons. Southeast Alaska-based boats move around Southeast Alaska waters to take advantage of fishing opportunities as they arise. When a major fishery is set to open, large fleets of boats arrive quickly, overwhelming facilities temporarily until they go fishing over a wide area. The boats gather again, where they deliver their catch to buyers and canneries.

Utility and service boats continually move about the Inside Passage: tugs with and without tows, and barges of every description hauling logs, cargo containers, and petroleum products.

There are also cruise ships during the season, ranging from huge vessels that carry five thousand passengers and crew to their smaller, older predecessors with half the complement of the latest liners. There are the much smaller cruisers, adventure travel, and eco-tourist ships that cater to a hundred or fewer passengers. A fairly recent breed of small cruise ship is the kayaker mothership that serves as home base to six-to-fifty kayakers during a week or more of travel.

There are few sailboats cruising the Inside Passage, but those that do generally have hulls over thirty-five feet with relatively large engines and are typically under power most of the time. Such vessels are usually classed as motor-sailors.

High-speed boats making the trip typically slow down to ten knots or under to conserve fuel and use their high speed sparingly. Small, fast trailer-able boats often arrive by ferry, but may cover great distances quickly to avoid bad weather, traveling from fuel stop to fuel stop.

I reimbursed Jim for the cost of the provisions I consumed, and left *Home Shore* before the remainder of the fishing crew arrived and flew home from Sitka. I was nearly overwhelmed by all I had seen and heard. As daunting as some aspects of the Inside Passage could be, having it explained to me mile-by-mile by a skipper with forty years of experience with it, and knowing its history and important nautical features, I was confident I could do the voyage myself. What I didn't account for, I would discover, was that as a passenger, I failed to see all conditions or process all information as a skipper must. But there was only one way to see the Inside Passage as a skipper, and that was to be one.

Alone to Alaska

For years, I had considered how to reduce Shearlean's stress of operating a boat in her role as first mate. At the end of any voyage, she was intensely proud of what we had done and where we had taken a boat, and forgave or willfully forgot the fear and anxiety she often experienced at sea under difficult conditions. She was a perfectionist: addicted to perfection, some would say. If I could routinely do everything on the boat myself, unassisted, she would enjoy herself more. When I bought *Sweetie Pie*, I organized and rigged the boat for single-handed operation by one person. Many boats had been single-handed around the world; surely, I could figure out how to single-hand a powerboat in sheltered waters.

I have to confess that I was also motivated to organize myself and the boat for single-handing in order to accomplish a single-handed voyage, an achievement I'd been coveting as much as making the long-distance passage with *Aorangi*.

I didn't tell Shearlean any of this; I just began doing it by involving her less in the routine operation of *Sweetie Pie*, though, so far, it had been under mild conditions. If I could take *Sweetie Pie* to Ketchikan by myself, I could prove to myself that I was a real single-hander.

Anchoring is the only brake a boat has for stopping. To be able to stop quickly, securely, anywhere, and under any conditions was the most critical safety action a skipper could take. I long considered anchoring to be the quintessential boating skill to master and believed it to be the key for safely single-handing. I was satisfied that I had proven my anchoring skills in Baja.

Long-time friend Earl Hinz, an engineer and skipper of *Horizon,* a Morgan Out Island 41, said in his definitive volume, *The Complete Book of Anchoring and Mooring*, that he believed that anchoring was the most critical boating skill a cruising skipper could master.

If Shearlean had a reservation about me single-handing to Alaska, she didn't confront me about it. She'd seen me off on other boating adventures to rescue *Lilli Sohex* at the Cook Islands, returning *Aorangi* from Hawaii, and taking *Cheyenne Summer* through the Panama Canal. The voyage on *Home Shore* to Sitka may have sealed the deal for her.

Determined to keep a proper log of this voyage, I bought a blank book, "Pilot Log," such as I had seen Jim using. The left page was for recording details of piloting and navigation, time run, and places of departure and arrival. On the right page, I recorded engine hours to track fuel-and-oil consumption, and in the Remarks column, I made brief comments about the daily weather, my activities, and where I anchored.

This log is the source of this narrative about my single-handing passage to Ketchikan, and Shearlean's and my voyage from Ketchikan to Glacier Bay and our return to Bellingham.

May 27

Sucia Islands is a contiguous group of islets among the San Juan Islands, twenty miles northwest of Bellingham Bay where the Squalicum Yacht Club held its 2002 Memorial Day rendezvous cruise. I chose it as the departure point for single-handing to Ketchikan for the bon voyage atmosphere, such as the Ensenada race provided for the Baja cruise.

Shearlean and I were both tearful as our friend Mike Heintz brought his boat, *Rebound,* alongside *Sweetie Pie* for Shearlean to step aboard to return to Bellingham. I continued to wave until *Rebound* was out of sight.

Shearlean would meet me in Ketchikan on July 2, 2002, when her university summer vacation started. We would cruise to Glacier Bay and return home together in time for her to resume her university duties.

I was glum. The autopilot, which had been working perfectly, failed when we left for Sucia on May 24. That was reason enough to postpone my departure, but I'd long ago vowed to never turn back from an adventure for anything less than a life-threatening reason. I hoped to get the device repaired at Port Sidney on Vancouver Island on my way north. Without it, I would have to steer every minute underway to Ketchikan.

With Shearlean and my yacht club friends gone, Fossil Bay, where I had celebrated my sixty-fourth birthday on May 25, was gray, desolate and depressing. I was reminded of how I felt in Ensenada Bay when all of the race participants had departed, and Shearlean and I remained behind on *Symbiont* eighteen years earlier.

I didn't feel fit to start now for Ketchikan, but thought I should make an effort to begin my voyage, so I motored over to Echo Bay, thirty minutes away, and anchored for the night.

May 28

Leaving at dawn, I motored six hours, forty miles, and got a slip in Port Sidney Marina. The next day, I learned that parts were no longer stocked for my old autopilot and no technician offered to come to the boat to check it out. From books, I knew that single-hander predecessors had traveled the Inside Passage without autopilots, so I decided I could, too.

So, I kept going, crossing the Strait of Georgia to Montague Bay and working my way north the following days up the west coast of British Columbia.

In preparation for this voyage, I had gathered published cruising itineraries and talked with experienced cruisers to compile my own itinerary. It was important, I felt, to have destinations and an idea of distance to be covered and fuel consumed before starting each day.

It was a great convenience to have the Douglass' Inside Passage cruising guides detailing piloting and navigation information about every anchorage along every mile of the passage. With electronic charts, GPS, and the guides, I could find and enter any harbor, marina, bay, cove, or anchorage easily and safely.

June 9

Approaching the first major detour from the marine highway, to avoid Johnstone Strait, I was reading charts and cruising guides about such challenging sounding destinations as Blind Channel, Yuculta Rapids, and Whirlpool Pass. But I preferred the risk of the unknown to the strait's notorious weather; I was trusting this detour's benign reputation.

I did lose my nerve momentarily when I confronted Whirlpool Pass and anchored nearby, where I could watch for a boat to come from the opposite direction to prove the whirlpool was tame. When I traversed the pass, I saw the whirlpools were small and harmless; they formed and dissipated quickly.

I arrived at the north end of Johnstone Strait, beyond the tumultuous area, after two days, with other things on my mind.

June 11

I was having frequent computer problems which jeopardized the reliability of my navigation software. While I had backup paper charts, I much preferred the convenience of electronic navigation. Underway to Port McNeill, on Vancouver Island, the computer failed completely.

Fortunately, I made it a practice to always have the paper chart for my next destination ready at the helm and steered by compass to the harbor.

I was unnerved by my failed computer and was in no mood to deal with the turbulent wind-and-water conditions of Port McNeill. Since it wasn't yet noon, I decided to continue on to Port Hardy and arrived at Quarter Deck Marina, without incident, at 5:30 p.m., very tired but feeling secure.

I was stranded here for five days, many times fearing my voyage was at an end and dealing with a series of bizarre computer and software problems.

I was determined to buy a new laptop, but discovered personal computers were in the midst of an upgrade cycle and I could find nothing on Vancouver Island compatible with my navigation software. Unwilling to be turned back, I bought a desktop computer and monitor, with the latest version of navigation software installed for $1500 on my credit card from a marine electronics store. Because of how and where I was traveling, my credit cards had repeatedly been declined due to fraud alerts against my account. I rented a motel room for all-day access to a telephone to clear up my accounts.

June 16

Exhausted by the nervous tension of solving my computer problems, I found myself nevertheless looking forward to being underway again and to the challenge of crossing Queen Charlotte Sound.

My crossing was uneventful.

> LOG ENTRY: Encountered some ocean swell near cape caution, but the sea is calm. Visibility deteriorating, low ceiling, rain squall ahead, but sea perfect for crossing.

I anchored in Fury Bay at Penrose Island near the entrance of Fitzhugh Sound at 4:50 p.m. and poured myself a celebratory scotch:

> LOG ENTRY: Maybe I'll make it after all.

I was now back to cruising and on my way to Prince Rupert, B.C., through Fitz Hugh Sound and on to Grenville Channel to Dixon Entrance and the last leg to Ketchikan and meeting Shearlean.

I stopped for fuel at Hartley Bay, a native village, with boardwalks throughout the village, used as sidewalks by pedestrians and as streets for ATVs. It was a high-energy, busy village with a thriving fishing fleet. Shearlean's birthday was the next day, June 21. I wanted to wish her a happy birthday and to confirm I was alive and well. I had found a pay phone on the dock when I stopped for water at Klemtu village, but it was out of order. There was no pay phone at Hartley Bay, but someone said there was a phone at the community center, so I went there and coaxed the manger to let me use her phone, putting the call on my prepaid phone card. Shearlean sounded relieved to hear from me and confirmed her flight and arrival time for Ketchikan, July 2. I spent a rainy night anchored behind Promise Island, a disappointingly busy site, uncomfortable because of wake from lots of fishing boat traffic.

Because of its waterfall, Lowe Inlet was on every cruiser's itinerary, so I had planned far ahead to spend the night there. Countless waterfalls populate the Inside Passage, and this one was among the best, but what impressed me most about Lowe was far back in the inlet. Before leaving the next morning, I decided to motor to the end of the inlet, out of sight around a dogleg in the channel. There was nothing known to be back there, but that was the appeal. Here, in the middle of nowhere, was an out-of-the-way body of water that I imagined maybe no human being had ever visited; I could be the first. Since it was uncharted, I kept the engine at idle and eased into the basin formed by the surrounding mountains. I shut down the engine and let *Sweetie Pie* drift to a stop in mid-basin. The silence was powerful, tangible. The stillness was unlike anything I had ever encountered, and it made me uncomfortable. I had always sought solitude, but this was overwhelming, and I scanned the surrounding forest, as though I'd find a tangible source of what I felt.

Suddenly, a ragged, raucous call from an invisible raven reverberated around the basin and it continued, obviously outraged at my intrusion. It told me I didn't belong here, and I agreed. It was more of nothing than a modern man such as I could tolerate. I started the engine and was immediately soothed by the sound, and left.

There were many encounters similar to this throughout my voyage, which in smaller doses, I savored.

I meandered on, stopping frequently, not just for fuel or water, but also to linger in particularly beautiful and scenic spots. Sometimes, I suspected I was dallying to delay my confrontation with Dixon Entrance, the gateway to Southeast Alaska.

June 22

Inevitably, I arrived at the amazing hub of civilization that is the city of Prince Rupert, a thriving grain-and-coal exporting port on Canada's west coast. I tied up at the Prince Rupert Rowing & Yacht Club marina.

Founded in 1909, the yacht club occupies the same site within the harbor today, and has been in continuous operation since its inception. It retains the "Rowing & Yacht" part of its name to acknowledge its heritage in the early twentieth century before marine internal combustion engines were readily available in 1910.

The region experiences big tides, creating powerful currents that must be accounted for any time you are maneuvering a boat. These conditions are routine the farther into Alaska you go, but this was the first time I had entered the confines of a marina since Port Hardy. I was unprepared for the effects of big tides and strong currents when moving among other boats and marina slips. With a single engine, maneuvering is limited and must be anticipated far ahead.

Others, unaware of the extreme tides, made the marina hazardous. I got rammed once while in my slip by an out-of-control boat, but suffered no damage.

The club itself is friendly, comfortable, and accommodating, and it qualifies as a major maritime crossroads between the U.S. and Canada, between Alaska and British Columbia, and as a major milestone on the Inside Passage.

June 24

I'd been underway for one month.

> LOG ENTRY: Becoming addicted to computer solitaire. Changed my mind about moving. Staying in slip another day. Rain, gusty winds. Don't want to move. Weather worse, occasional severe gusts, steady rain. Decided to clean up boat interior—shook rugs, vacuumed, dusted helm, and wiped surfaces with damp sponge. Spaghetti tonight.

June 25

It was time to face Dixon Entrance.

> LOG ENTRY: Twenty-one-foot tide, current fierce. Go to fuel dock when it slackens. Definite weather change. Forecast good for crossing. Maybe Ketchikan tomorrow. Warnings about lots of debris because of rain in mountains. One broadcast warned of thirty-foot tree, three feet in diameter at entrance to Prince Rupert. After fuel, moved to Russell arm, other side of harbor. Good to be out of marina.

June 26

There are options available when crossing Dixon Entrance; it is not all or nothing. I think it is better not to start if you have doubts. Dundas Island and other locations are places that offer shelter if you have to abort your crossing without returning to Prince Rupert.

LOG ENTRY: Underway in Dixon. Very calm conditions. May cross Dixon w/o stopping. Sun, blue skies to west, still heavy overcast overhead. Gloom. Gray. Good speed avg 9 knots. 10 a.m. slowed to 6.5 knots. Amazed how flat Dixon entrance is—never know from forecast. Back to 9.5 knots. Re-entered USA. Lord islands. Took wrong turn almost into Nakat Bay. Lost about an hour. Wonderful anchorage. Foggy bay.

June 27

Foggy Bay is nearly landlocked and is secure under all imaginable conditions—a good feeling if you've experienced an especially rough crossing of Dixon Entrance. As it turned out, I was literally landlocked because of a minus tide. I was eager to start for Ketchikan, my ultimate single-handing destination, but didn't have enough water until 1:00 p.m.

When I finally made it to Ketchikan, seaplanes taking off and landing, huge cruise ships disgorging thousands of passengers, and heavy boat traffic coming and going in all directions greeted my arrival. I was nearly overwhelmed and unsure if I really wanted to be here. I called the harbormaster's office on the radio and requested a slip in Thomas Basin. To get there, I had to pass under the stern of one cruise ship and bow of another towering overhead like passing under a bridge.

There was a laundromat at the head of the ramp leading up to the street and a good market nearby, so I did a large load of laundry and reprovisioned. The cruise ships had swallowed up their passengers and departed for another destination, and so this side of town was now deserted and the marina quiet.

It would be four days before Shearlean arrived, and I didn't want to sit around in a marina (I had developed an aversion to marinas unless they had a practical purpose; some were just floating slums, the last stop for derelicts—hulls and humans.) So, after checking my cruising guides and itinerary, I elected to go to Yes Bay, about which the Douglass guide said it not only offered secure anchoring and good fishing, but also offered civilized accommodations, such as phone service, and a bar and restaurant. The guide also included the explanation that the bay's name derived from the Tlingit word for mussels—*yas*.

On the way, I noticed there was a Forest Service float in Naha Bay and decided to check it out. There was no one there, and so I decided to spend the night. A ramp from the dock led into the dense, old-growth forest, so I took a walk in the woods. I found a picnic area littered with trash and gathered it all up and brought it to the trash can on the dock.

At daybreak, I set off again for Yes Bay.

I anchored near the lodge, and put the dinghy in the water, and cleaned up and dressed up and went to the lodge for dinner. I felt a little strange and out of place, but ultimately enjoyed the plush surroundings and excellent food.

There was plenty to explore in the extensive bay and I heard there were crabs and shrimp there. I lost a crab trap when a knot parted just as I was bringing a loaded trap over the bulwark—there went fifty dollars in gear. I left a shrimp trap out overnight and was rewarded with a dozen decent-sized shrimp in the morning.

July 1

Back in Ketchikan, I decided to get a slip for the night at Bar Harbor Marina South, opposite the airport, which is across Tongass Narrows on Gravina Island. I could walk from there to the airport ferry to greet Shearlean at the terminal when she arrived.

July 2

Shearlean arrived and she said she was hungry. After much hugging and kissing, I took her bulging red duffle bag and we walked down the ramp to the ferry dock and crossed over to Ketchikan. When Shearlean says she's hungry, I have to act immediately or she gets very cranky, so we stopped at a coffee shop on the way to the marina and got her fed. She was in good spirits. She had a good flight and seemed raring to go, despite the huge transition from being a college professor one day, living in a nice waterfront condo, to arriving to explore the Alaskan wilderness on a small boat.

I was relieved and impressed that she settled right into *Sweetie Pie*, but we had used the boat a lot the preceding year and she felt at home on it.

I didn't like Bar Harbor. It was too "uptown," very busy on the water and on the street. We returned to Thomas Basin, even though it was for just one night.

July 4

I was relieved to get out of Ketchikan—even though it might have had everything a person needed, it also had what I and many others want to escape—and went to Meyers Chuck ("Chuck" is a Chinook word meaning water), an island in Clarence Strait and anchored behind Meyers Island. A man in a skiff came by the boat and invited us ashore for the Fourth of July celebration, including fireworks. We were grateful, but declined, feeling too tired to be good guests.

At Meyers Chuck, I reviewed my itinerary with Shearlean and revised it to ensure we would arrive at Glacier Bay on the day of our reservation. She scanned cruising guides about our destinations for the next two weeks. It was effectively the last time I had free access to the guides, as she took custody of them for the remainder of voyage. Having it always open in her lap reassured her she had some control over things.

Single-handing, I had been in the habit of exploring an anchorage before settling on a spot to anchor. Shearlean felt, I think, that this was just looking for trouble and prolonged being underway. She wanted to be settled on an anchor and not at just any spot, but on the exact spot where the guides' authors had placed the symbol of an anchor on their diagram of the anchorage—as though there was only one safe place to anchor in the entire cove.

As I steered the boat into a cove to anchor, she would watch over my shoulder as I followed the electronic navigation chart on the computer monitor and compared it the guide's anchoring diagram. I learned to live with it. (Later, I learned from the guide's authors that this was a common occurrence among cruising couples.)

We worked our way northeast, on and off the marine highway, covering some of the same ground we had on our 1995 ferry journey to Wrangell, Petersburg, and Juneau.

Glacier Bay

Glacier Bay National Park and Preserve, located on Icy Strait at the northern end of the Inside Passage, is home to seven tidewater glaciers and is designated a World Heritage site.

Icy Strait is seldom icy anymore. It got its name when Glacier Bay's glaciers extended all the way to the strait and icebergs from calving glacier floated into, and clogged, the strait.

We had made the required reservations for cruising Glacier Bay starting July 19. We tied up at the guest dock in Bartlett Cove and went to the Park Service office to check in and for our orientation about the bay, restrictions on boat operations, and advice about encountering wildlife. We were reminded our permit was for six days and expired on July 25, when we were required to leave the park. We could declare our departure by radio.

Getting here and being here were reason enough, I felt, for owning a boat and making this voyage. Others had done it, and more would follow, but doing it in your own boat on your own itinerary was a rare experience. I was proud to become a member of the unofficial 59 North Latitude club—private boaters who navigated themselves to the end of Glacier Bay.

Nearly all the wildlife that inhabits the Inside Passage inhabits Glacier Bay. To me, the most unexpected presence in the bay was mountain goats. I thought Jim Kyle was pulling my leg when he told me I might sight mountain goats. Just their name convinced they could only be seen on mountaintops, not at sea level. We did see three mountain goats standing on a rocky point, and I became a believer.

Here's an inventory of the wildlife Shearlean and I encountered in Glacier Bay: brown and black bears, deer, sea otters, Steller or northern sea lions, harbor and fur seals, Dall's porpoise, orcas, gray, minke, and humpback whales, bald eagles, ravens, puffins, cormorants, gulls, guillemots, and dozens of other birds. Various salmon could be spotted just by looking overboard and seeing salmon that revealed themselves with their jumping behavior.

Brown (grizzly) bears were common. They seem to be inveterate beachcombers, especially in the morning and particularly when the tide changes and they overturn rocks on the beach, looking for morsels. When we were anchored close to shore one morning, and Shearlean was cooking bacon for breakfast, we got some serious attention from a grizzly, and Shearlean asked whether I thought the bear could climb onto our boat. I said no, but they are good swimmers and capable climbers. It returned to browsing the thick grass that nearly hid it.

Glaciers are as big an attraction as the wildlife, though they are all mere remnants of their former selves. All were tidewater glaciers extending far into the bay and formerly endlessly calved icebergs (not of the Titanic sort). Though greatly diminished over the years, they were beautiful and tempting destinations for Glacier Bay yachts or cruise ships.

Reid Glacier kept us fascinated for two days. It had retreated far enough that it now sat behind a mucky beach too far back from the tidewater to calve bergs.

> SHEARLEAN'S LOG ENTRY: Clear, some sun. Anchored directly in front of Reid Glacier, just off the beach. Utterly magical to sit alone in bay looking at glacier right in front of the boat. Gulls and ducks around. A waterfall roaring behind us.

We launched the dinghy and motored over to the glacier. We were wearing knee-high rubber boots and landed the dinghy in the mud and stepped out onto the gooey beach and trudged to the face of the glacier and touched it and examined the ice. Calving glaciers are dangerous to get near, but Reid appeared stable now that its front edge was supported by the land beneath, instead of the sea. By the time we'd tramped around, the muck was weighing down our boots and the tide was coming in, so we hopped back into the dinghy, which was now coated with mud, inside and out, and motored back to *Sweetie Pie*. We spent nearly an hour cleaning our boots and dinghy with brushes and sea water.

We went to Grand Pacific and John Hopkins glaciers, but couldn't approach closely, because they were still in the tide water. We were surprised to find a cruise ship at John Hopkins and wondered how we missed seeing it pass Reid. The decks were crowded, and cameras were in every hand. Passengers waved to us, and I wondered what they thought of tiny *Sweetie Pie*.

We returned to Reid to spend a second night, because we liked the waterfall and evening light on the glacier.

We saw all we hoped to see in Glacier Bay and without hurrying. Only thirty-six vessels of all types were allowed in the bay on any given day and twenty-five were yachts, but we seldom saw another yacht. Blue Mouse Cove was purportedly the most popular anchorage in the bay, but we were alone there, overnight.

Our permit expired on July 26, so we moved to Berg Bay, one mile inside the bay's entrance and the site of discoverer John Muir's camp when he explored the bay. I thought of it as a mere waiting room, but it turned out to be one of our most enchanting anchorages.

> LOG ENTRY: Berg Bay is like a marine Eden, pilot whales, sea otters, porpoise, and birds from eagles to ducks. The water swirls with the changing tide. Curtains of rain and mist come and go hiding and revealing our surrounding. We're the only boat here!

In the back of the bay was a very still, lushly wooded lagoon. We were still towing the dinghy, so it was ready for use. When the sun broke through, we motored to the lagoon. As we approached, the muted hum of the motor was overwhelmed by the sound of a whale spouting. I stopped the motor and our momentum allowed us to glide into the lagoon. I could hardly conceive of a whale being in such a confined space, but a humpback lazily broke the surface, spouted, and disappeared, barely disturbing the surface. The whale surfaced twice again nearby, and after about ten minutes, we realized it must have left the lagoon. What a rare moment it had been.

I celebrated my second month underway and it was time to head back to Bellingham. I radioed my farewell to the Forest Service, and we headed south for Hoonah Harbor for fuel, water, groceries, and a phone. Conditions were dead calm and heavily overcast, and several fishing boats were moving around. There must have been a fishing opening soon, because Hoonah Harbor was full, so we motored to nearby Neka Bay to anchor for the night. Crabbing was good there, providing us with six Dungeness crabs for dinner—all over eight inches.

We had headed north up the east side of the Passage from Ketchikan and our plan was to go south down the west side and not to hurry. I wanted to explore and show Shearlean Ell Cove on Baranof Island. Until we reached Ketchikan, it was all new territory for us both. From Ketchikan on south, I would be backtracking my trip north, but it would all be new to Shearlean until we got to Montague Harbor in British Columbia.

Ell Cove is a glorious little pocket of water that is a great anchorage, but it isn't included in the government's *Coast Pilot*. The Douglass guide provides a perfect description:

"Its name comes from its L-shape, which gives it full protection in all weather. The small cove has steep granite sides with cascades that descend from snowy ridges above. Old-growth spruce, cedar and hemlock cover its slopes. Immediately north of Ell Cove is a beautiful waterfall with a large sandy beach. Beware of the shoal that extends much farther from shore than what is shown on the chart."

Fascinating to me was the optical illusion created by the still water's reflection of the banded granite sides of the cove, causing the sides to appear twice as high as they were.

Venn Passage Fog

Departing Foggy Bay to cross Dixon Entrance, it was smooth-going on a clear, sunny day as we approached Venn Passage. As we emerged from the narrow, twisting passage, we were surrounded by commercial fishing boats with nets in the water. A fog to the west was moving toward us rapidly, faster than I could comprehend, and suddenly, the whole area was enveloped. We were near shore and approaching a shoal and among fishing boats setting and retrieving nets. I became immediately disoriented. I sent Shearlean out on deck with an air horn to warn away any other boat she might spot. I tried to maintain my original course away from hazards using my electronic charts, a big mistake. I should have started steering with the compass course, because the compass responds immediately to changes in direction, unlike electronic charts, which have a built-in delay. I did two three-hundred-sixty-degree turns trying to maintain my original course, and wondered what fishing boats, seeing me on radar, must have thought of these maneuvers. I feared a collision or fouling someone's net was imminent or that a boat twice my size would suddenly appear out of the fog and we'd collide. I glanced repeatedly at my own radar display and saw nothing nearby, but that was of little solace. I was out of control. At last, my brain kicked in and I switched my attention to watching my compass and was able to maintain a steady course at dead slow speed.

This all happened in less than ten minutes and the fast-moving fog soon disappeared.

Whiterock Passage

Whiterock Passage is a dredged channel that provides a significant shortcut from Blind Channel to Rebecca Spit, where we intended to anchor for the night. The cruising guide provides a grave warning about the hazards of this channel and prescribes that skippers steer toward an amber light visible at the far end of the channel, but as I entered, I saw no amber light. Instead, I saw what I took to be a range marker, two vertical white poles that when lined up, one behind the other, indicate you are on the right course. Shearlean said she saw a white post, too, and pointed it out. I proceeded to maneuver the boat to line them up, but she and I were looking at different objects.

Passengers in a skiff passing in the opposite direction waved wildly as they went by, and suddenly they returned waving us in their direction and I turned sharply to port and slowed to idle. They all gestured towards themselves, indicating to me that the channel was over there, and not where I was heading. It turned out that the poles we saw were not range markers, but one was a single, white pole that had replaced the defunct amber light. If I had aligned the two poles, I'd have been hard aground on rocks. More attention to my charts and confirming exactly what Shearlean and I were looking at would have kept us in the channel. I was extremely grateful to the skiff's passengers, who guessed the mistake I was making.

Montague Harbor

Familiar Montague Harbor, on British Columbia's Galiano Island, provided our last anchorage before Bellingham. We spent the afternoon cleaning up *Sweetie Pie*, packing our duffle bags, and getting ready to disembark the next day toward our slip in Bellingham's Squalicum Marina, where all of this started back in May.

Bellingham

We arrived back in our slip in Squalicum Harbor after fifty-one days underway for Shearlean, and ninety days for me, twenty-five miles short of a three-thousand-mile round trip, with twenty-three days in marinas and sixty-seven days anchored out.

Cruising is never without some excitement (it is often described as days of boredom interspersed with moments of sheer terror), but if you're prepared for those moments, they can pass as benign, colorful events and great learning experiences, such as we encountered on the way home.[22]

---

[22] See "Inside Passage Voyage Statistics" in the Appendix for a statistical summary of the Glacier Bay cruise and a list of boating lessons learned from the experience. See "Getting Underway Daily Checklist" in the Appendix for a checklist of the steps necessary to get the boat underway every day.

Sweetie Pie Survives a Landslide

"Of all the ways I've imagined dying on a boat, I never thought I'd be killed in a landslide," Shearlean said, following our July 11, 2006, night in Turnbull Cove.

Publisher and friend Robert Hale said in his introduction to the article I wrote for his 2006 edition of his publication, *Waggoner Cruising Guide*, that landslides were common in the area due to the thin layer of soil covering the glacier-scoured mountainsides. Heavy rain was a lubricant that broke a tree's grip on a steep slope.

It had been raining for days, but on July 11, the rain turned into a torrent. When Shearlean and I went to bed at 10:30 p.m., the rain was so heavy that the water's surface looked as though it were boiling.

At 11:30 p.m., we were wakened by an incredible roar that surrounded our boat. We rolled heavily to starboard, then to port. Shearlean and I bolted from our bed, staggering from the boat's motion. We were too stunned to act.

Trembling, I dressed awkwardly, grabbed a powerful flashlight, and went outside and up to *Sweetie Pie's* bow. The water around us was full of small debris and the air was heavy with the smell of freshly dug earth. I could see broken trees in the water about a hundred feet away, but the heavy rain reflected most of the lantern's light back, dazzling me.

I didn't know what had happened, but I knew I wanted to move the boat. I started the engine, raised the anchor and steered toward the opposite shore. I sat up for two hours to stand watch and calm down. I was certain the roar and fallen trees had been caused by a freak wind associated with the heavy rainstorm, maybe a williwaw or a microburst.

At dawn, a heavy mist had settled near the sea's surface. Beneath the mist, I saw broken trees in the water but little else. Later, after the mist cleared, I saw a stripped triangle of rock on the hillside, its base at the water's edge. It was about a hundred feet wide and the gash rose about two hundred feet up the mountainside. Trees had been there for sixty-to-eighty years. Now, there was an ugly wound of bare rock bleeding mud-blackened water. It was as chilling as seeing a human victim's red blood and white bone.

In the water, a fifteen-foot-high island of broken trees, soil, and rocks lay near where we had been anchored. The night's roar and mini tsunami had been a landslide.

By 9:00 a.m., a parade of boats arrived at Turnbull Cove with crew with video and still cameras. Another boat in the cove had seen the landslide and radioed the Coast Guard.

We left Turnbull Cove and moved to nearby Clayton Cove. Passersby in dinghies asked if we had heard about the previous night's landslide.

"We certainly did," we replied, the roar still ringing in our ears.

Three thousand miles and three months voyaging the Inside Passage to Glacier Bay hadn't diminished Shearlean's or my desire to keep cruising in *Sweetie Pie*.

At our very doorstep, near enough for overnight, holiday, weekend, and weeklong cruises lay a cruising wonderland between the east coast of Vancouver Island and the west coast of British Columbia's mainland.

I doubt that in a lifetime of active boating anyone could experience everything within a hundred miles of this segment of the Inside Passage north of Bellingham, Washington. The protected waters are packed with islands and the shorelines crammed with bays and coves, so inviting that each successive one seems like the best yet. Enchantingly, though you might suppose they will be all the same, each one proves itself to be special in some way—and memorable. Writing about them all would be inadequate, so I've selected the Broughtons to stand for them all and encourage you to see them all for yourself.

There's Broughton Island and North Broughton Island, but the term, "the Broughtons," is a bit arbitrary as to which of the plenitude of surrounding islands are included. The Broughtons are east of Port McNeill at the southern edge of Queen Charlotte Sound and at the northern terminus of Johnstone Strait.

Their proximity to Port McNeill makes refueling and reprovisioning easy for extended stays in the area.

Among my reasons for going there, aside from the obvious attractions (though I wasn't seeking landslides), resulted from reading the novel, *I Heard the Owl Call My Name*.

I had been reading a lot of literature about the Inside Passage in preparation for my voyage to Glacier Bay and recalled this best-selling 1967 novel by Margaret Craven. The novel tells the story of a young Anglican vicar named Mark Brian who, unbeknownst to him, has not long to live. He learns about the meaning of life when he is to be sent to a First Nations parish in British Columbia.

The book opens with a doctor addressing an unnamed bishop. The doctor tells the bishop that one of his candidates for ordination has no more than three years to live. The bishop replies that he will delay telling the candidate, lest he "try too hard" in the time he has left to him. The bishop further states that the candidate has much to learn in a short period, so he will send him to his most difficult parish, a First Nations village named Kingcome, in British Columbia. The bishop explains that it is the place he himself would choose to go if he were young, with little time left to live.

I was curious to compare the actual scene of the novel with how it was portrayed in the book, and it was an opportunity to visit an area historically occupied by First Nations people (the Canadian term for indigenous persons) and see how it might have changed since the novel was written.

Kingcome is a fjord one-and-a-half miles wide and twenty-two miles long. In the forty years since the book's publication, the former cannery town was largely deserted, but it was worth the trip for its stimulation of my imagination of a doomed young vicar arriving here when it was thriving.

We remained in the area for a week or more, exploring all day, every day, finding picturesque coves for dinner and a good night's sleep. My only complaint about the general area was the proliferation of fish farms, raising salmon in captivity, which involved machinery, night lighting, and industrial activity that to me belonged somewhere else, especially when it spoiled a pretty cove either by occupying it or polluting nearby coves with light and noise. Fortunately, it was possible to avoid the farms if you kept moving until you escaped them.

Shearlean and I continued this near-home cruising for the next six years, when we finally tired of life at seven knots, and taking one-to-two days to get anywhere and being exposed to bad weather more than we could tolerate any more—I was seventy years old and Shearlean, sixty-two. We weren't done with boating yet. I was even more involved than ever, as I will soon explain.

In 2007, I traded *Sweetie Pie* for *Duchess*, a speedier, gasoline-egine-powered Tollycraft 26, smaller, cheaper, and handier. We reduced our cruising to only nearby destinations only an hour or two away at sixteen knots.

Salmon, $0.12/Pound

When the price of salmon plunged to twelve cents per pound at the processing plant, it was no longer profitable for seiners, such as Jim Kyle, to catch them. Desperate to continue earning a living with *Home Shore*, Jim decided to offer ocean kayaking charters out of Sitka, Alaska. His challenge was to convert *Home Shore* from carrying thirty-five tons of salmon to carrying six paying passengers in comfort on a rustic wooden seiner.

What I learned during my reconnoiter with Jim was that the videographer and still photographer onboard were there to produce images needed to publicize *Home Shore's* upcoming conversion to an ocean kayaking mothership—a vessel that shelters, transports, and feeds six kayakers for a week in Alaska's wilderness.

Ocean kayaking was booming, and there were already motherships ranging from luxury motor yachts to dormitory boats carrying fifty passengers.

Few paying passengers would pay to sleep in the fo'c'sle as the fishing crew did, so Jim had two portable self-contained staterooms designed and constructed to install on the seiner's aft deck, and relinquished his captain's cabin to guests. Jim would sleep on the pilothouse helm berth.

It worked gloriously well, and saved the Kyle family and *Home Shore* until they could return to fishing, Jim's preferred way of life. It was a big and expensive gamble, and must have been nerve-wracking to accomplish.

Meanwhile, I had an idea for Jim that I thought would help his profitability.

As he had done for years, Jim "deadheaded" (no paying guests or cargo) from Bellingham to Sitka and return. *Home Shore* guzzled a gallon of diesel fuel per mile, a round trip of about two thousand miles.

Based on my reconnoitering trip to learn my way through the Inside Passage to Alaska, I told Jim that I thought he could sell such a trip to other recreational boaters who aspired to take their own boats to Alaska. He could have six passengers paying for fuel and more going to and from Sitka.

He couldn't adopt this idea right away, with so much else happening with converting *Home Shore* to kayak chartering, but agreed it was worth trying, someday.

Someday arrived in 2005. We called the course for recreational boats the Inside Passage Training Cruise (IPTC).[23]

I suggested my *Tips & Tactics* book as a supplementary text for the Inside Passage training, but neither Jim nor I wanted a textbook approach to training. We wanted it to be hands-on, over-the-shoulder, personal instruction every day, all day, at the helm of *Home Shore*.

To structure and describe the course, I wrote an instructional curriculum and syllabus that itself was a forty-three page document, but it allowed for individual guests' training demands. For example, a dentist from Hawaii wanted to spend his time learning all he could about using radar, because his wife made his mastery of radar a condition for going cruising with him. A couple wanted experience entering an anchorage at night, so we did that a couple of times.

---

[23] See "IPTC Abridged Curriculum, Learning Objectives and Labs" in the Appendix.

I participated in every IPTC, traveling both north and south, until 2008, when I resigned from *Home Shore's* crew because I thought that at seventy years old, I could no longer perform my crew duties as I thought they should be done.

Alaska on the *Home Shore*

I was a passenger, crew, and paying guest aboard *Home Shore* in Alaska, from my 2001 reconnoiter of the Inside Passage to a final commercial fishing trip in 2011. I made twenty-two Alaska trips, plus a couple of Puget Sound excursions.

At first, I saw myself as a supernumerary, happy to have been included. At the end of charters, guest tipped the crew, sometimes a thousand dollars per crew member. Being a naturally helpful person, but having no sense of obligation to the guests, I was shocked the first time I received an envelope of cash. I divided these first tips among what I considered the legitimate crew—cook, hand, and kayak guide.

I was especially charitable to our cook that year, because she had unpaid parking tickets in Seattle, which were revealed when we went through Canadian customs, much to her embarrassment.[24] When we started the IPTC and I was an instructor, I accepted tips, feeling I'd

---

[24] Guests were warned that if they had DUIs or other offenses, they may not be admitted entry to Canada, a matter of Canadian law. Parking tickets didn't count, but they were a matter of record.

earned them, and realizing a thousand dollars was a useful sum, though I'd have kept doing it without compensation for the love of it. A new audience for my old stories was a major benefit.

IPTCs were offered only for the voyages to and from Sitka. Ocean kayaking was offered only out of Sitka, corresponding with the salmon fishing season from late May through August. For most of my birthdays, May 25, for a good ten years, I was onboard *Home Shore*—the perfect birthday present.

Ocean Kayaking

I tried ocean kayaking, but I had two serious drawbacks—big feet and a bad back. My size fourteen shoes didn't fit under the deck of a kayak, and paddling with my legs extended and using lower back muscles was too painful for me to enjoy the experience. If I were on a kayaking charter, I would stay with *Home Shore*, so Jim and the crew could go kayaking with the guests.

The kayakers I remember best were six women. I don't know how they got together, because they all barely knew each other, but they all found that kayak chartering was an incredible bonding experience. Two of the ladies tried to convince Jim that he should advertise his charters as "bonding opportunities." The only friction on that charter was the inclination of the ladies to want to cook in the galley and to offer "advice" to our cook.

We did a special kayak cruise one time, which I enjoyed tremendously, that was an unusual charter by Alaskan kayaking legend Audrey Sutherland, then eighty-five, who had solo-kayaked more than eight thousand miles through Southeast Alaska in the past twenty-six years. There were places she always wanted to go, but had been prevented by age and circumstances, so she chartered *Home Shore* to accomplish her personal itinerary. Audrey was energetic and enthusiastic, and she bragged of her many encounters with grizzly bears, claiming that they understood her peaceful intentions. She was accompanied on the charter by her son Jock, fifty-five, a big-wave surfer in Hawaii, their home. Somehow, I was assigned to keep track of Audrey on our shore excursions, because Audrey frequently disappeared down paths, probably created by grizzlies, secure in her peaceful intent. I wasn't so confident, and tried to enlist Jock to help me, but he was dismissive.

Trying to persuade me to her point of view, Audrey told me she had been within a hundred and fifty feet of a grizzly bear more than fifty times. She presented it as a form of counting coup (a nonviolent demonstration of bravery once practiced by Native Americans). Singing, she insisted, as she wandered the wilderness, was an effective way to warn bears of her presence and to soothe them; she recommended "Alouette" and "Waltzing Matilda."

Son Jock, quiet and withdrawn, had his own passions. To pass the time underway, Jock sat at the galley dinette while everyone else was in the pilothouse sharpening every knife in the knife rack and cutlery drawer to an edge that he proved by shaving hair off his forearm. He used his personal whetstone carried in a sheath on his belt, along with his hunting knife.

On the last leg of "Audrey's celebration charter," we exited the Inside Passage into the Gulf of Alaska—open ocean—to go to storied Lituya Bay, a place Audrey had long dreamed of visiting.

I first heard of Lituya Bay when I read a *Reader's Digest* story nearly fifty years earlier of a tsunami there, caused by an earthquake, and I remembered it vividly.

Before the tsunami, Lituya was infamous for French explorer Jean-François de Galaup's loss of two boats and twenty-one men at Lituya's tricky entrance in 1786. The entrance opens to the west to the Gulf of Alaska and is unprotected. With a twelve-knot outgoing current opposed by windblown waves, perilous seas can develop quickly. No bodies were recovered in the incident. The event was commemorated by a cenotaph on the bay's Cenotaph Island.

I was apprehensive about approaching the entrance to the bay, despite my confidence in Jim, who had been here before. Entry was smooth and simple, as conditions were benign. Naturally, Jim had accounted for the state of the tide for our time of arrival.

The picturesque bay is attractive in an area where anchorages are scarce. No other boats were there, and we headed directly to the anchorage where a boat that survived the epic tsunami had anchored.

On July 9, 1958, an earthquake caused a landslide at the head of the bay, generating a massive mega tsunami to a height of 1,722 feet, taller than the Empire State building. There were three fishing boats anchored in Lituya Bay. The *Sunmore* was sunk by the wave and debris as it attempted to exit the bay, killing the two people aboard. The *Badger* was carried across the La Chasseuse, spit into the ocean, and sank, but the crew, in spite of injuries, managed to board a skiff and were rescued. The third boat, the *Edrie*, crewed by father and son, was anchored at the opposite side of the bay's entrance. The father turned the boat to face the wave, which picked it up, snapping the anchor chain, and carried it above the treetops out of the bay, but washed it back into the bay with no major damage. Estimates of the time it took the wave to reach *Edrie*, after overtopping Cenotaph Island, indicate the wave was traveling a hundred and twenty miles per hour. When the wave reached the open sea, it dissipated quickly.

As I looked around, I was stunned to see obvious evidence of the tsunami after fifty years. The trees that replaced those torn out by the wave were smaller and a lighter shade of green, making a dramatic comparison with the old-growth forest.

I continued to stare, wide-eyed, and strained to imagine the sight the crew of the three boats must have seen as a wave suddenly stood 1,722 feet tall and began to rush toward them. That the *Edrie's* skipper had the presence of mind to start the boat's engine and turn toward the wave is a staggering thought. The wonder of that event returned many times during our four days in Lituya Bay; it was a dark and troubling sensation.

Three of us took the skiff to the back of the bay, where there were remnants of the landslide, and stepped ashore. As I looked up the steep mountain face, I sensed a gentle rain of small pebbles trickling down the mountain and gathering at my feet, a sign of some incredible force still at work inside the mountain, eternally shaking fine debris down the slope.

The next day, we upped anchor and motored around Cenotaph Island to the shore of the long, low spit jutting towards the bay's entrance. As the anchor chain rattled loudly overboard, a large, beautiful grizzly broke from cover and dashed the length of the spit into the wooded mainland. There was a bright sun that morning, which illuminated the bear's shimmering coat as it flexed its mighty muscles to propel itself in long strides in full view of us on the boat. Its whole body rippled in the sunlight, displaying, simultaneously, great grace and power.

Where there was one bear on the spit, there could be another, so we planned accordingly. Ben, Jim's thirty-two-year-old son, advised us to stay together and wait at the shore for the arrival of our second group to be ferried ashore.

"Don't go off by yourself, stay away from the thickets along the spit," he said, motioning towards two thickets between the end of the spit and where the skiff would land.

I hoped Audrey was paying attention. This time, Audrey was not my responsibility, and knowing Jock's attitude, Ben volunteered to look out for Audrey.

Walking up the spit's boulder-strewn beach proved challenging, even for the young and fit of us. The brush was thick, requiring effort to push through it. At the spine of the spit, larger boulders rose above the brush and Audrey settled between two of them, out of the wind, pulling her hat over her eyes to rest. Ben stayed with her.

I and others were stepping from rock to rock, moving in unison to the tip of the spit (Alaskan bear lore advises that grizzlies wouldn't attack groups of three or more humans). Looking down to see where I could safely step next, I saw that I was standing above an eight-foot circle of matted grass and brush, forming a shallow depression. Piles of fresh bear scat were scattered around the perimeter of the circle. It was reassuring that the scat looked like a horse's road apples, which indicated a vegetarian diet.

While the rest of us were at the spit's end, a hidden grizzly had broken from one of the thickets and run past Ben and Audrey, hightailing it for the mainland.

"He gave us a good look as he ran by, but never slowed," Ben said. "He passed within fifty-to-a-hundred feet from us."

"Well, what was that, Audrey? Coup number fifty-four or fifty-five?" Ben asked.

She gave him a quizzical look. "Oh, that bear?" she said, trying to suppress a gleeful smile. "Something like that."

From this adventure, I wrote my last-ever boating article, titled "Singing to Grizzly Bears," which was published in the March 2007 issue of *PassageMaker* magazine.[25] I didn't know that was my last, then, but discovered it while writing this memoir.

The article was inspired by and organized around the lyrics of a bear safety song Shearlean composed when we visited Glacier Bay. She overheard a neighboring boat's bear song and thought she could do better by making it a useful reminder of bear encounter protocol. She based it on the Park Service's bear education brochure.

As a result of my trips to Southeast Alaska aboard *Home Shore*, and my professional involvement in the IPTC, I gradually lost interest in any other boating activity. Though I continued writing general content for *Dockside* magazine through 2004, I had little desire to write features about what I was now doing.

It seems I was absorbed in and fulfilled by instructing and promoting the IPTC, and felt that after thirty-eight years of writing about boats, I had written it all.

---

[25] See "Song: So You Don't Surprise Bears" in the Appendix.

All Inside Passage Training Cruises were superficially the same, though unique from a participant's point of view. I've picked one IPTC to represent all, and peopled it with persons and circumstances from other training cruises. All the people and the conditions were real, but a few situations, mainly involving people, happened on other cruises. The weather and sea conditions depicted all that occurred on this one cruise.

If you want to follow the course of the training cruise (or scout kayaking locations), I recommend *Alaska & Canada's Inside Passage: Cruise Tour Guide*, a map which includes substantial text about the history of the Inside Passage. For those more interested in piloting and navigation, there are north and south route planning maps of the Inside Passage available from FineEdge.com.

Training Cruise

Day 1, May 3

The crew for this IPTC was Jim Kyle, me as hand and co-instructor, and Kristin Hoelting as cook and hand. We were going to be ten days to Sitka (weather permitting, always a proviso).

Guests were five, paying: Couple Kurt and Donna, Silicone Valley techies, in their mid- to late-forties, with a load of pricey still and video gear, who were looking to buy a boat and going cruising; Couple Mike and Ann, in their sixties, from the Seattle area, who were preparing to take their own boat to Glacier Bay; Solo Richard, who was cruising for adventure travel and had no interest in do-it-yourself cruising, though he demonstrated intense interest in the motivations of other guests.

Non-paying was "Woody," a lively fifty-something, who lived in neighboring Anacortes. He was accommodated in the fo'c'sle and was going only as far as Ketchikan. He was a magazine editor researching an article on Inside Passage charters.

Guests were asked to come to the boat the afternoon prior to departure and were shown their accommodations. After unpacking, luggage was stowed in the fish hold. Guests met each other and the crew, and were shown around the boat. Those who wanted to could spend the night onboard in preparation for the 0500 departure.

Nevertheless, Richard showed up the previous afternoon wanting a tour, but I talked him out of it on the dock. He was worried about what clothing would be appropriate and so I repeated what our brochure said and he asked if there was a laundry onboard, to which I replied, "no."

"Ricardo, please," Richard said, grinning broadly, bringing his hands up to his chest in a prayerful posture.

"Oh," I said, confused, "your registration says Richard."

"I prefer Ricardo," he said. "It's more interesting, more romantic-sounding."

"Okay, *Ricardo*," I replied with emphasis, thinking, whatever! Then I reminded him when to return the next day to board and tour the boat.

Every guest was a story, ranging from ass-patting prevention to a virtual cell phone tour to a bottled water drama to a powdered sugar explosion.

Living with a woman, I had the habit of including a pat on the ass with most hugs, but I thoughtlessly did it once when hugging a female guest, and nearly did it too many times. I brought this up with a Protestant minister on a later cruise, and he sympathized and advised me to do what he did, and that was to turn sideways to female parishioners to prevent unfortunate familiarity.

Cell towers were few and far between in the Inside Passage, and as we approached towns, one of the female passengers would rush to the top deck, her arm thrust high, waving her cell phone about. When she got a signal, she called her daughter in New Jersey and updated her about the cruise and streamed a video of our location.

A Vietnam vet became highly agitated when there was no more bottled water in the drinks' ice chest. After I went into the fish hold and set a case of water on the deck, he visibly calmed down and relaxed. It made me wonder what kind of experience could trigger such a fierce reaction.

The cook surprised a guest celebrating a birthday during one cruise with a cake with several candles on it, frosted with powdered sugar. Filling his lungs, he blew mightily on the cake, raising a sugary dust cloud that powdered everyone around the compact galley dinette.

Every guest was keen about feasting on fresh seafood, but for one lady, seeing me break the tails off living shrimp was too brutal, and she said so. From then on, I put a drop of chlorine bleach into the pan of water where we kept shrimp alive until dinnertime, which instantly killed them.

Ricardo wore pajamas to bed and often lounged in the companionway outside his stateroom, staring through the windshield of the former helm station. He was about six-feet tall, very slender, and there was nothing particularly Latin-looking about him to complement his chosen name. With steering moved to the pilothouse, the former helm station consisted only of shelves and lockers where the crew and guests now stored their cameras, and charged their computers and cell phones. It was a tight space, where the steps to the pilothouse and the door to the foredeck were located. Standing there, he was an obstacle to everybody and everything. He seemed deaf to courteous urges to move out of the way and to outright shouts of "Coming through," but thanks to everyone's persistent harassment, he stopped loitering there.

Though Ricardo had no interest in learning to navigate the Inside Passage, he was eager to learn all he could about the passage, wildlife, and Alaskan history (as were most guests). What appalled Ricardo (and again, most guests) was clear-cut logging that made many mountainsides look as though the forest had been bombed into oblivion. Special umbrage was expressed over helicopter logging, which we'd once stopped to watch for a while. What was good about helicopter logging was that it occurred out of sight on the backside of mountains (and what may have been bad about it was that it occurred out of sight).

A helicopter logging operation resembled an amphibious military invasion, consisting of several barges for a dormitory, helicopter landing pads, and log delivery and processing, a few tugs and utility boats, and the *whop-whop-whop* soundtrack of helicopters coming and going.

Helicopter logging is an expensive method of harvesting timber and can be done only in areas of high-quality, high-volume timber, (usually old-growth, never previously harvested). One helicopter charter company reported that logging helicopters were billed at twelve thousand dollars an hour. Reportedly, each tree harvested this way cost the logger $322 per thousand board feet in 2007.

When Ricardo caught on to how we were navigating *Home Shore*, he could see for himself exactly where we were by glancing at the electronic chart. One day, he confronted Jim about spending too much time in the Inside Passage on the marine highway. Ricardo felt he could have had the same trip on the Alaska Ferry, a lot cheaper.

But nothing could be said or done on *Home Shore* that could visibly ruffle Jim's composure. Jim's demeanor would have you believe nothing unanticipated ever happened on *Home Shore* for which he was unprepared. He pointed out to Ricardo that there was no avoiding the main route, but we were on and off the ferry route frequently every day, throughout the day. Even along the marine highway, we entered bays, coves, and small harbors off-limits to the ferry, because of its size and schedule. To cap off his point with Ricardo, he explained that the ferry made the trip to Sitka in sixty hours, and *Home Shore* took ten days. Ricardo was obviously mollified.

Every guest was asked for health-and-medical information to accommodate any special needs, dietary or otherwise. Ricardo failed to forewarn us about his sleep apnea, and nightly used a CPAP machine to assist his breathing. His first night onboard *Home Shore* was at the dock, plugged into 110VAC shore power. The second night was underway. Because Jim prized a quiet anchorage, *Home Shore* had no generator to provide 110VAC household-type power. Instead, 110VAC came from an inverter powered by a big bank of batteries in the engine room. With careful management, there was plenty of 110VAC power, but to conserve the batteries when demand was minimal, Jim, the last to turn in for the night, turned off the inverter. Luckily, Jim, sleeping nearby, heard Ricardo struggling to breathe and rushed to help him and turned the power back on.

The next day we reviewed every guest's questionnaire with each guest to confirm they had made a full disclosure.

Cuisine

It is impossible to overstate the importance of food and beverages to guests, so I've let stand log and journal references to the menu provided over the ten days of the cruise. Reviewing dozens of journals, diaries, notebooks, and ships' logs for this memoir, it seemed as though every voyage, cruise, passage, or charter was all about weather, fuel, anchoring, and food, except for a few instances of excitement and stress.

Knowing the importance of food to guests (and crew), every effort was made to deliver on "Alaska on the Home Shore's" brochure claim that it offered "sumptuous and gourmet" meals, accompanied by a selection of wines.

And, I felt we delivered on our promises. Only one of a handful of cooks misfired on our boasts, and that failure was on the side of excess. That cook's specialty was cheesecake, and she produced one delicious daily cheesecake after another until we begged her to stop; they were irresistible, but too much of a good thing.

The galley was the center of *Home Shore*, and the galley range was its heart. The galley range was a traditional Alaska fishing boat's cast iron monster that operated on diesel fuel fed to it by its built-in carburetor. It took a lot of getting used to in order to produce predictable results, but once mastered, it was beloved. Besides being an oven and cooktop, the range was the sole source of heat for the boat's main cabin.

Convection carried the dry heat throughout the main cabin and up to the pilothouse. Except for the propane barbecue grill on deck, all meal preparation occurred on this galley range.

The refrigerator/freezer was built into the galley and operated from a compressor in the engine room. The freezer would keep ice cream frozen but couldn't make ice cubes. Organizing and filling it were major chores on provisioning days, and later, finding items was a challenge.

This built-in refrigeration was supplemented with on-deck ice chests for which we bought block ice or better yet, harvested icebergs. Ice chest number one was the large drink cooler in the lounge area, which was to be kept full at all times, and everyone was welcome to help themselves to beer, wine, sodas, water, and juice. Keeping it replenished was one of my jobs. No liquor was available on the boat.

Opposite the refrigerator, sink, and range was an L-shaped dinette, that, with a supplemental bench, could seat nine compactly.

Alaska is famous for its seafood, and guests anticipated and were promised plentiful fresh seafood. Often what landed on their plates for dinner was landed on the boat only hours earlier. We caught and bought seafood. We rod-fished for salmon, cod, and halibut, and trapped Dungeness crab and shrimp. We bought what we needed, sometimes from local fishers, as Jim did in Lund. Except for crab, the preferred method of cooking seafood was on the grill. Chicken and steak were also offered.[26]

Day 2

Jim gave his standard safety briefing, mentioning the meaning of alarms, how the intercom worked, and the fire drill and abandon-ship procedures. He emphasized that *Home Shore* was a round bottom displacement hull and often rolled twenty degrees in heavy seas, but that was normal and not dangerous—it was the nature of round bottom boats (boats with hard chines resist rolling, but can produce a quick, unpleasant movement).

---

[26] For examples of the meals served, see "Cuisine" in the Appendix.

On the way out of Bellingham Bay, Jim explained the steering mechanism and autopilot operation, and demonstrated the computer navigation software as he plotted our course for the day.

By the time we passed Lummi Island heading north into Rosario Strait, guest Kurt was steering for our stop at Nanaimo, Vancouver Island, before going on to Secret Harbor, our first night's anchorage.

Any time a guest was at the helm, either Jim or I was present and sometimes tutoring the guest about steering, navigation software, and maintaining watch for debris in the water. I believe every guest was surprised, maybe shocked, to find themselves at the helm of a seventy-tons displacement, sixty-two-foot commercial fishing boat within an hour of getting underway.

Much to everyone's confusion, Jim maintained clocks on *Home Shore* on Alaska time, one hour earlier than Bellingham; always had and wouldn't change. There were also two stereos onboard, one at the helm and the other in the galley. Jim listened only to his preferred music, but anyone could play anything they wanted in the galley. Jim preferred his coffee near boiling, so after pouring it from the coffeemaker's hot plate, it went into the microwave for thirty seconds. While kayakers seldom came up to the pilothouse, IPTC guests seldom left the pilothouse, so Jim considered putting a rope across the pilothouse stairs to indicate it was temporarily closed to guests, but he never followed through with the idea.

The autopilot did most of the steering, so watchkeeping was the main occupation of being at the helm, though Jim insisted everyone (except Ricardo, who was just along for the ride) take turns actively steering, which was more difficult than most people realized, creating an embarrassing "snake-wake."

Donna's turn at steering proved that practice and training were essential. Donna was inclined to swerve—oversteer—to avoid debris, causing *Home Shore* to suddenly roll enough to throw a person off his or her feet and for items to slide off the counters. With some tutoring and urging her to watch farther ahead of the boat for debris, she settled down nicely to the relief of the rest of us.

Debris is a serious hazard throughout the Inside Passage, though the amount varies by area and the weather. Deadheads (nothing to do with Grateful Dead fans) are probably the worst of the debris, because they can sink a vessel. A deadhead is a whole tree, maybe forty-to-seventy feet long, sunk vertically in the ocean, that if hit can hole a boat's hull, quickly sinking it. Jim sighted a very dangerous fresh deadhead and paused the boat to point it out, saying it was one of the worst he'd ever seen, with just a few inches of a whole tree showing above the water. He reported its location to the Coast Guard.

We arrived at Nanaimo around 1:00 p.m., after passing through Dodd Narrows. Crew and guests cleared customs and got brief shore leave, while Kristin did the balance of grocery shopping for items that could not be brought across the U.S.–Canadian border. With all aboard, we headed east across the Strait of Georgia to anchor in Secret Cove, arriving just at dark.

Day 3

I'm usually the first up (4:30 a.m.), but on this day, Woody was up, too. I slept well, despite my coughing and leg cramps. I made a pot of coffee and toasted an English muffin because it would be a while before breakfast.

I put away dishes, washed some others, and made a second pot of coffee while Woody chattered about yesterday, today, and tomorrow.

At 6:20 a.m., we departed Secret Cove with a light, help-yourself breakfast of cereal, toast, fruit, coffee, tea, and juice; later, a hot breakfast was served. We docked in Lund for an hour for a walk and look around. Jim bought seven pounds of shrimp for eight dollars a pound from a local boat delivering its catch to the harbor.

In honor of Cinco De Mayo, lunch was making your own hard and soft tacos, with refried beans, rice, ground beef, shredded chicken, salsa, sour cream, cheese, and guacamole.

We passed through Desolation Sound (which isn't desolate at all, Vancouver was just depressed when he named it) and continued north through Yuculta and Dent tidal rapids. Here, training focused on tides, rapids (not white water, tidal), and boat-handling to make the most of a rapids running experience.

We anchored for the night in Douglas Bay, in Forward Harbour, with other recreational and fishing boats.

Day 4

From Douglas Bay, we headed down Sunderland Channel and into Johnstone Strait. Some guests got up early to enjoy the sunrise. Traffic in the strait was light, because it was still early in the cruising season.

When the daily wind came up, a guest became queasy, so we anchored early in Millbrook Cove at the entrance to Smith Sound. As they got their sea legs, guests were seldom bothered by motion sickness under normal sea conditions.

Day 5

Guests decided to bypass a side trip to Ocean Falls in favor of exploring Open Bight and stopping in Shearwater, on Denny Island, for shore leave, while we took on some fuel and water.

After a walk and a beer in the Shearwater pub, we continued north to anchor in Nowish Cove, near Klemtu. Dinner was finished off with a perfect lemon meringue pie for dessert.

Day 6

Exiting the cove at 5:40 a.m., the late risers were still able to share the morning's freshly baked coffee cake. We arrived at the ruins of Butedale at 11:30 a.m., and we swung bow to the dock to talk with one of the squatter residents for a few minutes, before backing off for a closer look at the waterfall, which still generated hydroelectric power for the ghost town.

Just before dark, we arrived at Chalmers Anchorage at Elliott Island. We had decided to eat the lasagna dinner underway, instead of waiting to anchor.

Day 7

I attended to getting the anchor up at 3:25 a.m. Conditions were lumpy and bumpy as we approached Dixon Entrance because of unusual north-northeast winds right on the nose. Crossing this thirty-mile stretch of open ocean was mildly uncomfortable. We went into Thomas Basin in Ketchikan, where Shearlean and I had often been, and stayed onboard until Jim cleared the boat and all of us with U.S. customs. When he returned, we all got shore leave to explore the city. Kristin went shopping to replenish our provisions. With everybody but Woody back onboard and worn out from the noise and bustle of the big city, we headed north again in calm conditions.

Because of job pressures, Woody had to return home from Ketchikan. He said endless goodbyes. I thought, ten times, he was leaving before he left. Really an emotional guy. I thought I saw tears.

When we were leaving Ketchikan, we passed the airport ferry float and there was Woody waiting for the ferry, waving wildly at us as *Home Shore* passed by. He raised his camera and took a photo of us waving back.

The guests had voted to travel and anchor at night, so we continued on north, eating dinner underway, to Ratz Harbor. After dark, everyone gathered in the pilothouse to take turns running the boat at night under blackout conditions to maximize night vision. *Home Shore* was equipped with two radars. Running at night or in low visibility, both radars were used, one adjusted for long range and the other for short range. Properly tuned short-range radar detected birds and debris directly in front of the boat. Some guests went on deck to observe our entry into Ratz Harbor, where we anchored at 11:17 p.m.

Day 8

At dawn, we saw *Alaska Secret* anchored, a charter boat like ours headed north for the season in Sitka. We were underway by 4:30 a.m.

Day 9

We traveled all day under typical conditions: small sea chop, overcast, with sun breaks and little wind.

A pod of eight-to-ten humpback whales greeted us on our arrival in Frederick Sound. They put on a big display, leaping and thrashing for about a half-hour as we drifted nearby with the engine off. Their antics rivaled trained Sea World porpoise. Just as we thought they were done with their show and we were about to start the engine, two whales broke from the pod and circled *Home Shore* twice from about twenty feet away. They rolled on their sides as they swam, so that one of their eyes could see us.

After anchoring in Cannery Cove, a defunct salmon cannery and now stylish sportfishing lodge on Admiralty Island, at 7:30 p.m., Jim grilled the dinner salmon, something he'd perfected over the years. After dinner, we listened to the tape of a National Public Radio (NPR) broadcast cook Kristin had done about salmon fishing in Alaska when she was ten years old and living in Petersburg, Alaska.

Kristin was a recent Harvard graduate in her mid-twenties, from an Alaska fishing family acquainted with the Kyle family. She was our cook several times and I got to know her well. She was a good cook, sometimes disorganized and on the brink of disaster, but always managed to overcome her self-inflicted problems. Once, she forgot to defrost the frozen chicken in time to prepare dinner. Jim did finally have to talk with her about making the whole galley uninhabitable when preparing a meal. Since the galley was supposed to be a "common room" for guests and crew, she couldn't take over the dinette to the exclusion of everybody else. She needed to better organize her meal preparation activities so the galley could be used simultaneously by others. Though I sometimes thought she was courting disaster, like choosing to make a pot of soup while *Home Shore* was wallowing through heavy seas, I was always mistaken; she never failed. It must have been that Harvard education.

Day 10

This was crew-overboard training day, and Kristin had volunteered to go into the water in an exposure suit to give us practice rescuing someone overboard. While rehearsing overboard procedures, everyone took a turn donning a one-size-fits-all exposure suit on deck. In the Inside Passage, exposure suits are preferred over an inflatable life raft (though *Home Shore* had one), because land is always nearby and you can swim in an exposure suit, though awkwardly.

All the guests wanted a turn at maneuvering the boat to recover the practice float target. So, as we neared Baranof Island for a dip in the hot spring, each person took a turn at the wheel under Jim's direction, and attempted to steer the boat back to the overboard float. It was harder than they'd thought.

We docked at Baranof Warm Springs, where some guests hiked up the trail to the source of the hot spring, and others elected to soak in the galvanized steel tubs at the head of the dock.

After a few hours, we cast off and headed for our last anchorage of the cruise, near peculiarly named Partofshikof Island in Neva Strait.

Day 11

As we traveled toward Sitka, we fell into a discussion about whether it had rained during the cruise. No one could remember, and so we checked the ship's log to discover there were showers one day.

Approaching Sitka midafternoon, training continued, with guests learning how to contact the harbormaster for a slip assignment. Once we had our slip number, we checked the cruising guide for a diagram of New Thomsen Harbor to locate our slip, and then looked for slip numbers, so we knew where to turn. At the marina, departure packing began for the trip to a local B&B or to the airport.

There were two IPTCs per season, the one north to begin the season, and the one south to conclude the season. The cruise south one season included the only child guest during my time aboard *Home Shore*, and my only near-emergency medical episode.

I was in the pilothouse instructing guests, when I heard a dreadful sound I recognized immediately, though I'd never heard it before. Everyone in the pilothouse recognized it, as four pairs of eyes locked onto each other, all acknowledging the sound. It was the sound of a human body collapsing on the cabin sole of the companionway at the foot of the stairs to the pilothouse.

Though *Home Shore* was underway, making her usual nine knots, the big diesel engine in her bowels growling strenuously, and the bow wave hissing along the hull, the distinctive sound was loud and clear. I immediately dropped down the stairwell, hardly touching a stair tread, and found John in a motionless heap, passed out in the passageway.

John and Johnny, forty-plus-year-old father and twelve-year-old son, were on what I interpreted to be a bonding holiday. John had for days been obviously pushing himself physically to impress his son, and Johnny was having the time of his life, a blond and eager darling of the crew. He was clearly wowed by this side of his dad he had probably never seen before. And he was enjoying new, exciting sights and activities every day, as our training cruise made its way back to *Home Shore's* homeport of Bellingham, Washington.

Except for Jim at the helm, the other three guests were staring at the scene from the stairwell. "Let us down, let us down," pleaded Ames and Celia, "We're ski-patrol trained. We can help."

I rose and stepped over the unresponsive John, hoping this wasn't a heart attack, but was something we could deal with here and now. We were a day away from any medical facilities.

Johnny was unaware, playing a computer game in the lounge area of the boat on the far side of the galley. Our cook was distracted by assembling a recipe at the galley's dinette table.

Without seeming to have done anything, Ames and Celia had John sitting up, looking confused and disoriented, but talking coherently. I think he realized that all of his strenuous activity and contrived excitement over Johnny's activities had taken a toll, and he'd stressed himself to the point of collapse.

John got to his feet and went to sit with Johnny in the lounge, and for the remaining three days of the cruise backed off a little and stowed away the super-dad persona he'd been displaying. All eyes were now on him in case he showed signs of overdoing it again.

The IPTC training curriculum is extensive and diverse, sometimes extemporaneous.[27]

I had been crewing aboard *Home Shore* for the past few years, during which, Jim and I, and the whole Kyle family, had become close friends. Besides sharing *Home Shore*, Jim and I were part of a larger community of charter providers. There was a lot of interest in cruising the Inside Passage in the first decade of the twenty-first century.

With my book and participation in the IPTC, and Jim's years of experience in Southeast Alaska, we were welcome guest speakers at many Alaska cruising events: boat shows, kayaking gatherings, yacht clubs, and boating seminars sponsored by other Inside Passage experts. Occasionally, I even represented kayaking on *Home Shore* when Jim was chartering from May through August.

---

[27] See "IPTC Abridged Curriculum, Learning Objectives and Labs" in the Appendix.

Shearlean to Alaska and Africa

When I resigned as crew, I booked a kayak charter for Shearlean and me on *Home Shore*. I wanted her to experience what I had for so long, and I wanted her to see more of the wonderland that is Southeast Alaska, without enduring the demands of couples cruising as we did to Glacier Bay in 2002.

So, I paid full fare and selected the port stateroom and took a silent oath not to participate in *Home Shore's* operation and to behave as a paying guest. We had a great time, and at the end, I delivered an envelope of cash to the crew, like other guests. I kept my oath, offering no advice to any crew, but knowing where everything was stored and how everything operated, I did help myself to whatever I wanted—silently.

Shearlean learned to handle a kayak and went kayaking with other guests, though I didn't because of my big feet and bad back. We saw a lot of wildlife, including a pair of curious bear cubs watching the kayakers from a rocky point fifty feet or so above the water. Whales and porpoise were plentiful, along with kelp beds populated by sea otters and large colonies of sea lions sunning on isolated islets.

Soon after kayaking, Shearlean left, in July 2008, for Kenya, Africa, for two weeks, to lead Western Washington University's international service learning program at the Ombogo Girls Academy to help train girls orphaned by AIDS for clerical jobs.

I stayed home and decided that when she did this again the next year, I would join her for a safari after she'd fulfilled her university obligations. I was eager to see Africa's animals before they were gone (or at age seventy-one, before I was gone).

In 2009, we lived in a Maasai village for three days, where young spear-carrying warriors took us on bush walks, demonstrated how traditional huts were lion-proofed, and showed us what were otherwise invisible features of the savannas. For tourists, the village offered individual cabins with a common bathroom. Getting up at night to go to the toilet was a singular adventure, walking an unlit path and looking for lions lurking in the shadows.

Next, we spent a week in a safari camp, doing game drives every day. On our way from breakfast to the safari wagon, Shearlean stopped in an outdoor restroom. I recognized her screams when she ran to a crowd of other tourists, saying she'd been bitten by a snake. I ran back to her but found no signs of snake or insect bites. She recovered her composure, and we went on our game drive, but in the following days, she was plagued by pain.

Back home, her doctor said those pains were seizures caused by a terminal brain tumor, a stage-four glioblastoma. With surgery, radiation, and chemo, she learned she might survive for eighteen months.

We immediately put everything else in our lives aside and undertook full-time treatment and care. On February 2, 2011, eighteen months after her diagnosis, Shearlean died at home, in bed beside me, at age sixty-four. She had been hospitalized only four days for brain surgery and four days in ICU preceding her death; otherwise, I was her sole caregiver the entire time.

Our difficulties with acute healthcare inspired me to write a book in the hope of improving care and treatment for terminally ill patients, titled *Waking Up Dying: Caregiving When There Is No Tomorrow*. For the next ten years, until January 2020, I wrote healthcare articles for a monthly newspaper column and my blog. Simultaneously, I worked as a community activist in Bellingham to reform local healthcare, raise funds to combat brain cancer, and improve care for terminally ill patients. My blog, also titled "Waking Up Dying," at robertaduke.com, is still active.

Shearlean was fortunate to be able to remain active during nearly her whole period of survival. We traveled by car twice from Washington to California in 2009 and 2010. She maintained office hours at the university, she drove, and entertained guests at home. Cancer hadn't forced us to quit boating. We still had *Duchess* and took occasional day trips to nearby anchorages.

It wasn't until Thanksgiving 2010 when there was a noticeable decline in her condition. Even so, we drove to Palm Desert, California, for Christmas with her sister and nephew, but we returned home earlier than planned as her decline became severe. She died twenty-one days later.

By 2010, the price of salmon had recovered, and *Home Shore* was salmon fishing again. I asked Jim if I could spend a week aboard *Home Shore* while he was fishing, in an effort to distract myself from my loss.

He said, "Of course, come on up."

So, I flew to Sitka and took a small plane to a town near where Jim was fishing, and joined the crew. I was mainly a passenger, but occasionally, they would let me operate the hydraulics to recover the net.

Later, in 2011, still seeking distractions and healing, I went to Thailand for a month to a cooking school and did tourist things, such as riding an elephant and dining literally in the streets of Bangkok where, at night, restaurants move tables and chairs into the street, restricting traffic to one congested and threatening lane. During this journey, I experienced a hairline fracture of my left hip, not the result of a fall, rather a consequence of too much walking for old bones. Though painful, I followed my traveling mantra to "never turn back," and bought a heavy-duty umbrella to utilize as a cane. Back home in November, a doctor said the facture would heal itself with rest. I began writing *Waking Up Dying*.

Swallowing the Anchor

While I cared for Shearlean, I felt twenty years younger. With the loss of her inspiration, I began a rapid physical decline. Though my overall health was great, my physical disability grew worse, and it became difficult and painful to walk, but I persisted. I thought that with my disability a small boat would be more suitable, but twenty-six-foot *Duchess* proved me wrong; every move onboard was precarious, because its motion was too frequent and sudden.

I made the mistake of buying another boat in 2012. It was the nicest boat I'd ever owned, other than *Symbiont*. I had decided a bigger boat would be easier to get around on at anchor or underway, and since I had perfected single-handing, I kept cruising locally and remained an active boater until January 2015.

My disability (peripheral neuropathy of both legs from knee to foot) was becoming severe, and either because of my disability or from other causes, I was making a lot of mistakes, and believed I was becoming a hazard to myself and others. For example, on returning to my slip, I got off the boat, leaving it in gear, in reverse, and it started backing itself out of the slip. I managed to grab the bowdock line before it was out of reach, but the boat was picking up speed, and I was lucky to get the line around a dock cleat to stop it. But *Sea Change* was out in the fairway now, still in gear. Fortunately, either the tide or wind swung it sideways up against the neighboring dock, and I was able to climb onto the stern and put the gear in neutral. I went to the bow, and with the cleated dock line, pulled *Sea Change* into her slip.

On other occasions, I calculated that I had only a fifty-fifty chance of getting in or out of the dinghy without falling into the water. This was irresponsible. I was unfit to be boating anymore, and decided to swallow the anchor (give up the sea and boats) and sell *Sea Change*. I would go RVing.

At the time I was confronting the end of my boating career, Jim was confronting giving up fishing. He was turning over *Home Shore* to son Ben, but Jim didn't want to give up boating. I sold *Sea Change* to Jim in January 2015. I thought *Sea Change* was the perfect boat for Southeast Alaska, and though Jim knew little about recreational boats, he knew I knew, and so he purchased it. He would become a recreational boater and continue annual trips to Southeast Alaska with friends and family. The last I heard from Jim, he was planning on leaving *Sea Change* in Sitka, intending to fly there from then on.

This was the end of my forty-five years' obsession with boating. Besides my disability, I was growing older and weaker every day. That's life, what some call *elderhood*, a predictable and natural state.

With the proceeds from the sale of *Sea Change*, I purchased a four-wheel drive Toyota Tundra and an off-road-rated Arctic Fox travel trailer, and set off to explore the western states—off-road—from Montana to Arizona, but that's another story.

Time is Money

There's a financial term: "time is money." Financially speaking, that sentence means that money *now* is more valuable than money *later*. As I experienced it, it also meant to me that time is *as valuable as*, and a *substitute for*, money; and time now is more valuable than time later.

    Sometimes you have to put a dollar value on your time in order to measure its value. With time, in every area of my life, I was able to do for myself what others had to pay someone else to do for them. I did my own house and boat maintenance and improvements. I managed complex transactions and projects, such as being my own home and boat renovation general contractor and project manager. As a marine surveyor, I oversaw repairs to other peoples' boats for individuals and insurance companies, at the time at $65/hour. In one twenty-year period, I bought and sold five homes and three boats, functioning as my own broker, saving the six-to-ten percent selling price commissions. In a troubled, six-unit condo where I lived, I led a lawsuit against the insurer and won a $1.5 million award, and was then paid $1,800 per month by the other owners to oversee the nearly year-long remedial reconstruction.

As an adult, I don't think I ever earned a salary greater than $40,000 per year. Neither did I have many salaried jobs; rather, I was a freelancer, consultant, part-timer, temp, or an entrepreneur, or self-employed. Shearlean was all of these things, too, but with a master's degree, she preferred salaried jobs with benefits (thank you, Sweetie Pie), but she made career choices that gave her lots of time off (as a college professor, she was in an office or classroom only a thousand hours annually—half of a work-year).

Choosing to have no children and having no other obligations was critical to our lifestyle choices. (Other couples, though, with children, lived aboard boats and cruised for years, home-schooling at sea.[28])

Shearlean, eight years younger than me, intended to work until she qualified for Medicare, on her birthday, June 21, 2011.

Though I lost her far too early, I was convinced that the ocean of time we'd shared—forty years of freedom and adventure—had been the best of times: a wonderful life.

---

[28] See "Family Cruising Books" in the Appendix for a list of titles and authors.

Appendix

Islander 36 Specs

So, let the Islander 36 stand in for all the other modest, affordable cruising sailboats in your imagination. Here are its basic specifications from Boat.com:

- **Designer**: Alan Gurney
- **LOA**: 36'—the longest measurement from the bow stem to the farthest part of the hull at the stern.
- **LWL**: 28'3"—the length of the boat at the waterline, the living space within the hull.
- **Beam**: 11'2"—width of the hull at its widest point.
- **Draft**: 6'—the depth of the lead or iron keel and the submerged portion of the hull.
- **Ballast**: 5,450 lb.—the weight of the above keel, makes the sailboat self-righting.
- **Displacement**: 13,450 lb.—total dry weight of the vessel (no fuel, no water or gear).
- **Sail Area**: 612 sq. ft.—main and headsail area combined.
- **Fuel**: 30 gallons—gasoline or diesel fuel for auxiliary engine.
- **Water**: 56 gallons—potable water.

Between seven- and eight-hundred Islander 36s were built between 1973 and 1986. Designed as a performance family cruiser, it was sloop-rigged, with a standard Atomic Four gasoline auxiliary engine. It had a fin keel with a skeg-mounted rudder. The alternative to this arrangement is a full (length of the boat) keel with the rudder attached to the keel.

List of Improvements to *Symbiont*

My random approach to a series of improvements lead to the following impressive list of modifications to *Symbiont*. Thanks to my surveying and yacht brokerage contacts, I had met many shipwrights and maritime craftsmen capable of implementing the improvements I envisioned. Having the time to look over their shoulders in their shops and to watch as they worked on *Symbiont*, I acquired a wealth of knowledge and made several lifelong friends, such as the talented Bill Eisenlohr.

Propane Locker—For a generous supply of propane for cooking, I needed two propane tanks, but they had to be stored on deck to eliminate the risk of explosion in case of a leak. I'd already given up space at the transom to a solar panel and steering vane. The tanks would be out of the way on the foredeck up against the forward end of the trunk cabin, but I wanted them hidden in a stylish locker that conformed to the boat's sleek lines. I asked my shipwright friend Bill Eisenlohr to construct a teak locker that blended into the deck and superstructure. He used teak staves that could be easily tapered and angled to conform to the necessary shape. He built a sturdy box that looked like it was an original part of the boat. I installed a one-piece copper supply line to the galley range and an electrically actuated shutoff valve at the tanks.

I once witnessed a boat's propane explosion as I was eating lunch at a window table in a waterfront restaurant. I saw the deck and superstructure of a passing forty-foot motor yacht lifted several inches into the air and settled back on the hull, a bit askew. I'd also found so many defective propane systems while surveying that I would only trust my own installation.

Waterproof Cockpit Hatch—All of a small sailboat's propulsion machinery and steering gear is crammed into the least accessible part of the boat—the cockpit bilge. *Symbiont's* original access was through a small cockpit storage locker (tough to get my six-foot-four-inch frame into) and through hinged companionway steps at the front of the engine. On my own, I installed a flush-mounted watertight aluminum deck hatch in the fiberglass cockpit sole over the top of the engine to facilitate immediate access and to let in plenty of air and light for easy maintenance.

My early experience with nearly sinking because of a leaking engine shaft log had demonstrated the need for immediate and easy access to the engine gear and through hulls in this area.

Giant Anchor Roller Trough—Unless a cruiser intends to cruise from marina to marina (as some do), "world cruising" as I wished for it would require anchoring securely every night under all imaginable conditions.

I concluded anchoring was the most critical cruising skill I could master. I wanted to anchor confidently anywhere, anytime, and under any conditions. I would have an oversized anchor with three hundred feet of larger-than-required chain, backed up with three hundred feet of hefty rope, ready to deploy, easily handled on deck under any load or force, and retrievable even if the windlass failed. This would be too heavy for the bow of most boats, and *Symbiont's* finely shaped clipper bow lacked the required load-carrying buoyancy. The load would have submerged the bow below the design waterline, causing her to plow dangerously into head seas.

I redesigned the chain locker so most of the anchor rode could be stowed farther aft under the forward cabin's V-berth. I installed the large manual windlass farther aft on the foredeck than was customary, leaving only the roller trough and stowed anchor to be supported by the farthest forward portion of the hull. When I finished, *Symbiont* still floated on her original lines.

My roller trough was fabricated as a stainless steel box, which slipped over the existing bow pulpit. It was frequently characterized by others as a "battering ram," or sometimes just "ugly," but I was proud of it. The forty-five pound CQR anchor nested securely in the trough and the chain moved easily over the five-inch diameter bronze roller set between two chafe-proof flared trough cheeks.

Convert Sewage Tank to Fuel—With fuel sometimes unobtainable and sanitation requirements nonexistent where we were going, I converted the stainless steel holding tank under the starboard settee to a fuel tank, increasing our range under power by about two hundred miles or twenty hours of engine operation. With minor plumbing changes and the addition of a shutoff valve, I connected the tank to the main fuel tank. It could easily be converted back to its original purpose.

Solar Panel—My only purpose for a solar panel was to ensure the batteries were kept charged if the boat was left unattended. Cruisers seeking more substantial supplemental power chose wind generators, alternators with propellers attached, hoisted high up the mast to catch the wind. They were popular, but noisy and dangerous in high winds or if their rigging got fouled.

Among my waterfront acquaintances was a Hollywood special effects technician who moonlighted as a direct current (DC) marine electrician solving complicated 12-volt problems on boats. He made integrating a solar panel into my alternator/battery system a mere thirty-minute job.

Computer—In 1984, I put my Kaypro II personal computer, an early, so-called portable computer, an 18"x18"x15.5" metal box weighing twenty-nine pounds, on the boat. It was my first personal computer, purchased in 1983, for the equivalent today of $4,800. Because Shearlean and I expected to earn cruising money by writing, we also had a dot matrix printer to go with it. Both were powered with our portable Honda generator. We used to joke about how many words per gallon of fuel we got from the generator. I'd get up first and write every morning until Shearlean fixed breakfast. After we ate, Shearlean would write for a couple of hours while I cleaned up.

Rub Rail—Few sailboats of any type are built with a real rub rail, intended for warding off some serious knocks. The few rub rails I can recall were little more than topside trim. I wanted a "real" rub rail, approximately two-inch square teak, properly shaped and through-bolted to the hull. With it, I didn't worry about who or what came alongside, and an unanticipated bonus was that it provided a useful step for getting on and off from a dinghy. Along with the boom gallows, the rub rail transformed the dainty-looking *Symbiont* into a world-wise, no-nonsense cruiser. Here again, Bill Eisenlohr stepped in, casting custom bronze fittings, shaping and finishing large pieces of costly teak, and bending thirty-foot lengths of two-inch-square teak to *Symbiont's* curved hull.

Boom Gallows—Almost as useful as the rub rail, the boom gallows was a very nautical-looking teak-and-bronze structure arching over the cockpit, giving the mainsail boom a solid resting place. The gallows also provided a strong point for securing the aft edge of a windproof cockpit sun awning that could be deployed underway.

Portable Generator—A 600-watt Honda generator, one of the first such portable generators, was inexpensive, reliable, and quiet. It lived out of the way in a garbage bag in the cockpit, along with a three-gallon jerry jug of gasoline. It would be crucial to us earning about $14,000 during our year in Baja.

Auto Pilot—The idea of an autopilot was irresistible, but its reality was disappointing as we learned the hard way coming south—when it was most needed, it was least capable. Much the same was true of the self-steering wind vane I chose. Both could be made to work reliably, but it would take more knowledge and care than I had as an inexperienced cruiser. Neither worked properly when we needed it most. I was mainly relying on the autopilot, but it functioned through a belt attached to the boat's steering wheel, and the belt slipped when steering was difficult. The autopilot worked best when it wasn't needed. My wind vane was an afterthought, and I fooled myself into believing I would figure out the vane's operation while underway. (For most vanes to work as claimed, you have to be a better sailor than I was, able to adjust sails to balance forces on the rudder).

Dodger—*Symbiont's* dodger was the typical structure of stainless steel tubing and canvas that shields the companionway hatch and the cockpit aft of the companionway bulkhead from the wind, spray, rain, and sun. Atypical, though, my dodger didn't fold, it had no transparent windshield, and its trailing edge connected to the leading edge of the sun awning on the boom gallows. It was stoutly built to withstand use as a handhold for crew getting in and out of the cockpit or persons falling on it.

I had to take my ideas and requirements to several harbor canvas shops before one shop owner would hear me out about exactly what I wanted and why. He didn't exactly embrace my concept, but he didn't oppose it, either, and agreed to do what I'd asked.

SatNav—Only days before our departure to Baja, Magnavox released an affordable SatNav, an electronic device that displayed latitude and longitude based on satellite signals (affordable, GPS-based electronic chart navigation was still years away). Though I'd been practicing for two years with my sextant, I gladly surrendered to the convenience of SatNav, despite making my navigation dependent on a source of electricity. At $3,000 in 1983 (equivalent to $7,900 in 2020), it was a big expense to swallow on the eve of being unemployed, but I never regretted one cent of it—I would always know precisely where I was.

Huge Alternator—An original propulsion engine's alternator is typically tiny, maybe twenty-five amps, good only for recharging the engine's small starting battery. For cruising, a bank of hefty deep-cycle house batteries is installed, and a large, new starting battery replaces the tired old original. Shore power is rarely available to cruisers, which takes the powerful battery charger out of the picture, leaving most battery charging to the engine driven alternator, requiring long hours of engine operation even with the biggest alternator (one-hundred amps and up).

Boarding Ladder—Unless you have the physical means immediately available and have practiced with it, the chances of recovering someone who falls overboard are nearly zero. There are many reasons, but chiefly it is a matter of being unable to lift a waterlogged person three-to-five feet from the ocean's surface to the deck of the boat. My preparation consisted of mounting a long, folding boarding ladder to the transom where it could be unfolded from the water and extended deep enough for a person in the water to put their foot onto the lowest rung.

Bending stainless steel tubing into infinite geometric configurations, from ladders to deck railings to antenna arches, is a marine fabrication specialty that answers many safety and utility requirements on recreational boats.

No Radar—I can't explain my failure to outfit *Symbiont* with radar. I can only suppose that at the time I understood radar's value only in terms of navigating in poor visibility. Years later, I learned under the tutelage of Jim Kyle, an Alaska salmon seiner's captain, of the many uses of radar as a general navigation tool. Jim would prefer radar as a navigation aid over GPS electronic charts, he said.

Sweetie Pie's Specs and Improvements

Mainships were a line of lightly built, affordable, and popular powerboats built by Mainship Corporation in Midway, Georgia, and sold nationally:
- The engine was a venerable Perkins 6-354 diesel turning a four-bladed propeller.
- Overall hull dimensions were thirty-four feet long, eleven-feet, eleven-inches beam, and had a draft of three feet.
- Two aluminum fuel tanks held a total of two hundred and twenty gallons, giving me a range of approximately eight hundred miles at a speed of seven knots.

- Disappointingly, the water tank held a pathetic and unacceptable forty gallons.
- There was a 4-kW, 110VAC diesel generator.
- A rigid bottom inflatable eight-foot dinghy, with a six-horsepower outboard motor, was stowed on the transom swim step.
- Electronics consisted of radar, global positioning system (GPS), two depth finders, and three marine VHF radios, of which one was portable.
- Navigation included Nobeltec electronic charts on a laptop computer, on which I could plot a course to steer. As the chart scrolls, the boat icon progresses along the plotted course. I also had approximately sixty paper charts and copies of the Douglass' Exploring series of cruising guides, and *Marine Atlas*, volumes one and two.
- I chose a forty-four pound Bruce-style anchor and three hundred feet of 5/16" chain, and three hundred feet of 5/8" nylon rope rode.
- As with *Symbiont*, I added a hinged boarding ladder that could be accessed from the water. I added a twenty-five-gallon bladder water tank for a total of sixty-five gallons, and I fashioned a rain catcher on the flybridge to replenish my water tanks.

Inside Passage Voyage Statistics

- Duration, 90 days.
- 2,975 nautical miles traveled.
- 425 engine hours.
- 772 U.S. gallons of fuel consumed.
- Average speed, 6.94 knots.
- Cruising RPM, 1,600.
- Fuel consumption average 1.85 gallons per hour, with generator, two hours daily.
- Range per gallon was 3.86 nautical miles.
- Anchored 67 days.
- Marina slips, 23 days.

Getting Underway Daily Checklist

- Latch sliding cockpit door open.
- Close forward deck hatch over berth.
- Stow items on counters and close locker doors.
- Use toilet.
- Open electronic charts.
- Open side window at engine controls for fast access from deck.
- Turn on anchor windlass circuit breaker.
- Turn on depth finder.
- Turn on VHF radio.
- Get out paper charts.
- Check cruising guides, tides, etc., for day's course.
- Tie back window curtains.
- Take in items drying on clothesline.
- Sponge off FB helm seat.
- Swab decks dry.
- Hoist anchor enough to remove bridle.
- Remove chain stopper.
- Raise anchor.
- Replace chain stopper to secure anchor.
- Start generator to chill freezer.
- Set freezer control.
- Make log entries.
- Put boat in gear.
- Discharge holding tank when clear of anchorage.

Single-Handing Lessons Learned

- Never enter a difficult channel without first knowing exactly how you will get through it.
- Don't accept the lookout's sighting without confirming you're both looking at the same thing.
- Never arrive at a destination exhausted because you don't know what you might encounter.
- Always accept help. Always offer help.
- Don't attempt quick tight maneuvers using electronic charts. Too much delay between boat's movement and depiction on electronic chart.
- The instant you see fog, check your compass course and write it down. In the excitement of being enveloped, you may forget.
- Travel in poor weather so you are at attractive destinations when the weather clears.
- Buy fuel at every opportunity and run off only the top half of your tank. Keep a 50 percent reserve.
- Don't get so focused on your destination that you blind yourself to other opportunities or facilities.
- Always delete old course tracks so they are not confused with the current course when using electronic charts.
- Check your bilge every day. No telling what you'll find.
- Pay attention to what you can see around you. Don't obsess over electronic charts.

Song: So You Don't Surprise Bears

Shearlean composed her own bear song at St. James Bay, Alaska, in 2002, because she thought she could do better than someone else's overheard song. Shearlean used Park Service literature from the service's bear education brochure. Originally published in *PassageMaker* magazine, March 2007.

Bear, bear, bear, always aware.
Bear, bear, bear, always aware.
Bear, bear, bear, always aware.

They may be neat
But you don't want to meet.
Bear, bear, bear, always aware.

They may look slow
But oh they can go.
Bear, bear, bear, always aware.

Quick on their feet,
Don't run, can't beat
A bear, bear, bear.

Looking for bear, always aware.
They may be neat
But you don't want to meet
A grumpy old bear.

Strolling on shore
Bears we adore.
When we're safe on our boat
We watch them and gloat.
That's the way to view bears.

IPTC Abridged Curriculum, Learning Objectives and Labs

Goals—provide trainees with a realistic training cruise of sufficient duration for six individuals to personally live through an actual cruise of nearly the whole length of the Inside Passage (approximately 1,000 miles over 10 days). In so doing, trainees are able to encounter nearly all of the circumstances and conditions *normally* found on an Inside Passage cruise on a recreational boat during the prime cruising season.

After completing the cruise, trainees should be able to:
- Understand and use marine radar for navigation in coastal waters.
- Manipulate electronic charts sufficiently to accomplish limited piloting objectives.
- Understand the use of depth finders in piloting and anchoring.
- Understand and apply marine weather radio broadcasts.
- Plan a recreational cruise.
- Select an anchorage.
- Know at all times the location of their vessel.
- Read and apply tide tables.
- Enter a marina and tie up a boat.
- Acquire a working knowledge of Nobeltec electronic charting and navigation software.
- Use a GPS.
- Interpret weather and sea conditions as they evolve.
- Operate an autopilot.
- Hand-steer a vessel in open waters relative to traffic, aids-to-navigation, and obstacles and hazards.
- Use cruising guides and nautical references.
- Understand paper navigation charts.
- Stand watch.
- Read a magnetic binnacle compass.
- Perform boat-keeping, housekeeping, and underway operational procedures.
- Understand crew overboard recovery procedures.

In the context of the IPTC curriculum, lab sessions are periods when trainees can use equipment or materials for practice, experimentation, or intensive learning without direct supervision or sharing of equipment.

Sometimes, trainees choose to work in teams, purposely sharing equipment in order to learn from each other.

Radar

Turn on, adjust, and use the radar to practice adjustments and functions. For example, choose an existing radar target, set the EBL on the target, and watch to see whether the target diverges from the EBL. If it doesn't, it is on a collision course with your vessel and you should inform the captain immediately. Another radar Lab example is to change the radar's range and to compare the resulting differences between the radar screen image and what can be observed with the naked eye. Ask the captain for suggestions for independent study.

Electronic Charting

Review the electronic charting section of the exercises covered previously by the captain. Choose tools, functions, commands, and operations of particular interest, and attempt to use them to determine whether you understand them completely and to develop proficiency in their application. For example, turn the Tide Bar Display on or off, and then with it on, compare the local tide information with a printed tide table so see similarities and differences in the data.

GPS

Find the currently displayed GPS latitude and longitude on the paper chart for the area currently being navigated. Alternatively, switch the GPS from its main display of latitude and longitude to other functions that are available from the units menu in order to see what other uses there are for the typical GPS unit's capabilities.

Depth Finder

Switch the depth finder's depth measuring scale and notice how the graphic display changes with the change in scale. As with the GPS, switch from the basic depth-indicating display to the other menus available to see what other data the unit is able to provide and to see alternative ways of displaying basic depth data. Many depth finders interface with other navigation electronics (such as the GPS) or with knot meter and sea temperature transducers.

Steering

When the boat enters different bodies of water (from narrow channel to broad sound) with different physical characteristics, request a turn at the wheel or switch to manual steering in order to use your limited steering experience in different surroundings than you may have experienced previously. Take opportunities to gain additional steering experience when there are changes in visibility, sea conditions, or buoyage.

VHF Radio

Turn up the volume on the VHF radio when it is time for a weather forecast, and pay particular attention to the content of the report and compare it to local conditions. Try calling another vessel, bridge-to-bridge, to request information about the vessel's intentions or conditions in its immediate area. Prior to calling another vessel, review good radio procedures and then practice the procedure in talking to another vessel on the appropriate channel. Acknowledge that there is no such radio procedure as "over and out," you are either over, or you are out, but you can't be both.

Cuisine

"Galley Greats," favorite mothership recipes from *Alaska on the Home Shore Cook Book*, 2007.
- Slav Garlic-Dill Baste Salmon
- Apricot-Chili Glaze Salmon
- Khaz Bay Salmon with Soba Noodles and Lime-Ginger Sauce
- Salmon with Tomatillo Salsa
- Rhubarb Halibut
- Stuffed Halibut with Brie Sauce and Roasted Garlic Mashed Potatoes
- Shrimp with Coconut-Curry Risotto
- Flash Sauteed Prawns with Angel Hair Pasta
- Simple Crab Pasta
- Blue Cheese-Pear Salad with Caramelized Pecans
- Broccoli and Red Cabbage Salad
- Nany's Curried Spinach Salad
- Zucchini Rollatini
- Teriyaki Rice
- Rhubarb Muffins with Cinnamon-Sugar Topping
- Golden French Toast Baked with Berries
- Hearty Baked Oatmeal
- Shrimp Omelet with Spinach and Tomatoes
- Pepper-Onion Home Fries
- Killer Mocha Cheesecake
- Spiced Poached Pears with Vanilla Ice Cream
- Whidbey's Best Chocolate Cake
- Molasses Ginger Cookies
- Graham Wafer Bars

Family Cruising Books

Many sailors have cruised with kids onboard for weeks, months, and years. Considerations are home-schooling, socializing, isolation, and a kid's own dinghy, among a thousand-and-one other considerations.

When I was writing *Cruising to Alaska*, I specifically interviewed Alaska cruisers about having kids onboard for any time. For Alaska cruisers, kids were generally visiting teen grandkids. Comments were mixed, but one suggestion stood out: If you invite your grandkids to come cruising in Alaska with you, require that their parents provide a prepaid return airline ticket.

Here are a handful of titles to get you started, but there are many more available. I've read the first three in the order listed. They are interesting and entertaining, whether considering cruising with kids or not.

- *Blown Away* by Herb Payson.
- *All in the Same Boat* by Tom Neale.
- *The Curve of Time* by M. Wylie Blanchet.
- *Into the Light* by Dave & Jaja Martin.
- *Boat Girl* by Melanie Neale (Tom's daughter).

About the Author

Robert "Bob" Duke has been a full-time nonfiction writer his entire professional life. He has written marketing, training, and technical material for nuclear weapons maintenance, the aerospace industry, computer hardware and software, manned spacecraft, and the petroleum industry. His clients included Northrop Corporation, McDonnell Douglas Aerospace, IBM, Xerox, GTE Information Systems, Control Data Corporation, Unisys (nee Burroughs), and other Fortune 500 companies.

Duke made his way into freelance writing in 1979, ran his own publishing business, and supplemented his income by producing articles for national and regional newspapers and magazines. His favorite subject? Boating. Since 1982, he's authored more than six hundred boating, fishing, and travel articles. He was a regular writer for *Sea* magazine's Hands-On Boater, Mexico Report, and Stem to Stern columns. He was Northwest Editor for *Dockside*, and contributed features about renovating, commissioning, and repowering yachts.

In an effort to "have his cake and eat it too," Duke managed corporate communications for the world's largest avocado growers' cooperative in Santa Ana, California, where he worked twenty-five hours per week with summers off for nine years. This allowed him to pursue his boating interests and to travel all summer with his professor wife, Shearlean, who also had summers off.

Eventually the couple relocated to Bellingham, Washington, where Duke began writing course material and sales and marketing literature for Alaska on the *Home Shore*, a Southeast Alaska sea kayak charter business. He developed and co-instructed *Home Shore's* Inside Passage Training Cruise.

In August 2009, when Shearlean was diagnosed with terminal brain cancer, Duke became her full-time caregiver and advocate, working 24/7, 365 days a year for eighteen months, managing her treatment and care. He wrote *Waking Up Dying* and devoted most of his recent writing to raising funds for the Shearlean Duke Memorial Public Relations Scholarship, which he founded at Western Washington University where she was working as chair of the Journalism Department when she died.

www.ingramcontent.com/pod-product-compliance
Lightning Source LLC
Chambersburg PA
CBHW072146100526
44589CB00015B/2119